WITHDRAWN

WITH CHARITY TOWARD NONE

AN ANALYSIS OF

AYN RAND'S PHILOSOPHY

WITH CHARITY TOWARD NONE

AN ANALYSIS OF
AYN RAND'S PHILOSOPHY

CARL A. RUDISILL LIBRARY
LENOIR-RHYNE COLLEGE

WILLIAM F. O'NEILL

University Of Southern California

1977

LITTLEFIELD, ADAMS & CO.
TOTOWA, NEW JERSEY

Reprinted 1972, 1977
by
LITTLEFIELD, ADAMS & CO.

Manufactured in the United States of America

CONTENTS

PART ONE

THE PHILOSOPHY OF OBJECTIVISM

Chapter I

THE PHILOSOPHY OF AYN RAND: A FEW
INTRODUCTORY CONSIDERATIONS

> The Red Queen shook her head. "You may call it 'nonsense' if you like," she said, "but *I've* heard nonsense, compared with which that would be as sensible as a dictionary!"
>
> *Alice in Wonderland*

Writing about Ayn Rand is a treacherous undertaking. In most intellectual circles, she is either totally ignored or simply dismissed out of hand, and those who take her seriously enough to examine her point of view frequently place themselves in grave danger of guilt by association.

This is unfortunate, because—for better or worse—Miss Rand has refused to shut up and go away, and many of her ideas seem to possess a peculiar fascination for those who are more or less oblivious to the esthetic limits of legitimate intellectual debate. On the freeways of Southern California, for example (and while they have scarcely replaced Triple A decals as yet) the hero of Miss Rand's *magnum opus, Atlas Shrugged,* has recently become the subject of automobile bumper stickers which occasionally loom up through the contaminated air to pose the insistent question, "Who is John Galt?" In a similar respect, in many of our colleges and universities, undergraduates are beginning to show a disconcerting enthusiasm for the bold, iconoclastic and uncompromising "individualism" which Miss Rand so stridently propounds.

In a sense, then, and regardless of whether certified academics formally choose to acknowledge her presence, Ayn Rand has made a rather significant impact on contemporary American culture. Whether or not she is to be deemed intellectually respectable, she is an important cultural phenomenon who, if anything, seems to flourish from the concerted neglect of the "intellectual establishment."

3

Unfortunately, Miss Rand's philosophy, which she terms "objectivism," is difficult to grapple with. This difficulty arises for a variety of reasons. For one thing, her philosophy is perhaps best and most eloquently expressed in her works of fiction and, particularly, in her two major novels, *The Fountainhead* and *Atlas Shrugged.* In addition to this, most of her nonfiction consists of brief articles and essays of a highly polemical nature which were originally written either for her syndicated newspaper column or for *The Objectivist,* a monthly publication which Miss Rand publishes (until recently in collaboration with her erstwhile disciple, Nathaniel Branden). Finally, and as Miss Rand herself is well aware, her philosophy is, as yet, incomplete, unsystematized and largely implicit within pronouncements which are scattered widely throughout her various publications.[1]

Much of what Miss Rand says is open to attack on a variety of different grounds—logical, linguistic or purely empirical. It is far too pat, however, simply to dismiss Ayn Rand as the progenitor of some new and exotic type of intellectual lunacy. She may be precisely this, but merely "labeling" her as such scarcely establishes the point, and, if she is to be judged guilty of some kind of philosophical felony, she should at least be presumed innocent until the evidence has been presented in some legitimate arena of intellectual enquiry.[2]

THE IMPACT OF OBJECTIVIST PHILOSOPHY

The scope and impact of Miss Rand's philosophy of objectivism is very impressive. She is, by any objective standards, one of the most widely discussed philosophers of our times. Eight years after its initial publication in 1959 her most important work, the novel *Atlas Shrugged* has sold over a million copies, and her other well-known novel *The Fountainhead,* published over twenty years ago, has sold in excess of two million copies. Each continues to sell between one hundred thousand and two hundred thousand copies every year.[3] In addition, Miss Rand's novels have been translated into over a dozen foreign languages and are read widely throughout the rest of the world. Her major works of non-fiction—*For the New Intellectual; The Virtue of Selfishness* and *Capitalism: The Unknown Ideal*—have enjoyed astonishing success for works dealing exclusively with philosophical problems and abstruse theoretical questions. *The Virtue of Selfishness* which was published in 1964, has gone through several printings in both paperback and hard cover and has now exceeded sales of over one half million. Nathaniel and Barbara Branden's book *Who is Ayn Rand?* has also managed to sell over one hundred thousand copies.[4]

The popularity of Objectivism is by no means reflected solely in book sales, however. As of 1966, the Nathaniel Branden Institute was sending materials to over 60,000 persons.[5] The pamphlet-newsletter *The Objectivist* presently goes out to over 15,000 subscribers. In 1966 the Nathaniel Branden Institute offered lecture courses in over eighty cities in the United States and Canada and was negotiating to begin operations in such varied places as Germany, Greenland, Viet Nam, Pakistan and the trusteeship area of the Marshall Islands.[6] At the University of Denver a noted objectivist (who is also a Ph. D. in philosophy) Dr. Leonard Peikoff, conducted a graduate course entitled "Objectivism's Theory of Knowledge."[7] During several months of 1964, the Nathaniel Branden Institute's introductory course, "The Basic Principles of Objectivism" was offered on board a United States polaris submarine located somewhere in the mid-Atlantic.[8]

In 1966, approximately five thousand people—up 30 per cent from the previous year and up approximately 50 per cent from 1963—attended the courses given by the Nathaniel Branden Institute.[9] During this same year, several thousand others attended individual lectures on the objectivist philosophy. In New York City alone approximately two hundred students were enrolled in the basic course in the principles of objectivism.[10] Approximately two-thirds of these people are reported to be professional adults,[11] and some of Miss Rand's most visible followers are highly trained people who are involved in the intellectual professions. These include physicians, professional writers, attorneys, psychologists, psychiatrists, economists, historians, and even professional philosophers.[12]

In addition to these considerations, Miss Rand's influence has been significantly augmented by the coverage which she has been able to obtain in the mass media. For a period of time, she wrote a newspaper column which appeared in the *Los Angeles Times*.[13] She has, on occasion, contributed a regular radio program entitled "Ayn Rand on Campus," for the Columbia University Station WKCR (FM) in New York City[14] and currently has a program entitled "Commentary" on radio station WBAI (FM) in New York City.[15] In what is perhaps the supreme accolade which our society is capable of bestowing upon a public personality, she was made the subject of an interview in *Playboy* for March, 1964.

Miss Rand's influence is, of course, particularly well-established at the college and university level. Approximately one-third of her readers are reported to be in the college age-group, and she has frequently been chosen as a hero or "most admired person" on polls conducted among contemporary college students.[16] Her book *The Virtue of Selfishness* was selected as book-of-the-semester at Rice University during 1965.[17] She has received the honorary degree Doctor of Humane Letters from Lewis and Clark College in Portland, Oregon, where the entire faculty and student body devoted their attentions for a period of time to conducting a thorough discussion of Miss Rand's ideas.[18]

Popularity is not verification, of course, but the fact remains that—however anyone may feel about them—Miss Rand's ideas are very popular today. For better or for worse, she is winning the free competition of ideas, not only in many parts of the public arena, but, significantly, in many parts of the academic marketplace itself. Objectivists, as *The Catholic World* indicates, "are far more zealous and numerous than it is comfortable for us to admit.[19]

"Objectivism"

Man needs a philosophy, states Rand, whether he is aware of his need or not.[20] He needs a "frame of reference, a comprehensive view of existence, no matter how rudimentary . . . a sense of being *right,* a moral justification of his actions, which means: a philosophical code of values."[21]

Ayn Rand's answer to this need is her philosophy of "objectivism," which is, in the words of Nathaniel Branden "a philosophy for living on earth."[22]

The term "objectivism," as it is used in this study, refers to the philosophy of Ayn Rand. The only authentic sources of information with respect to this philosophy are, by official pronouncement (1) Miss Rand's own books, (2) the book *Who is Ayn Rand?* which was written by Nathaniel and Barbara Branden, (3) *The Objectivist Newsletter* and (assumedly) its somewhat revised successor *The Objectivist,*[23] (4) the courses on Objectivism offered by the Nathaniel Branden Institute, and (5) the publications of the Nathaniel Branden Institute.[24] As Nathaniel Branden indicates: *"No group, organization, newsletter, magazine, book or other publication—with the exception of those named above—is endorsed or recognized by us as a qualified spokesman for*

Objectivism."[25] In accordance with this designation of the official scripture, this study is restricted to a consideration of these materials.

In a public announcement contained in *The Objectivist* of May, 1968, Miss Rand formally dissociated herself from the Brandens. As she states: "I hereby withdraw my endorsement of them and their future works and activities. I repudiate both of them, totally and permanently, as spokesmen for me or for Objectivism."[26A]

At a later point in the same announcement she adds the following qualification: "I must state, for the record, that Mr. and Mrs. Branden's writings and lectures up to this time were valid and consonant with Objectivism. I cannot sanction or endorse their future work, ideas or ideological trends."[26B] Accordingly, the Nathaniel Branden Institute (which was reported to be closing in 1968) is no longer associated with Ayn Rand and no longer represents the "official" Objectivist point of view. *The Objectivist* is now edited by Miss Rand herself in collaboration with Dr. Leonard Peikoff. Because of Miss Rand's formal disavowal of Nathaniel Branden's recent work, his current book *The Psychology of Self-Esteem* (Los Angeles: Nash Publishing Company, 1969) is not used as a source of information about Objectivism in this study.

The only portions of the officially-sanctioned sources which were not utilized were the courses offered by the Nathaniel Branden Institute (which are now available from other Objectivist sources). These were not used for two basic reasons. First, because they consist primarily of tape transcriptions and occasional lectures which are not reproduced in print and which do not therefore (barring literal transcription) lend themselves readily to effective critical scrutiny and subsequent objective verification by means of precise and specific citations. Second, a sampling of the materials offered in these courses does not suggest that they provide any significant additions to, or variations from, the materials otherwise available in print.

THE ORGANIZATION OF THE STUDY

Any comprehensive discussion of Ayn Rand's Objectivism necessarily encompasses three basic areas: (1) an exposition of what Ayn Rand's philosophy actually *is,* (2) a critical analysis of what such a philosophy *means* in terms of generally-accepted criteria for evidence and verification, and (3) a discussion of the major social implications of such a point of view.

The study which follows is divided into two major sections. The first part presents Ayn Rand's philosophy of Objectivism. It is, in turn, subdivided into three separate subsections: (1) knowing and the known, (2) personal value and the nature of man, and (3) the ethics of Objectivism.

The second half of the study, which follows the same general organizational scheme as the first, constitutes a critical analysis of Miss Rand's philosophy. It is concerned primarily with examining the truth and validity of Miss Rand's philosophy and with determining the major social implications which grow out of her overall point of view.

I am not an Objectivist, and I do not purport to be a spokesman for Objectivism. I have attempted to separate carefully my views from those of Miss Rand and her associates, ascribing to them only positions which they take or which are clearly implied on the basis of those statements which they make. In several instances, and particularly where the basic meaning of Rand's point of view is obscure and requires lengthy analysis (as is the case, for example, when it comes to discussing the self-evident nature of her "axiomatic concepts," the relationship between wealth and morality, and such), a full explanation of the principles summarized in the first part of the study must necessarily await information and arguments which are developed in the later chapters.

I have made every attempt throughout this study to be accurate, objective and fair. This is not always easy in dealing with any body of philosophical thought. It is particularly difficult in dealing with Rand, because she has not written her philosophy as an overall and systematized whole but, rather, as a series of discrete pieces which frequently deal with specific problems which are only indirectly related to the usual sort of philosophical issues. Even where she deals with purely philosophical problems—as, for example, in the essays that are contained in the book *For the New Intellectual* and in her articles (now a separate monograph) which comprise her "Introduction to Objectivist Epistemology," she does not, on the whole, deal with these topics in the usual step-by-step academic way but tends to veer off into polemics and digressions of various kinds. In addition, and quite in common with virtually all other philosophers, she is guilty of occasional inconsistencies, contradictions and ambiguities.

Where Miss Rand is not entirely clear about significant points, I have attempted to resolve the confusion by a sort of analytical triangulation-process, using context and emphasis as well as general coherency with respect to her overall position as my guides. This has not always resolved all doubt—particularly with respect to some of her more basic assumptions—but it has worked quite well in most instances.

Wherever I have found myself in strong disagreement with Miss Rand in the initial, or non-critical, phase of this study, I have attempted to "suspend disbelief" and become, empathically, a temporary objectivist in order to make the most persuasive and sympathetic presentation of her basic point of view. In almost all instances, I have attempted to document my presentation of the objectivist position by citing appropriate quotations from the writings of Miss Rand and her primary exponents. I have never purposefully used quotations which would misrepresent the objectivist position by being taken out of context. Where this seems possible, I have attempted to make the context of the quotation quite explicit.

I have used many quotations from the objectivist literature in an effort to corroborate my statements. I have done this for two reasons. First, I wanted, where possible, to preserve the flavor—and particularly the polemical nature and the air of emotional commitment—which pervades most of the objectivist writings. Second, I have worked to avoid, wherever possible, paraphrasing positions which, being extreme, might have a strong tendency to appear caricatured if rephrased by a less than sympathetic eye.

There is nothing particularly sacred about the way in which I have subdivided Miss Rand's philosophy into an ordered sequence of particular points. These points simply provide a classification scheme which provides a somewhat greater degree of clarity than is ordinarily present in Miss Rand's own organization and which therefore facilitates a more ready grasp of the concepts involved. As is always true with conceptual classifications, the points themselves are somewhat arbitrary and could well have been fused into larger points or even, if necessary, further fragmented to provide an even longer list of particulars. Also, and as in any conceptual breakdown of an otherwise integrated system, there is a certain amount of unavoidable redundancy among the points themselves.

The second half of this study consists of a critical analysis of Miss Rand's philosophy of objectivism. This analysis must necessarily be prefaced by three important considerations.

To begin with, I assume that the reader has read the first part of the study and is therefore generally familiar with the objectivist philosophy before progressing on to this latter section. While I have, in several

9

instances, attempted to rephrase the gist of the positions discussed in summary form prior to undertaking any sort of critical analysis, these paraphrases are necessarily less satisfactory representations than those presented in the preliminary non-critical presentation of the objectivist point of view where I have drawn more heavily upon Miss Rand's own words.

In addition, it is important to note that this critical analysis is not intended to be either exhaustive or definitive. The intention throughout is quite expressly to deal with Miss Rand's *basic premises* and not to become side-tracked into an interminable discussion of her secondary and derivative points of view with respect to less basic philosophical problems. I have, in short, and quite in line with Miss Rand's own directives, sought to "check her premises" on the assumption that, if such premises are discreditable, it is scarcely worthwhile to engage in lengthy disquisitions with respect to the secondary manifestations of error. In line with this, then, and as I hope will be quite evident in the critical phase of the study, I have centered my attention on Miss Rand's more basic philosophical propositions and have been only incidentally concerned with how these propositions have been expressed in such specific areas as politics or economics, education or esthetics.

Finally, insofar as possible, I have tried to be objective in my analysis and have attempted, wherever feasible, to operate by means of *internal criticism.* I have, in other words, tried to criticize Miss Rand's philosophy, not so much from *my own point of view,* but, wherever possible, *from her own,* applying the generally accepted principles of logic to the various objectivist positions. This means that I have been concerned, not so much with the *content* of Miss Rand's philosophy *per se*—not, that is, so much with *what* she says—as with the more basic question of whether or not *whatever she says makes sense.* This has entailed a consideration of two basic questions with respect to all of the more fundamental objectivist principles: (1) Are they *rational* (valid) with respect to other fundamental objectivist principles? (2) Are they *true* in the sense of being verifiable (at least in principle) with respect to accepted standards for the empirical confirmation of knowledge?

I have attempted to assess the rationality underlying Miss Rand's ideas in two ways: (1) by determining whether her statements are *directly* coherent in and of themselves—whether, that is, they are consistent and non-contradictory when viewed as an integrated whole (and prior to any sort of deeper analysis with respect to what they *mean*)—and (2) whether they are *indirectly* coherent—whether, in short, any of the statements, taken either singly or in conjunction with others, imply a position which would necessarily preclude the truth or application of other aspects of objectivist thought.

The *truth* of objectivist theory is, of course, a substantially more complicated thing to determine than its *validity* (rationality) vis-a-vis its own basic assumptions. Here again two basic procedures have been used: semantic analysis and scientific verification.

It is very difficult to apply semantic analysis to Miss Rand's statements without rejecting all claims to objectivity. It can, after all, be said that Miss Rand's theory *is* precisely the way she *defines* her basic terms and that any attempt to alter or invalidate these meanings is necessarily an implicit rejection of her own fundamental assumptions about truth and value. This is quite true and, accordingly, I have not attempted to dispute the *meaning* of any of Miss Rand's terms or statements on substantive grounds. Instead, the only semantic criteria which have been used are criteria which Miss Rand herself quite explicitly approves of—ie; that the term or statement should be *explicit* (i.e., capable of being consciously comprehended in non-ambiguous terms), that it should be employed *consistently* in the same way, or (in lieu of the two above criteria) that it should at least not purport to be otherwise. In line with this, for example, it will be seen that my basic argument with Miss Rand's interpretation of the formal law of identity in logic is not that it is opposed to my own but, rather (1) that it is *ambiguous*—acting implicitly as an empirical principle and not merely (in the traditional sense) as a law of procedural logic—and (2) that it is used *inconsistently*—frequently being applied in the traditional sense as a purely formal principle and, at still other times, being used as an empirical criterion for the establishment of extra-logical self-evident facts. In both of these ways, Miss Rand's concept of rational "identity" deviates quite markedly from the Aristotelian principle which it purportedly represents. Phrased somewhat differently, then, my objection to Miss Rand's definition of the law of identity—to anticipate but one particular instance of disagreement—is not that it is irregular, or non-Aristotelian, but, rather, that it is ambiguous, that Miss Rand is guilty of being both inconsistent and contradictory in its use, that it purports to be that which it is not, and, finally, that Miss Rand herself seems largely oblivious to the fact that all of these things are true.

Still another area in which Miss Rand is open to vast criticism is that of empirical verification. Here, it must be admitted, it is necessary to drop all pretense of purely *objective* analysis in dealing with Miss

11

Rand's philosophy. The objectivist philosophy is fundamentally anti-scientific. It begins, not with *evidence* or hypotheses, but with *Truth*. Its first principles deal, not with the way of validating knowledge, but with the substantive nature and content of knowledge itself.

I would like to indicate quite explicitly, then, that I shall be criticizing Miss Rand's fundamental assumptions on empirical bases and that the criteria I am using are the accepted procedures for the scientific verification of knowledge. As a result, I have chosen to reject any statements or assumptions which are nonverifiable *in principle* (because they violate one or more of the fundamental conditions necessary for the application of scientific procedures for enquiry and verification) or which are scientifically discredited by virtue of being overwhelmingly disconfirmed by contemporary scientific findings.

In all likelihood, Miss Rand and her followers are not going to be dissuaded by this kind of evidence, because the basic assumptions of the scientific worldview are quite explicitly opposed to some of the most fundamental objectivist assumptions. Science has no *empirical content* of a non-procedural nature, and the only "absolute" scientific principles are those which comprise the experimental protocol of the scientific verification process itself. Science is, as Rand quite correctly senses, radically empirical, relativistic and—ultimately—pragmatic.

On the other hand, the advantages of approaching Miss Rand's philosophy from the point of view of scientific verification are compelling, for to use any philosophical criterion which are not fundamentally pragmatic and relativistic would be merely to accede to Miss Rand's own basis philosophical assumptions. It is pointless to argue dogmatism dogmatically on the basis of a counter-dogmatism which presupposes the same general sort of authoritarian philosophical assumptions with respect to the general nature of reality and which differs only in relationship to specific descriptions of absolute "Truth." It would, for example, be relatively fruitless to undertake a traditional Christian critique of Rand's philosophy, for, ironically, both Rand and the Christians are fundamentally variations of the same mystical and absolutistic *Weltanschauung* which starts with *a priori* concept of absolute truth and which remains totally inviolable in the face of any new evidence whatsoever.

Contemporary science has no fundamental argument with Rand's naturalism. Most scientists—if they are not merely compartmentalized technicians who fail to apply their scientific principles to the more

12

humanistic areas of existence—would probably be quite willing to accede to Miss Rand's propositions that all truths are restricted to statements about natural (empirical) phenomena and that all values are, in a similar respect, grounded in the conative or affective aspects of human nature. Indeed, most would probably be quite willing to concede that Miss Rand has every right to oppose the use of scientific verification procedures in determining fundamental truth if she likes. They would also maintain, however, that, in so doing, she relinquishes her right to deprecate the absence of a "scientific ethic"[26] or to talk as if her own anti-scientific orientation were in some peculiar way compatible with, or even supported by, the findings of modern science itself.

The only alternatives to using scientific verification as one of the criteria for criticizing Miss Rand's position, then, are twofold. One possibility is to accept Miss Rand's own basic definitions and assumptions, thereby restricting oneself to *interior* problems with respect to such purely procedural matters as logic—for example, "Does the law of identity, as defined by Rand, necessitate the doctrine of enlightened selfishness?"—or legitimacy—e.g., "Does Rand's concept of identity correspond to Aristotle's concept of identity?" The other alternative is to accept her basic position of metaphysical absolutism and merely to object to her particular descriptions of reality—e.g., "Granting that truth is absolute, how can one say that God is not self-evidently 'real'?" In the first case, one concedes virtually her entire argument. In the second, one concedes her general position *vis-a-vis* the nature of truth and disagrees only with respect to its particular content—e.g., "Does God exist or not?" "Should men be treated as means or as ends?" and so on.

A Few Additional Considerations

Before discussing Miss Rand's philosophy—and particularly in view of the somewhat negative critique which comprises the latter part of this study—I would like to make several qualifying and, I hope, generally positive remarks with respect to her overall point of view.

First of all, and what might otherwise go unremarked, there are many nice things which can be said about Miss Rand's ideas which unfortunately tend to become obscured in the process of long and, I am afraid, somewhat negative analysis.

To begin with, and while Miss Rand's *answers* may be wrong, her *questions* are frequently right. She is occasionally very acute in her

13

diagnosis of contemporary intellectual pathologies and cultural disorders. She also has a number of relevant and provocative things to say about such questions as alienation, conformity and the deteriorating state of modern philosophy. Right or wrong, she "speaks" loud and clear to many people, and she is obviously addressing herself to real areas of concern. This is reflected in the enthusiastic reception she is currently receiving, particularly among members of the younger (pre-thirty-five) generation. Miss Rand's answers may not be appropriate, but she has obviously tapped a real need for deep and intelligent discussion of such topics as "commitment," "individualism," "free will" and the nature of moral responsibility. She has properly assessed the popular discontent with the current vacuum in such areas as moral philosophy and relevant religion. Like the existentialists whom she abhors, her negations tend to be far more profound than her affirmations. On the other hand, a negation is also a sort of reverse affirmation. Even disagreeing with Miss Rand, one is frequently aware of a more fundamental and visceral agreement with her identification of the problems and with her deep sense of urgency in working toward some kind of solutions.

Still another point which should be made in Miss Rand's favor is that she has provoked many people into thinking—frequently for the first time—about their most basic assumptions with respect to such primary considerations as the nature of reality and the good life. It is no indictment of either altruism or democracy to suggest that most people are neither altruistic nor democratic *on principle* but merely out of unreflective habit based on prerational emotional conditioning. One of the great virtues of the objectivist point of view—and quite regardless of its truth or validity—is that it provides us with a place to stand outside of our ordinary ways of looking at things and, in so doing, it gives us precisely that sort of intellectual perspective which is required to fully comprehend, and possibly even reaffirm, our own non-objectivistic patterns of belief. Whatever else Miss Rand may have achieved, she continues to serve as a useful intellectual catalyst in a society which frequently suffers from philosophical "tired blood."

In addition, of course, Miss Rand is frequently guilty of being "right" for the wrong reasons. Many who would, for example, be in fundamental agreement with her doctrine of rational egoism would also disagree rather violently with the vague and somewhat mystical premises upon which she establishes her position. In a similar sense, she occasionally comes up with a very interesting and highly plausible idea—as, for example, her concept of the "sense of life"—which is fundamentally inconsistent with the gist of her overall theory or, on other occasions, with a highly plausible and significant insight—as, for example, her concept of psycho-epistemology—which she effectively distorts beyond recognition to suit the purposes of her more specific moral commitment to *laissez-faire* capitalism.

Whatever criticism one may have of the objectivist philosophy, however, it is difficult to accuse Miss Rand of any lack of either intellectual or moral courage. Considering the strong psychological relationship which typically exists between the extreme sort of economic conservatism which Miss Rand espouses and a variety of old-fashioned authoritarian attitudes with respect to most other significant social issues, it must be said that Miss Rand has demonstrated remarkable restraint by making no attempt to court favor with established right-wing groups and has consistently refused to ameliorate her singularly unorthodox opinions with respect to race, religion and country—opinions which are scarcely designed to elicit vast enthusiasm in most traditional "conservative" circles. She continues to reject the Judeo-Christian ethic, to look upon the national collective as a necessary evil, and to regard racism as "the lowest, most crudely primitive form of collectivism."[2][7]

In a world of increasingly innocuous philosophies, Miss Rand's point of view is refreshingly abrasive. Objectivism is not an ingenuous philosophy which is designed to attract popular approval in a culture which is largely founded on diametrically-opposed principles of belief and action. This may explain part of its popularity, for it provides a marvelous source of "protest commitment" which has a strong appeal to the more youthful members of the middle-class who find themselves suffering from the anguish of over-adjustment and who seek the outrageous as an antidote for the banality of their everyday lives. The fact remains, however, that Miss Rand has persistently avoided capitulating to either her enemies or her friends. However "extremist" her ideas may be, she has avoided the traditional extremist techniques of directing emotional invective and vilification against all of those who take exception to her point of view, and she has been equally opposed to adopting the expedient course of making common-cause with all of those fringe groups who happen to agree with some aspect of her program for the wrong reasons.

Finally, it must be conceded that Miss Rand has accomplished a formidable task. Whatever its imperfections, she has completed a systematic theodicy of capitalism, a theoretical rationale for the free enterprise system. Despite vast and fatal flaws, she had succeeded in presenting a philosophy which is simple, original, clearly defined and (at least implicitly) systematic. Within its own established context of assumptions, it is also surprisingly comprehensive, coherent and consistent. It addresses itself to the solution of significant problems, and it culminates in a practical plan of action. If it were *true*, it would be a masterpiece. It is, at the very least, an impressive failure.[28]

AYN RAND AND POLITICAL CONSERVATISM

Miss Rand is frequently regarded as a type of extreme right-wing conservative. There is an element of truth in the contention, but it is far from being entirely accurate.

In a general sense, Miss Rand has very little sympathy with traditional reactionary conservatism. She is not an admirer of the late Senator McCarthy[29] or of the John Birch Society[30] and she expresses vast reservations about the positions espoused by such an exemplar of contemporary conservatism as Barry Goldwater. What she seems to be primarily distressed about is the passivity and superficiality of contemporary conservatism. "It took," she states, "the so-called 'conservatives,' the alleged defenders of capitalism, to create the Antitrust laws. And it takes the intellectual superficiality of today's 'conservatives' to continue supporting these laws, in spite of their meaning, record and results."[31] She particularly deprecates the sort of political activity which has no ideological basis except habit and expediency, the sort of activity which results in "that embarrassing conglomeration of impotence, futility, inconsistency and superficiality which is loosely designated today as 'conservatism',"[32] and which has, as its common denominator, "a folksy 'cracker-barrel,' mass oriented kind of anti-intellectual reliance on faith ('the heart') and on 'tradition.' "[33]

The followers of objectivism are not, then, "conservatives" in the usual sense of the word. They are, rather, "radicals for capitalism [who are] fighting for that philosophical base which capitalism did not have and without which it was doomed to perish."[34]

As Miss Rand sees it, the basic problem which faces the world today is "the conflict between capitalism and altruism [which] has been undercutting America from her start and, today, has reached its

16

climax."[35] "The basic issue in the world today is between two principles: Individualism and Collectivism."[36]

The fundamental problem confronting the contemporary world is "the role of mind in man's existence."[37] As Miss Rand states, ". . .the basic conflict of our age is *not* merely political or economic, but moral and philosophical . . . the so-called 'redistribution of wealth' is only a superficial manifestation of the mysticism-altruism-collectivism axis . . . "[38] An inevitable corollary of this problem is the redefinition of public morality—the formulation of a new ethics of rational self-interest.[39]

The only solution to this problem is to revive the basic principles of laissez-faire capitalism, for "these, implicitly, were the political principles on which the Constitution of the United States was based . . ."[40]

The difficulty with capitalism is that it has always lacked any sort of sufficient philosophical justification or moral defense. "As a resurgent tide of Mysticism engulfed philosophy in the nineteenth century, capitalism was left in an intellectual vacuum . . . Neither its moral nature nor even its political principles has ever been fully understood or defined."[41]

What Miss Rand proposes is at basis a *"moral revolution,"*[42] a revolution fought *"ideologically,* on *moral-intellectual* grounds."[43] This revolution will be hastened by the fact that ". . . statism . . . has collapsed as an intellectual power or a cultural ideal. The altruist-collectivist creed has run its course . . . In today's intellectual vacuum, it holds a position of leadership only by default."[44] "Today, [the liberals'] perfunctory advocacy of collectivism is as feeble, futile and evasive as the alleged conservatives' defense of capitalism. The fire and the moral fervor have gone out of it."[45]

This moral revolution will not be won by the old-fashioned conservatives, however, for the real "conservatives," are those in their mid-fifties and beyond who grew up before the first world war and who took capitalism as a self-evident truth "refusing to take notice of its cracking ideological foundations, maintaining an attitude of stubbornly stagnant anti-intellectuality, [trying] to stem a philosophical flood by means of a few stale slogans—and [letting] freedom slip through their limp fingers."[46] In a similar respect, it will not be won by those in the 35 to 50 age-group, for these have been brainwashed by the New Deal era and "are riding a dead intellectual horse."[47]

It is those under 40 who will be the champions of the new radical capitalism,[48] and they will be guided by the objectivist philosophy, a philosophy which Miss Rand synopsizes as follows:

1. *Metaphysics:* Objective Reality
2. *Epistemology:* Reason
3. *Ethics:* Self-interest
4. *Politics:* Capitalism[49]

(In less formal terms, Miss Rand paraphrases this synopsis as follows: "1. 'Nature, to be commanded, must be obeyed' or 'Wishing won't make it so.' 2. 'You can't eat your cake and have it, too.' 3. 'Man is an end in himself.' 4. 'Give me liberty or give me death.' ")[50]

As Rand sees it, the required course of action is apparent: "The road is now left clear for those who know that the battle has to be fought on *moral-intellectual* grounds, those who are willing ... to build the philosophical foundation which freedom and capitalism have never possessed ... "[51] "The power of Objectivism ... lies in the fact that its adherents ... have a rational, consistent and comprehensive frame-of-reference in which to judge ideas and events—and who are moved by an authentic *moral* enthusiasm."[52]

AYN RAND AND CONTEMPORARY PHILOSOPHY

Miss Rand holds virtually all of modern philosophy in the utmost contempt. This contempt extends in large part to most contemporary "intellectuals" as well. As she states: "... it was the intellectuals who reversed the trend toward political freedom and revised the doctrines of the absolute State ... of the government's right to control the lives of the citizens in any manner it pleases."[53]

The treason of the intellectuals is perhaps best exemplified by the vacuous and sterile wasteland of modern philosophy. "... never before has the world been clamoring so desperately for answers to crucial problems—and never before has the world been so frantically committed to the belief that no answers are possible."[54]

Partly by default, partly by commission, then, we find ourselves devoid of standards, deprived of any sort of satisfactory moral and intellectual vision. "A major symptom of a man's—or a culture's—intellectual and moral disintegration is the shrinking of vision and goals to the concrete-bound range of the immediate moment."[55]

18

We must regain the capacity to regard the world in terms of principles.[56]

While it is scarcely a new phenomenon, the deterioration of philosophy can be observed in almost all aspects of significant human experience. In the post-Kantian world a series of philosophical "anti-Aristotelian" heresies have done progressive violence to the cause of objective intelligence. Pragmatism strengthened irrational tendencies toward expediency and subjectivism. Logical positivism has sought to reduce Truth to a matter of semantic disputation. Finally, linguistic analysis has sought to restrict philosophy to the clarification of meaning in everyday speech. "This was the final stroke of philosophy breaking its moorings and floating off, like a lighter-than-air balloon, losing any semblance of connection to reality, any relevance to the problems of man's existence."[57]

Ranging from the incomprehensible mysticism of Zen to "the underlying irrationalism of the analytic movement,"[58] modern philosophy has descended "into a nightmare blend of neo-mysticism and unutterable triviality."[59] This collapse is perhaps best observed in the case of pragmatism, a philosophy admirably designed to produce "The psychoepistemological savage who believes that reality is indeterminate, that facts are fluid ... that concretes will not add up to a sum if he rejects abstractions and principles."[60] Pragmatism—a philosophy "which holds ... that objectivity consists of collective subjectivism, that whatever people wish to be true, *is* true, whatever people wish to exist, *does* exist—provided a *consensus* say so,"[61] has made it possible for intellectuals "to be *unprincipled on principle.'*[62]

The pernicious effect of this paralyzing relativity and chaotic subjectivism are readily apparent in our colleges and universities where more and more classes can be described as merely "words, words, words, paper, paper, paper."[63] Ironically, the worst victims of this pathological pseudo-intellectualism are the students of philosophy themselves. "Who are the neo-mystics victims?" inquires Nathaniel Branden. "Any college student who enrolls in philosophy courses, eagerly seeking a rational, comprehensive view of man and existence — and who is led to surrender the conviction that his mind can have any efficacy whatever."[64]

The tragedy is that the college years are precisely the time when some kind of general insight and overall commitment is required. It is also the time when the student is most receptive to *positive* intellectual suggestions, when he actively seeks a viable set of ideals to live by.

19

" . . . some never give up the quest; but the majority are open to the voice of philosophy for a few brief years. These last are the permanent, if not innocent, victims of modern philosophy."[65] "Most of them endure their college years with the teeth-clenched determination of serving out a jail sentence. The psychological scars that they acquire in the process are incalculable."[66]

The only solution, states Rand, is a philosophical renaissance. We must return to essential reality, to objective Being, and this can only be attained by returning to the philosophical principles first encountered by that "philosophical Atlas who carries the whole Western civilization on his shoulders," Aristotle.[67]

REFERENCES–CHAPTER I

1.   Miss Rand's major publications to date consist of eight works, her four major novels–*Anthem, We the Living, The Fountainhead* and *Atlas Shrugged*–and the four major works of nonfiction–*For the New Intellectual; The Virtue of Selfishness: A New Concept of Egoism, Capitalism: The Unknown Ideal*, and *The Romantic Manifesto: A Philosophy of Literature*. There are, in addition to these, a variety of materials available on the philosophy of objectivism which are available in article and pamphlet form. A complete listing of the available pamphlets as well as back issues of *The Objectivist Newsletter* and *The Objectivist* can be obtained by writing *The Objectivist*, 201 East 34th St., New York City, New York (10016). In addition to these, The Objectivist Book Service, Inc: (210 East 34th St., New York City, New York (10016) recommends additional reading (going as far afield as Sir Walter Scott and Victor Hugo) for serious students of objectivism. The Objectivist organization also offers a number of lecture series, among them *The Basic Principles of Objectivism: The Philosophy of Ayn Rand*. This course, which costs $40.00 (1966) for the entire series was offered by the Institute in over eighty cities in the United States as well as overseas. Outside the New York City, the courses are given primarily through the medium of tape transcriptions. At present several courses are being sponsored by *The Objectivist* (mostly in the New York City area), and tapes of lectures are available to groups of ten or more interested people on a rental basis. Information about these lectures and lecture courses can be obtained by writing Dr. Robert Hessen, Box 165B, Skillman, New Jersey (08558).

20

2. Nathaniel Branden maintains that Ayn Rand's antagonists pay her the highest tribute possible because they misrepresent her ideas in order to attack them. "No one," states Branden, "has dared publicly to name the essential ideas of *Atlas Shrugged* and to attempt to refute them." (Nathaniel Branden, *Who Is Ayn Rand?* New York: Random House–Paperback Library, 1962, page 51.)

Miss Rand herself is extremely sensitive to the rather cavalier treatment she has received at the hands of the academic community. She is particularly critical of what she terms the *Argument from Intimidation* which, according to Rand, is particularly prevalent in college classrooms where professors seek "to stifle independent thinking among the students, to evade questions they cannot answer, to discourage any critical analysis of their arbitrary assumptions or any departure from the intellectual status quo." (Ayn Rand, "The Argument from Intimidation," *The Virtue of Selfishness,* New York: Random House–Signet, 1961, pp. 142-3.) The Argument from Intimidation consists of *"substituting* moral judgment for intellectual argument." *(Ibid.)* "All smears are Arguments from Intimidation: they consist of derogatory assertions without any evidence or proof, offered as a substitute for evidence of proof, aimed at the moral cowardice or unthinking credulity of the hearers." *(Ibid.)*

It should be added that the difficulty involved in analyzing Ayn Rand's philosophy is compounded by several special problems. To begin with, Miss Rand is extremely reluctant to have her ideas expressed by anyone who is not an officially-sanctioned spokesman for "Objectivism." She and her supporters tend to view any unsympathetic and therefore unauthorized presentations of the Objectivist position as verging on a violation of copyright and implicitly trespassing on her intellectual property. This difficulty is augmented by the fact that they are inclined to denounce any paraphrase as either inaccurate or misrepresentative of her actual views. (One cannot, for example, analyze Miss Rand's position vis-a-vis "reason" without using other terms unless one is willing to concede Miss Rand's point of view to begin with, because she tends to use the term quite improperly to encompass a variety of quite separate operations which are commonly described by a number of other words. (See Chapter V.) This throws the potential critic into something of a "double bind" situation: if he quotes beyond the barest requirements of textual criticism or factual corroboration, he runs the risk of litigation. If he does not quote, he places himself in jeopardy of being charged with gross inaccuracy or willful falsification. This difficulty is further exaggerated by the fact that many of Rand's ideas (see Part II) are often ambiguous, inconsistent or contradictory. This is particularly true of her epistemology where she has gone to the extraordinary length of developing a highly involved and very relativistic epistemological theory (her *Introduction to Objectivist Epistemology)* in order to backstop earlier epistemological and metaphysical contentions which not only bear little relationship to such a posteriori analysis but which are fundamentally inconsistent with, and even contradicted by, it. (In a sense, this is a clever defensive maneuver, because she can now use the formal ep-

21

istemology—which is inconsistent with her overall position—to refute those who criticize her basic assumptions on the grounds that they do not make good epistemological sense. Most Objectivists, however, could not care less about her labored, after-the-fact epistemological speculations and are quite content with the far more naive ideas that undergird her original position. At the same time, however, she has the advantage of being able to counter her intellectual critics by referring them to her more recent epistemological speculations *as if* they were germane to her overall point of view and provided some sort of intellectual rationale for it.)

This is not to say that Objectivists are willing to recognize such inconsistency in Miss Rand's work. For many of her followers, Rand functions very much like a Rorschach test. It is precisely her vast ambiguity, disguised by misleading intellectual rhetoric, which allows them to project their own emotional predispositions into her open-ended pseudo-profundities like "Existence exists." For such people, any clarification of Rand's thoughts which exposes her underlying inner contradictions must be a misrepresentation, because Miss Rand's is "true" by definition. In short, she says she is, and they are quite willing to acquiesce to her self-evaluation. (It might be added that perhaps Miss Rand's favorite type of verification is self-quotation. She never tires of quoting her own eloquent words, frequently expressed by various characters in her novels, in order to establish a point. *Atlas Shrugged* frequently assumes the proportions of sacred writ in her subsequent writings.)

3. Nathaniel Branden, "A Report to Our Readers—1965," *The Objectivist Newsletter*, IV, 12 (December 1965), page 57.
4. Nathaniel Branden, "A Report to Our Readers—1964," *The Objectivist Newsletter*, III, 12 (December 1964), page 51.
5. Nathaniel Branden, "A Report to Our Readers—1965," *op. cit.*, page 58. The statistics cited here are somewhat dated but, to the best of my knowledge, no more recent information has been published about the scope and extent of the Institute's activities.
6. *Ibid.*, page 57; also Nathaniel Branden, "A Report to Our Readers—1964," *op. cit.*, page 51.
7. Nathaniel Branden, "A Report to Our Readers—1965," *op. cit.*, page 57.
8. Nathaniel Branden, "A Report to Our Readers—1964," *op. cit.*, page 51.
9. Nathaniel Branden, "A Report to Our Readers—1963," *The Objectivist Newsletter*, II, 12 (December 1963), page 47. Also Nathaniel Branden, "A Report to Our Readers—1964," *op. cit.*, page 51.
10. Nathaniel Branden, "A Report to Our Readers—1965," *op. cit.*, page 57.
11. Nathaniel Branden, "A Report to Our Readers—1963," *op cit.*, page 47.
12. *The Objectivist*, VI, 6 (June, 1967), page 16.
13. This column first appeared on June 17, 1962, and last appeared sometime in 1965.
14. *The Objectivist Newsletter*, III, 10 (October 1964), page 44.
15. *The Objectivist*, VI, 7 (July, 1967), page 15.
16. Nathaniel Branden, "A Report to Our Readers—1965," *op. cit.*, page 58.

17. *Ibid.*
18. *The Objectivist Newsletter,* II, 9 (September, 1963), page 36.
19. Nathaniel Branden, "A Report to Our Readers—1965," *op. cit.,* page 58.
20. Ayn Rand, "For the New Intellectual," in *For the New Intellectual* (New York: Random House—Signet, 1961), page 18.
21. *Ibid.,* pp. 16-17.
22. Nathaniel Branden, "An Analysis of the Novels of Ayn Rand," in Nathaniel Branden and Barbara Branden, *Who Is Ayn Rand?* (New York: Random House-Paperback Library, 1962), page 38.
23. In January of 1966, the monthly *Objectivist Newsletter* was enlarged, provided with a new format and retitled *The Objectivist. The Objectivist* is a profit-making and self-supporting publication. (The now defunct Nathaniel Branden Institute was owned solely by Nathaniel Branden, and Mr. Branden was for several years co-owner with Miss Rand of *The Objectivist.*)
24. Nathaniel Branden, "Message to Our Readers," *The Objectivist Newsletter,* IV, 4 (April, 1965), page 17.
25. *Ibid.*
26A. Rand, "To Whom It May Concern," *The Objectivist,* VII, 5 (May 1968), page 1.
26B. *Ibid.,* page 5.
26. Ayn Rand, "To Young Scientists." *The Objectivist Newsletter,* I, 10 (October, 1962), page 41. The term "science" is used here in reference to the "scientific process," to a particular type of verification-procedure used with respect to assertions about empirical fact. Miss Rand has no basic argument with particular scientific conclusions or with the use of the scientific process as a means of substantiating subordinate "technical" questions with respect to natural phenomena which pose no significant threat to her more basic "objective" assumptions about the nature of knowing and the known.
27. Ayn Rand, "Racism," in *The Virtue of Selfishness: A New Concept of Egoism* (New York: Random House—Signet, 1961), page 126. As Miss Rand sees it (and excepting the non-industrial and non-capitalist Southern states where state government was used to maintain slavery) the government's intervention into private business was very slight during the early years of American capitalism. " . . . the government's role was predominantly confined to its proper function: that of a policeman and arbiter charged with the task of protecting the individual citizen's rights and property." (Ayn Rand, *The Intellectual Bankruptcy of Our Age,* New York: The Nathaniel Branden Institute, 1961, page 10.)

     Miss Rand makes occasional comments which cast some doubt upon her professed contempt for collectivistic chauvinism. In her article "How to Judge a Political Candidate," for example, she expresses dismay "that the United States of America should be brought down to a level where it is being insulted and defied by Panama . . . ." (Ayn Rand, "How to Judge a Political Candidate," *The Objectivist Newsletter,* III, 3, March 1964, page 10.) "When Barry Goldwater keeps stressing the theme of 'national honor,' it is the first and only sound of hope–a sound of a human step–in the truly unbelievable abyss of a great nation's gratuitous, suicidal self-abasement." *(Ibid.)*

Her attitude toward racism also requires a certain amount of analysis and warrants a good deal of healthy skepticism. See Chapter VII.

Rand takes a particularly interesting stance with respect to women. On the whole, she is a staunch advocate of women's rights. On the other hand, she adds that she would not vote for a woman as President of the United States on psychological grounds. (Rand, "An Answer to Readers About a Woman President)", *The Objectivist* VII, 12 (December 1968), page 1). As she explains it, "The essence of femininity is hero-worship–the desire to look up to a man." *(Ibid.)* Such worship, she notes "is an abstract emotion for the *metaphysical* concept of masculinity as such–which [the woman] experiences fully and completely only for the man she loves, but which colors her attitude toward all men." *(Ibid.,* page 2). Since the President deals only with inferiors in terms of status and responsibility, *"this* would be an unbearable situation for a truly rational woman. To act as the superior, the leader, virtually the *ruler* of all the men she deals with, would be an excruciating psychological torture." *(Ibid.,* page 2).

28.   Interestingly enough, Miss Rand's philosophy, with all of its imperfections, is probably doomed to academic immortality. It meets all of the required standards to be included in the usual college curriculum in philosophy:

1) It is simple and therefore readily comprehensible.

2) It is extreme and therefore memorable.

3) It is dogmatic and can therefore be classified easily in relationship to other points of view.

4) It is a position which has been lacking in formal philosophy (ever since the recognition that science is implicitly founded upon a pragmatic base) to exemplify the formal philosophical category of what might be termed "non-theistic essentialistic realism."

5) It is untenable and can therefore be used for purposes of philosophical one-up-manship by professors of philosophy who can easily demonstrate their own intellectual superiority over all comers by disposing of still another patently implausible point of view.

29.   Ayn Rand, " 'Extremism' or the Art of Smearing," *The Objectivist Newsletter,* III, 9 (September 1964) page 37.

30.   ". . . I don't want to be lumped with anyone, and certainly not with the John Birch Society . . . I consider the Birch Society futile, because they are not *for* capitalism, but merely *against* communism." (Rand, *Playboy's* Interview with Ayn Rand," New York: Nathaniel Branden Institute, 1964, page 14.)

31.   Ayn Rand, "Antitrust: The Rule of Unreason," *The Objectivist Newsletter,* I, 2 (February 1962), page 5.

32.   Ayn Rand, "Choose Your Issues," *The Objectivist Newsletter,* I, 1 (January 1962), page 1.

33.   Ayn Rand, "It is Earlier than You Think," *The Objectivist Newsletter,* III, 12 (December 1964), page 50.

34. Ayn Rand, "Choose Your Issues," *The Objectivist Newsletter,* I, 1 (January 1962), page 1.

35. Ayn Rand, *Conservatism: An Obituary* (New York: Nathaniel Branden Institute, 1962), page 10.

36. Ayn Rand, *Textbook of Americanism* (New York: The Nathaniel Branden Institute, 1946), page 3.

37. Ayn Rand, "Is Atlas Shrugging?" *The Objectivist Newsletter,* III, 8 (August 1964), page 29.

38. *Ibid.*

39. *Ibid.*

40. Ayn Rand, *America's Persecuted Minority: Big Business* (New York: Nathaniel Branden Institute, 1962), page 5.

41. Ayn Rand, "What is Capitalism?" *The Objectivist Newsletter,* IV, 12 (December 1965), page 60.

42. *Ayn Rand, Faith and Force: The Destroyers of the Modern World* (New York: The Nathaniel Branden Institute, 1960), page 12.

43. Ayn Rand, "The Cashing-in. The Student 'Rebellion' (Part III)," *The Objectivist Newsletter,* IV, 9.

44. Ayn Rand, *The Fascist New Frontier* (New York: The Nathaniel Branden Institute.

45. Ayn Rand, *Faith and Force: The Destroyers of the Modern World* (New York: The Nathaniel Branden Institute, 1960), page 10.

46. Ayn Rand, "It is Earlier than You Think," *The Objectivist Newsletter,* 12 (December 1964), page 52.

47. *Ibid.*

48. Ayn Rand, "It is Earlier than You Think," *The Objectivist Newsletter,* III, 12 (December 1964), page 52.

49. Ayn Rand, "Introducing Objectivism," *The Objectivist Newsletter,* I, 8 (August 1962), page 35.

50. *Ibid.* In the opening lecture of this course "Basic Principles of Objectivism," Nathaniel Branden offers an excellent summary of the objectivist philosophy. In essence, he holds that it is characterized by seven principles: (1) that reality is "independent of anyone's knowledge," (Nathaniel Branden, from an advertising brochure, New York: Nathaniel Branden Institute, n.d.) (2) that reason is fully capable of comprehending the nature of reality as it is; (3) that man's perception of the facts provides the basis for his value-judgments and subsequent behavior; (4) "that man is an end in himself . . . he must live for his own sake with the achievement of his rational self-interest as the moral purpose of his life" (*Ibid.*); (5) that no one has the right to force another to sacrifice himself or his interests through the use of physical force; (6) that the socio-economic system implied by these objectivist principles is laissez-faire capitalism; and (7) that the neglect or negation of these principles is responsible for the dismal state of the contemporary world. (*Ibid.*)

51. Ayn Rand, "It is Earlier than You Think," *The Objectivist Newsletter,* III, 12 (December 1964), page 52.

52. Nathaniel Branden, "A Report to Our Readers—1964," *op. cit.,* page 51.

53. Ayn Rand, *Faith and Force: The Destroyers of the Modern World* (New York: The Nathaniel Branden Institute, 1960), page 10.
54. *Ibid.,* page 3.
55. Ayn Rand, "The Anatomy of Compromise," *The Objectivist Newsletter,* III, 1 (January 1964), page 1.
56. *Ibid.*
57. Ayn Rand, "The Cashing-in: The Student 'Rebellion' (Part II)," *The Objectivist Newsletter,* IV, 8 (August 1965), page 33.
58. Nathaniel Branden, Review of the book *Reason and Analysis* by Brand Blanshard, *The Objectivist Newsletter,* II, 2 (February 1963), page 8.
59. *Ibid.,* page 6.
60. Ayn Rand, "How to Judge a Political Candidate," *The Objectivist Newsletter,* III, 3 (March 1964), page 9.
61. Ayn Rand, "The New Fascism," *The Objectivist Newsletter,* IV, 6 (June 1965), page 26.
62. *Ibid.*
63. Ayn Rand, "The Cashing-in: The Student 'Rebellion' (Part II)," *The Objectivist Newsletter,* IV, 8 (August 1965), page 34.
64. Nathaniel Branden, "The Stolen Concept," *The Objectivist Newsletter,* II, 1 (January 1963), page 4.
65. Ayn Rand, "The Cashing-in: The Student 'Rebellion' (Part II)," *The Objectivist Newsletter,* IV, 8 (August 1965), page 34.
66. *Ibid.,* page 38.
67. Ayn Rand, Review of the book *Aristotle* by John Herman Randall, Jr., *The Objectivist Newsletter,* II, (May 1963), page 18.

Chapter II

KNOWING AND THE KNOWN

Ayn Rand's theory of knowledge centers about three basic
principles: the self-evident nature of *a priori* truth, the objectivity of
value and the "natural" (sense-empirical) basis of all knowledge.

SELF-EVIDENT TRUTH

There is only one reality, states Rand, and therefore one truth. This
reality is "objective" in the sense that it exists prior to being known
and is not therefore contingent upon personal experience. Such truth is
a priori, self-evident and indubitable. "Metaphysically," states Rand,
"the only authority is reality; epistemologically—one's own mind. The
first is the ultimate arbiter of the second."[1] "The concept of
objectivity contains the reason why the question 'Who decides what is
right or wrong?' is wrong. Nobody *'decides.'* Nature does not *decide* —it
merely *is;* man does not *decide,* in issues of knowledge, he merely
observes that which is."[2A] " 'Nature, to be commanded, must be
obeyed.' This means that man does not *create* reality and can achieve
his values only by making his decisions consonant with the facts of
reality."[2]

The basic axiom of Miss Rand's philosophy is that *existence exists.* [3]
As protagonist John Galt states in her epic novel *Atlas Shrugged:* "We,
the men of the mind, are now on strike against you [the parasites] in
the name of a single axiom, which is the root of our moral code . . . the
axiom that *existence exists.* "[4]

The principle that *existence exists* implies two corollary axioms:
"(1) that something exists which one perceives and (2) that one exists
possessing consciousness, *consciousness being the faculty of perceiving
that which exists."*[5] "Whether you know the shape of a pebble or the
structure of a solar system, the axioms remain the same: that *it* exists
and that you *know* it."[6]

For Rand the axiom that *existence exists* is substantially

synonymous with Aristotle's principle of identity. As she notes: "To exist is to be something, as distinguished from the nothing of non-existence, it is to be an entity of a specific nature made of specific attributes ... Existence is Identity, Consciousness is Identification."[7]

At basis, Miss Rand's fundamental position with respect to underlying reality (Truth) may be summarized in three points:

1) Reality is what it is—that is, what it is immediately apprehended to be.

2) Everyone comprehends that reality *is* what it is—that is, all men implicitly know the Truth.

3) The basic problem with respect to knowing stems, not from a lack of knowledge, but, rather, from a tendency to deny, or to avoid recognizing, true knowledge for what it is. "The extreme you have always struggled to avoid is the recognition that reality is final, that A is A and that the truth is true."[8]

To know the truth is simply to recognize reality *for what it is*. Truth is apprehensible, however, only by means of reason. Reason, " ... the faculty that perceives, identifies and integrates the evidence of reality provided by man's senses,"[9] is man's means for acquiring the knowledge he needs to deal with existence.[10]

The most important truths are those formative principles—those basic premises—which are inherent within the processes of reason itself, that is, the laws of logic.[11]

The ultimate principle of formal logic is the law of identity. Indeed, logic *is*, ultimately, "the art of noncontradictory identification."[12] According to Rand, Aristotle's foremost contribution lies in his elucidation of the fact that reality is an "objective absolute" which exists independent of consciousness,[13] "that there is only *one* reality, the one which man perceives ... that abstractions are man's method of integrating his sensory material—that man's mind is his only tool of knowledge—that A is A."[14]

All of the additional principles of formal logic: contradiction, excluded-middle—even causality—are corollaries of the basic principle of identity. The law of causality is, for example, "the law of identity applied to action."[15] "All actions are caused by entities. The nature of an action is caused and determined by the nature of the entities that act: a thing cannot act in contradiction to its nature."[16]

28

With respect to economic gain, for example, Miss Rand appears to subscribe to the following line of reasoning:

1) Productive (practical) reason[17A] applied to the solution of real (objective) problems gives rise to profit (which *is* "objective value").

2) Profit is, then, the *effect* caused (or logically entailed) by the nature of its two constituent conditions (productive reason and material problems).

3) Therefore, productive reason *causes* profit and, conversely, any "profit" arising under different conditions—i.e., in the absence of productive reason—is, by logical (metaphysical) necessity, not "profit" at all but, rather, "counterfeit profit" which does not possess real (objective) value at all.

"Money is the scourge of the men who attempt to reverse the law of causality—the men who seek to replace the mind by seizing the products of the mind."[17] Just as causeless wealth is implausible, there is no such thing as causeless love. "An emotion is a response to a fact of reality, an estimate dictated by your standards. To love is to *value*."[18] To love a person who is regarded as worthless is as impossible as to grow rich by consuming without producing. "The links you strive to drown are causal connections. The enemy you seek to defeat is the law of causality: it permits you no miracles. The law of causality is the law of identity applied to action."[19]

Frustration and failure are, then, the ultimate fate of those who believe "that causality is an illusion and that only the immediate moment is real."[20] "Whenever you rebel against causality, your motive is fraudulent desire, not to escape it, but worse: to reverse it."[21]

It goes without saying that Miss Rand is opposed to virtually all non-Aristotelian philosophy, whether traditional or modern. Plato's thought is, for example, characterized as "a monument to the Witch Doctor's metaphysics."[22]

Not all of her criticism, however, is leveled against the traditional "Witch Doctor's ideologies" of mysticism and theology. She is also unalterably opposed to the "neo-mysticism," relativism and "epistemological agnosticism" of the pragmatist, positivist and existentialist (to name but a few). "Theirs is a conspiracy against the mind, which means: against life and man."[23] "Withdrawing from reality and responsibility, the neo-mystics proclaim that no entities exist, only relationships ... that every datum is single and discrete ... that context is irrelevant, that anything may be proved or disproved in midair and midstream ...."[24]

Such thinkers, Rand continues, have solved their problems by conceding to the mystic or the theologian and " ... by surrendering to *him* the conceptual level of man's consciousness—a victory no Witch Doctor could have hoped to achieve on his own."[25]

OBJECTIVE VALUE

Value is an aspect of truth (objective reality). Truth precedes and determines value. Value is, therefore, factual, or "objective."

Values are not relative to choices. Choices are relative to values and can be objectively-determined on the basis of certain absolute and self-evident standards.

Emotions are not properly an aspect of the cognitive process. Truth is not determined by means of choice on the basis of instrumental action. Indeed, one of the fundamental principles which provided a "basic minimum" for any sort of intellectual resuscitation is the epistemological principle which holds that emotions are not tools of cognition.[26] "One does not have to be omniscient in order to possess knowledge; one merely has to know that which one does know, and distinguish it from that which one feels ...."[27] "What one *feels* in regard to any fact or issue is irrelevant to the question of whether one's judgment of it is true or false, right or wrong."[28] "In the psychology of a rational man, the relationship of cognition and evaluation—of reason and emotion—is that of cause and effect."[29] Irrationality consists of reversing this relationship, of allowing one's emotions to determine one's thinking.

Any true understanding of Rand's philosophy is based upon a recognition of the fact that the two basic laws of logic—the principle of identity and the principle of cause-and-effect—are not only *metaphysical* principles of the utmost importance but also *normative* principles of the first magnitude. The principle of identity—A is A—is, for example, not only *true*. It is equally important to understand that a conscious *recognition* of the fact that it *is* true provides the first and most significant step which is necessary in order to arrive at any sort of legitimate moral insights.

The law of excluded-middle is, similarly, not only *true* but of basic *ethical* significance as well. "There are two sides to every issue: one side is right the other is wrong, but the middle is always evil."[30] The man in the middle solves his conflict "by ordering the thinker and the fool to meet each other half way."[30 A] "The Law of Identity (A is A) is a rational man's paramount consideration in the process of determining his interests . . . he does not . . . imagine that the pursuit of a contradiction can ever be to his interest."[31] "When a person reaches the stage of claiming that *man's interests conflict with reality,* the concept 'interests' ceases to be meaningful—and his problem ceases to be philosophical and becomes psychological."[32]

In a similar sense, the law of causality holds reign, not only in matters of *fact,* but also in questions of *value.* Money (which signifies wealth) is, for example, good (and, in fact, constitutes "objective value") providing (1) that it is *earned* (and is, therefore, the natural *effect* of the natural *cause* of creative personal effort on the part of the recipient) and (2) that it has been earned *honestly* (and is, therefore, a *just,* or correct, effect which is congruent with the moral nature of the causal behavior involved). In essence, then, Miss Rand's position might be summarized to read as follows:

1) Value (happiness/pleasure) is caused by—and is therefore identifiable with—effective behavior.

2) Effective behavior is caused by true knowledge.

3) True knowledge is caused by right reason (which is, in turn, regulated by the principles of identity and causality). "Reason (the faculty which identifies and integrates the material provided by man's senses) is man's only means of perceiving reality, his only source of knowledge, his only guide to action, and his basic means of survival."[33]

4) Therefore, right reason is the cause of—and is basically synonymous with—value.

NATURAL KNOWLEDGE

There is no truth (ultimate meaning) except that which is self-evident on the basis of natural (sense-empirical) experience, and all truth is, at least potentially, knowable.[34]

Both traditional idealism and traditional materialism are in error. Matter is not mind and mind is not matter. In a similar respect, however, the traditional mind-matter dichotomy is also wrong. At basis, mind is a unique configuration of material (objective) reality which expresses itself as thought only in response to the challenge of concrete,

31

problematic situations. The true intellectual rejects the idea of a soul-body dichotomy with all of its related irrational problems pertaining to such issues as mind versus heart, thought versus action, reality versus desire and the practical versus the moral. A truly integrated man, he is the thinker as a man of action, "a reunion of the twins who should never have been separated: the intellectual and the business man."[35]

In a similar sense, Rand rejects all of the traditional supernatural and religious interpretations of reality. Life is rational, concrete and objective. There is no God, and there is no soul. The goal of life is ultimately the fullest experience of life itself.[36]

REFERENCES – CHAPTER II

1. Ayn Rand, "Intellectual Ammunition Department," *The Objectivist Newsletter,* IV, 2 (February 1965), page 7.
2A. *Ibid.*
2. *Ibid.*
3. Ayn Rand, *Atlas Shrugged,* in *For the New Intellectual,* pp. 124 and 128.
4. *Ibid.,* page 124.
5. *Ibid.* My italics.
6. *Ibid.,* page 125. 7.
7. *Ibid.*
8. Ibid., page 172.
9. Nathaniel Braden, "Intellectual Ammunition Department, *"The Objectivist Newsletter,* I, 1 (January 1962), page 3.
10. *Ibid.*
11. Ayn Rand, *Atlas Shrugged,* in *For the New Intellectual,* pp. 126-7.
12. *Ibid.,* page 126.
13. Rand, "For the New Intellectual," *op. cit.,* page 22.
14. *Ibid.*
15. Rand, *Atlas Shrugged,* in *For the New Intellectual,* p. 151.
16. *Ibid.*
17A. The term "productive reason" is not Miss Rand's term. It refers to rational thought directed to the solution of real problems and thereby yielding productive results (profit). See Chapter VI ρρ. 150 ff.
17. *Ibid.,* page 90.
18. *Ibid.,* page 147.
19. *Ibid.,* page 151.
20. Rand, "For the New Intellectual," in *For the New Intellectual,* page 40.
21. Rand, *Atlas Shrugged,* in *For the New Intellectual,* page 152. Nathaniel Branden, who was until very recently Miss Rand's foremost spokesman and interpreter, holds that the basic purpose of *Atlas Shrugged,* which is generally conceded to be Miss Rand's most important work to date, is to

dramatize "the importance of recognizing the ontological status of the law of identity." (Nathaniel Branden, "An Analysis of the Novels of Ayn Rand," in *Who is Ayn Rand?*, page 99.)

22. Rand, "For the New Intellectual," in *For the New Intellectual*, page 22. In Miss Rand's personal mythology, those who rationalize the use of brute force—false prophets, priests and most philosophers—are termed "Witch Doctors." The Witch Doctor frequently acts in conjunction with Attila—a man who seeks to rule by means of brute force. (Rand, "For the New Intellectual," in *For the New Intellectual*, page 41.)

23. Rand, *Atlas Shrugged*, in *For the New Intellectual*, page 162.

24. Rand, "For the New Intellectual," in *For the New Intellectual*, page 44.

25. *Ibid.*, page 30.

26. *Ibid.*, page 55.

27. *Ibid.*

28. Nathaniel Branden, "Intellectual Ammunition Department," *The Objectivist Newsletter*, I, 1 (January 1965), page 3.

29. *Ibid.*

30. Rand, *Atlas Shrugged*, in *For the New Intellectual*, page 173.

30A. *Ibid.*

31. Rand, "The 'Conflict' of Men's Interests," *The Virtue of Selfishness*, page 51.

32. *Ibid.*

33. Rand, "Introducing Objectivism," *The Objectivist Newsletter*, I, 8 (August 1962), page 35.

34. Nathaniel Branden, "Intellectual Ammunition Department," *The Objectivist Newsletter*, II, 1 (January 1963), page 3.

35. Rand, "For the New Intellectual," in *For the New Intellectual*, page 51.

36. Miss Rand has surprisingly little to say about religion. Mr. Branden states the position that "to be known as crusaders for atheism would be acutely embarrassing to us; the adversary is too unworthy". (Nathaniel Branden, "A Report to Our Readers—1965," *The Objectivist Newsletter*, III, 12, December 1965, page 58.) In general, however, the objectivists take the stance that religion is merely a primitive expression of philosophy (Ayn Rand, "Philosophy and Sense of Life," *The Objectivist*, V, 2, February 1966, page 1.) They reject agnosticism as epistemologically indefensible (Nathaniel Branden, "Intellectual Ammunition Department," *The Objectivist Newsletter*, II, 4, April 1963, page 15) and are explicitly atheistic. On the other hand, and as Nathaniel Branden indicates, objectivists " . . . are intransigent atheists, *not* militant ones. We are *for* reason . . . but atheism is scarcely the center of our philosophical position." (Nathaniel Branden, "A Report to Our Readers—1965," The Objectivist Newsletter, IV, 12, December 1965, page 58.)

Miss Rand reserves her most caustic comments for those "mystical conservatives" who seek moral justification in religion, who are willing to concede reason to their enemy and who, to quote Barbara Branden, "retreat into the world of the supernatural, surrendering *this* world to Communism." (Barbara Branden, "Intellectual Ammunition Department," *The Objectivist Newsletter* I, 3, March 1962, page 11.)

"Intellectually," states Rand, "to rest one's case on Faith means to concede that reason is on the side of one's enemies—so one has no rational argument to offer." (Ayn Rand, *Conservatism: An Obituary*. New York: The Nathaniel Branden Institute, 1962, page 11.) "To claim that capitalism rests on religious faith," notes Barbara Branden, "is to contradict the fundamental principles of the United States: in America. religion is a private matter which must not be brought into political issues." (Barbara Branden, "Intellectual Ammunition Department," *The Objectivist Newsletter*, I, 3, March 1962, page 11.) "The greatest single threat to capitalism today is the attempt to put capitalism, mysticism and original sin over on the public as one "package deal.' " *(Ibid.)*

Chapter III

PERSONAL VALUE AND THE NATURE OF MAN

The topics of personal value and human nature are intimately related in Ayn Rand's writings and must necessarily be considered together. As was true with respect to knowledge, the essence of Miss Rand's point of view can be summarized in a sequence of basic, if somewhat overlapping, ideas.

THE ULTIMATE VALUE OF HAPPINESS

Happiness—which Miss Rand defines as "a state of non-contradictory joy"[1] —is the ultimate value in life. "Pleasure, for man, is not a luxury, but a profound psychological need."[2] It is "a metaphysical concomitant of life, the reward and consequence of successful action—just as pain is the insignia of failure, destruction, death."[3]

The pursuit of happiness is the sole moral purpose of life.[4] "Happiness—not pain or mindless self-indulgence—is the proof of your moral integrity, since it is the proof and the result of your loyalty to the achievement of your values."[5] There is no moral substitute for happiness, and true happiness requires the most stringent kind of rational discipline. "Discard the protective rags of that vice which you call a virtue: humility—learn to value yourself . . . and when you learn that *pride* is the sum of all virtues, you will learn to live like a man."[6]

THE CONTINGENCY OF VIRTUE

Virtues have no *intrinsic* value. They possess value solely because they lead to the realization of the self by augmenting productive life-experience. *Life* is the reward of virtue—and happiness is the goal and the reward of life.[7] Virtue is always a means to the end of value (i.e., personal happiness).[8] The three cardinal values of objectivism — "the three values which, together, are the means to and the realization of one's ultimate value, one's own life—are: Reason, Purpose, Self-Esteem, with their three corresponding virtues: Rationality,

35

Productiveness, Pride."[9] These three values: reason, as man's only source of knowledge; purpose as his choice of happiness which reason necessitates; self-esteem "as his inviolate certainty that his mind is competent to think and his person is worthy of happiness, which means: is worthy of living,"[10] logically imply all of man's virtues, and these virtues—such things as honesty, justice, productiveness, pride—"pertain to the relation of existence and consciousness."[11]

All virtues are *good,* then, not because they possess value in and of themselves, but, rather, because they enhance rational action and therefore prepare the ground for productive work and sexual love which are "the two sources of greatest potential happiness for man."[12]

THE PRIVATISTIC NATURE OF HAPPINESS

Happiness is always a personal experience. "Every form of happiness is private. Our greatest moments are personal, self-motivated, not to be touched. The things which are sacred or precious to us are the things we withdraw from promiscuous sharing."[13]

To say that happiness is *private* is not, however, to say that it is *subjective* (or autistic). Objectivism is, as Nathaniel Branden states, in "total opposition to any alleged 'individualists' who attempt to equate individualism with subjectivism."[14]

THE CHOICE TO LIVE

Happiness is produced by a total commitment to *living.* The only significant choice is the choice *to live.* "My morality, the morality of reason, is contained in a single axiom: Existence exists—and in a single choice: to live. The rest proceeds from these."[15] "In psychological terms, the issue of man's survival [is] ... an issue of 'happiness or suffering.' Happiness is the successful state of life, suffering is the warning signal of failure, of death."[16]

As Miss Rand maintains, then, "the maintenance of life and the pursuit of happiness are not two separate issues."[17] *"This* is the fallacy inherent in *hedonism*—in any variant of ethical hedonism, personal or social, individual or collective."[17A] "Man's life is the *standard* of morality, but your own life is its *purpose.*"[18] "A being who does not hold his own life as the motive and goal of his actions, is acting on the motive and standard of *death*. Such a being is a metaphysical monstrosity . . . ."[19]

Life is an *end* and never a *means*. "An organism's life is its *standard of value:* that which furthers its life is the *good*, that which threatens it is the *evil.*"[20] "The Objectivist's ethics holds man's life as the *standard* of value—and *his own life* as the ethical *purpose* of every individual man."[21]

THE OBJECTIVE CONTEXT OF EXPERIENCE

Man has an objective (factual) nature, and this nature must necessarily express itself in an objective (factual) world.

SELF-ACTUALIZATION

The fullest realization of life is dependent upon the fullest realization of the objective (factual) self. "For each living species, the course of action required is specific; what an entity *is* determines what it *ought* to do."[22] "No choice is open to an organism in this issue: that which is required for its survival is determined by its *nature,* by the kind of entity it *is.*"[23] "The fact that a living entity *is* determines what it *ought* to do. So much for the issue of the relation between 'is' and 'ought'."[24]

THE OBJECTIVE BASIS FOR HAPPINESS

Happiness is the *effect* of two objective *causes* (entities)—man and the world—in proper relationship. It is invariably the "objective" product of "rational" (cause-and-effect) behavior. "Happiness is a state of noncontradictory joy . . . which is possible only to a rational man, the man who desires nothing but rational goals, seeks nothing but rational values and finds his joy in nothing but rational actions."[25]

HAPPINESS AND OBJECTIVE VALUES

Happiness occurs when one realizes *objective (ontological) values. (Ontological values* are values logically entailed, i.e., teleologically determined, by the objective nature of the entities—self and world—which interact.)

SELF-RENUNCIATION AS EVIL

A morality which advocates a voluntary renunciation of happiness also, indirectly, advocates a renunciation of the conditions necessary for happiness—that is, realism, rationality and active life-involvement. Every man exists for his own sake, as an end in and of himself. His highest purpose lies in realizing his own happiness. "A morality that dares to tell you to find happiness in the renunciation of your happiness—to value the failure of your values—is an insolent negation of morality. It . . . gives you . . . *death* as your standard."[26]

RATIONAL EXISTENCE

The essential nature of man is his capacity for productive reason. Man is a man because he possesses rational consciousness. *Life* in the human mode is *rational existence;* anything less than this is death.

THE PRACTICAL GOAL OF REASON

The highest value for man lies, therefore, in the fullest realization of his capacity for productive (practical) reason. The ultimate operational value is, then, the value of reason itself. Since reason is the *means* necessary to realize *all other ends,* it is the basic *practical value* required to live. The objectivist ethics posits a psycho-epistemological morality in which *rationality* is the foremost virtue—the virtue that is the basis for all of a man's other virtues.[27] The morality of reason is the morality proper to man, and *"Man's Life* is its standard of value."[28] "All that which is proper to the life of a rational being is the good; all that which destroys it is the evil."[29] "To the extent to which a man is rational, life is the premise directing his actions. To the extent to which he is irrational, the premise directing his actions is death."[30]

Reason is required, not only for survival, but also for any effective realization of happiness. It operates in two spheres: (1) as the basis for personal value (pleasure/happiness) and (2) as the criterion for the determination of ethical values (moral standards), values which can ultimately be justified only on the basis of their contribution to personal happiness.

The full realization of productive reason is necessarily contingent upon three prior conditions:

1) An acceptance of the principle of identity, complete with all of its logical implications and corollaries.

2) An application of rational principles to the solution of practical problems within the real world.

3) An acceptance of the self-evident nature of certain substantive (empirical) "truths"—for example, the ontological principle of independence (which holds that a "real" world exists apart from being known), the naturalistic interpretation of reality as restricted to sense-empirical phenomena, and so on).

REASON AND TRUTH

A commitment to productive reason necessarily implies a corollary acceptance of certain basic metaphysical assumptions. Reason is not merely a *process*. It also encompasses certain types of metaphysical *knowledge* and therefore functions as both a set of self-evident truths and as a way of relating these truths in order to arrive at derivative types of legitimate knowledge.

The principle of identity is beyond all doubt. All reason is ultimately based upon the credibility of certain self-evident truths.

To relativize thought is normally sufficient to paralyze action. Productive reason requires philosophy, and any attempt to derogate philosophy is an indirect attack upon reason itself. The basic trend of post-renaissance philosophy has been *"a concerted attack on man's conceptual faculty."*[32] "If America perishes, it will perish by intellectual default. There is no diabolical conspiracy to destroy it: no conspiracy could be big enough and strong enough."[33]

THE PRACTICAL NECESSITY OF THEORY

The fullest development of productive reason is to be found in philosophy. In this sense, philosophy both directs reason and is, at the same time, symptomatic of its nature and development; " . . . man needs an integrated view of life, a *philosophy*, whether he is aware of his need or not . . . "[34]

In essence, then, Rand's basic theory of value may be outlined as follows:

1) Happiness is predicated on a fully-realized life.

2) A fully-realized life is, in turn, based on an accurate perception of reality *as it is*.

3) An accurate perception of reality grows out of the acceptance of certain basic assumptions about the underlying nature of reality.

4) Therefore, happiness is contingent on the nature of behavior which is, in turn, contingent on the nature of belief.

SENSE AND SANITY

Most psychological disorders are predicated upon errors in cognition—and, fundamentally, upon errors with respect to the true nature of value. As Nathaniel Branden notes: "Contradictions in one's values result in contradictions in one's emotions. Philosophical conflicts are the base of *psychological* conflicts. A *neurotic* conflict is a philosophical conflict that has not been faced or resolved."[35]

"Neither mysticism nor the creed of self-sacrifice is compatible with mental health or self-esteem. These doctrines are destructive existentially and psychologically."[36] "For the rational, psychologically healthy man, the desire for pleasure is a desire to celebrate his control over reality. For the neurotic, the desire for pleasure is the desire to escape from reality."[37] To believe any idea which does not stem from reality and which is not capable of being validated by reason or which is inconsistent with one's fundamental understanding of reality *"is to sabotage the integrative function of consciousness, to undercut the rest of one's convictions and kill one's capacity to be certain of anything."*[38] As John Galt states in *Atlas Shrugged,* "the alleged shortcut to knowledge, which is faith, is only a short circuit destroying the mind."[39]

THE RATIONALITY OF MAN

Since man is rational by nature, all men are self-evidently aware of the real (ontological) nature of self and world. [39A]

THE CHOICE TO THINK

Man is also capable of free moral choice, and the one great moral decision which all men must ultimately make is the choice of reason itself. "That which you call your soul or spirit is your consciousness, and that which you call 'free will' is your mind's freedom to think or not . . . your only freedom, the choice that . . . determines your life and your character."[40]

Man has the capacity for rational consciousness, but he also has the capacity to realize this potentiality *by choice*. "The issue," states Nathaniel Branden, "is a *moral* one, because man is a being who has to be conscious *by choice.*"[41] "Man's particular distinction from all other living species is the fact that *his* consciousness is *volitional.*"[42]

Moral perfection is at basis "an unbreached rationality."[43] The basic error lies, not in making mistakes in judgment, but, rather, in volitionally misconceiving (falsifying) the true nature of underlying reality. An error of knowledge is not a moral flaw if one is willing to correct it. A breach of morality is, on the other hand, "the conscious choice of an action you know to be evil, or a willful evasion of knowledge, a suspension of sight and of thought."[44] "Morally," states Branden, "it is not the *degree* of a man's productive ability that matters, but his choice to exercise such ability as he does possess."[45]

MORAL FREEDOM

In a basic sense, then, immorality is *voluntary evil,* and that person is volitionally evil who subverts his own capacity for productive rationality or who denies his own intuitive awareness of the-world-as-it-is. The moral man is that man who is *voluntarily committed to reason.*

PRODUCTIVE REASON

The ideal man is the integrated thinker-doer who combines the virtues of "the twin-motors of progress . . . the intellectual and the business man."[46] A producer, he "is the Atlas who supports the existence of mankind."[47]

In an objective world of actual entities, thought is not an end-in-itself. *Productive reason* is always reason which is devoted to the realization of practical (material) goals. For Miss Rand, the intellectual and the practical, the moral and the intellectual, the moral and the practical, are indivisible spheres of activity.

REFERENCE – CHAPTER III

1. Ayn Rand, *Atlas Shrugged*, in *For the New Intellectual*, page 133.
2. Nathaniel Branden, "A Psychology of Pleasure," in *The Virtue of Selfishness*, page 61.
3. *Ibid.*
4. Rand, *Atlas Shrugged*, in *For the New Intellectual*, page 179.
5. *Ibid.*
6. *Ibid.*
7. *Ibid.*, page 131.
8. Rand, "The Objectivist Ethics," in *The Virtue of Selfishness*, page 25.
9. *Ibid.*
10. Rand, *Atlas Shrugged*, in *For the New Intellectual*, page 128.
11. *Ibid.*
12. *Ibid.*
13. Rand, *The Fountainhead*, in *For the New Intellectual*, page 70.
14. Nathaniel Branden, "Counterfeit Individualism," in *The Virtue of Selfishness*, page 138.
15. Rand, *Atlas Shrugged*, in *For the New Intellectual*, page 128.
16. Rand, "The Objectivist Ethics," in *The Virtue of Selfishness*, page 27.
17. *Ibid.*, page 29.
17A. *Ibid.*
18. Rand, *Atlas Shrugged*, in *For the New Intellectual*, pp. 122-3.
19. *Ibid.*
20. Rand, "The Objectivist Ethics," in *The Virtue of Selfishness*, page 17.
21. *Ibid.*, page 25.
22. Nathaniel Branden, "An Analysis of the Novels of Ayn Rand," in *Who is Ayn Rand?*, *page 26.*
23. Rand, "The Objectivist Ethics," in *The Virtue of Selfishness*, page 16.
24. *Ibid.*, page 17.
25. Rand, *Atlas Shrugged*, in *For the New Intellectual*, page 132.
26. *Ibid.*, page 123.
27. Nathaniel Branden, "Psycho-Epistemology," *The Objectivist Newsletter*, III, 11 (November 1964), page 47.
28. Rand, *Atlas Shrugged*, in *For the New Intellectual*, page 122.
29. *Ibid.*
30. *Ibid.*, page 127.
32. *Ibid.*, page 30.
33. *Ibid.*, page 46.
34. *Ibid.*, page 18.
35. Nathaniel Branden, "An Analysis of the Novels of Ayn Rand," in *Who is Ayn Rand?*, page 58.
36. Nathaniel Branden, "Mental Health versus Mysticism and Self-Sacrifice," in *The Virtue of Selfishness*, page 37.
37. Nathaniel Branden, "The Psychology of Pleasure," in *The Virtue of Selfishness*, page 64.
38. Nathaniel Branden, "Mental Health versus Mysticism and Self-Sacrifice," in *The Virtue of Selfishness*, pp. 37-8.

39. *Ibid.*
39A. The source and nature of human reason is one of the most confused questions in Rand's philosophy. In her book *For the New Intellectual* she hold that men have the ability to be rational, but they also have the ability to be otherwise. "Man is the only living species who has to perceive reality—which means: to be conscious by choice." (Rand, "For the New Intellectual," in *For the New Intellectual,* page 15.) The penalty of unconsciousness is destruction. "For an animal, the question of survival is primarily physical; for man, primarily epistemological." (*Ibid.*) On the other hand, men must choose by means of knowledge, and the choice not to choose (the choice to be irrational) must be founded on the basis of reason (objective knowledge) and not emotion (as indicated earlier in this chapter). An analysis of the epistemological inconsistencies inherent in Objectivism is to be found in Chapters V and VI, and the underlying rationale for this principle is established at that time.
40. Rand, *Atlas Shrugged,* in *For the New Intellectual,* page 127.
41. Nathaniel Branden, "An Analysis of the Novels of Ayn Rand," in *Who is Ayn Rand?,* pp. 61-2.
42. Rand, "The Objectivist Ethics," in *The Virtue of Selfishness,* page 20.
43. Rand, *Atlas Shrugged,* in *For the New Intellectual,* pp. 128-9.
44. *Ibid.,* page 179.
45. Nathaniel Branden, "An Analysis of the Novels of Ayn Rand," in *Who is Ayn Rand?,* page 29.
46. *Ibid.,* page 26.
47. *Ibid.,* page 20-1.

Chapter IV

THE ETHICS OF OBJECTIVISM

Miss Rand's ethical theory is largely implicit in what has already been said with respect to knowledge, personal value and the nature of man. In a somewhat more extended sense, however, her moral philosophy too may be said to center about certain basic principles.

THE NECESSITY OF MORALITY

Ethics—i.e., a knowledge of how to attain maximum productive reasoning—is "an objective necessity."[1] Man has no inherent moral knowledge. Such knowledge is, however, "an *objective metaphysical necessity of man's survival*—not by the grace of the supernatural nor of your neighbors' whims, but by the grace of reality and the nature of life."[2] Man requires "a defined hierarchy of *rational* values (values chosen and validated by a rational standard)."[3]

THE DERIVATIVE NATURE OF ETHICS

Ethical questions, relating to social responsibility, are always secondary, or derivative, questions which are logically subordinate to prior enquiries into the nature of personal values. Concern for others "is not the central focus of a rational code of morality nor the source of a man's virtue nor the justification of anyone's existence."[4]

THE NORMATIVE STATUS OF REASON

Personal happiness is the ultimate value in life. It is not, however, a proper *criterion* for determining ethical behavior. It is the "*purpose* of ethics, but *not the* standard."[5]

The good of the individual depends upon the attainment of a fully-realized life through the maximum development of productive rational action. Reason is therefore the proper standard for determining moral behavior.

Rational behavior is always and necessarily moral behavior. Morality is not "some separate endowment opposed to reason—man's reason *is* his moral faculty."[6] "Just as feelings are not a tool of cognition, *so they are not a criterion in ethics.*"[7]

MORALITY AND ANTI-MORALITY

Moral behavior is practical behavior which is directed toward the fullest realization of objective individual values.[8] Morality can be turned into a weapon for human subjugation only by divorcing it from the goal of rational self-interest. For "there is no way to degrade man's life on earth except by the lethal opposition of the *moral* and the *practical.*"[9]

The good of society as a whole is necessarily predicated upon the fullest realization of goodness (value) on the part of each individual *as an individual.* " . . . nobody's good can be achieved at the price of human sacrifices . . . when you violate the rights of one man, you have violated the rights of all . . . The public good be damned, I will have no part of it!"[10] "Only individual men have the right to decide when or whether they wish to help others; society—as an organized political system—has no rights in the matter at all."[11]

THE PHILOSOPHICAL ROOTS OF POLITICS

Politics is a branch of philosophy. It always and necessarily represents an application of prior philosophical principles to the determination of social policy.

The philosophy of objectivism is deeply concerned with political questions. As Rand states: "Objectivism advocates certain political principles . . . as the consequence and the ultimate practical application of its fundamental philosophical principles. It does not regard politics as a . . . goal that can be achieved without a wider ideological context."[12] In a sense, then, and as Rand indicates, "A change in a country's political ideas has to be preceded by a change in its cultural trends; a cultural movement is the necessary precondition of a *political* movement."[13]

"HUMAN RIGHTS"

A "right" is "a moral principle . . . defining and sanctioning a man's

45

freedom of action in a moral context."[14] "There is only one 'right,' man's right to live as a man—i.e., rationally."[15] All rights are merely conditions necessitated by the goal of rational self-satisfaction. As such, a right is never based upon permission. Rather, "a right is the sanction of independent action. A right is that which can be exercised without anyone's permission."[16] Objectivism " ... demonstrates that *rights are neither arbitrary nor 'stipulational' nor provisional, but are logically derivable from man's nature and needs as a living being ... the source of man's rights is ... the law of identity. A is A—and Man is Man.*"[17]

The right to a rational existence, however, logically entails other corollary "rights" as well. Man, for example, "cannot function successfully under coercion."[18] In a similar sense, "no man can have a right to impose an unchosen obligation, an unrewarded duty or an involuntary servitude on another man. There can be no such thing as *'the right to enslave.'* "[19] Property rights and the right of free trade are the only legitimate "economic rights," and these are ultimately *political* rights.[20] There are no "collective rights" which adhere to groups and not to individuals, and the idea that there are is symptomatic of the collectivist mystique.[21] A group, as such, has no legitimate claim to rights. "A man can neither acquire new rights by joining a group nor lose the rights which he does possess. The principle of individual rights is the only moral base of all groups or associations."[22]

A true recognition of man's individual rights is the surest guarantee against statist abuses. In this sense, "the most profoundly revolutionary achievement of the United States of America was the *subordination of society to moral law.*"[23] "The United States was the first *moral* society in history."[24]

THE PRECONDITIONS FOR REASON

The maximum development of productive rational action requires an atmosphere in which true intellectual freedom is both permitted and encouraged.

THE POLITICAL PREREQUISITES FOR OBJECTIVITY

Intellectual freedom requires political freedom. "The only good which men can do one another and the only statement of their proper relationship is—Hands off!" "Civilization is the process of setting man free from men."[25] *"Freedom,* in a political context ... does *not* mean freedom from the landlord or freedom from the employer, or freedom from the laws of nature . . . It means freedom from the coercive power of the state—and nothing else."[26]

In a similar sense, political freedom serves to guarantee intellectual freedom. A truly free society performs a valuable epistemological function, for it guarantees the unhampered pursuit of truth in any area of enquiry independent of "forced restrictions or legal barriers."[27] "[This] prevents the legalized enforcement of a 'monopoly on truth' by any gang of power-seekers—it protects the free marketplace of ideas—it keeps all doors open to man's inquiring mind."[28]

THE ROLE OF GOVERNMENT

The government is not a source of positive good.[29] "The difference between political power and any other kind of social 'power,' between a government and any private organization, is the fact that *the government holds a legal monopoly on the use of physical force.* "[30]

"The only proper purpose of a government is to protect man's rights, which means: to protect him from physical violence."[31] "The proper kind of government acts on the principle of man's self-defense."[32] It "may resort to force only against those who *start* the use of force."[33] "Men have the right to use physical force *only* in retaliation and *only* against those who initiate its use."[34] The only legitimate functions of the state are "the police, to protect you from criminals; the army, to protect you from foreign invaders; and the courts, to protect your property and contracts from breach or fraud by others . . . according to *objective* law."[35]

Miss Rand opposes anarchy both on the grounds of possible human immorality under conditions of total political permissiveness and also on the grounds that even a fully moral and rational society would call for some sort of government to establish *objective* laws to arbitrate reasonable disagreements among its citizens.[36] As she states, " . . . the use of force against one man cannot be left to the arbitrary decision of another."[37] *"A government is the means of placing the retaliatory use of physical force under objective control—* i.e., under objectively defined law."[38]

"The proper kind of government *does not* initiate the use of force. It uses force *only* to answer those who have initiated its use."[39] Thus, and as Rand indicates, if the government arrests a criminal, "it is not the government that violates a right; it is the criminal who has violated

47

a right and by doing so has placed himself outside the principle of rights, where men have no recourse against him except through force."[40] The criminal is punished, however, not for committing a crime against the state, but for committing an offense against some particular individual or individuals. Indeed, "there are no 'crimes against society'—all crimes are committed against specific men, against individuals."[41] Objective natural law requires retribution in the face of evil, for, as Nathaniel Branden states, "an unearned forgiveness of evil . . . is a shrug of indifference toward the pain of the innocent."[42]

Even capital punishment is morally justified under certain conditions. *Morally,* the murderer deserves to forfeit his own life. His execution is "the logical and just consequence of his own act."[43] On the other hand, apart from the moral duty to avenge wrong-doing, individual productive reason should be the sole arbiter of conduct within any society which is dedicated to the fullest expression of individual well-being. "Let no man posture as an advocate of freedom if he claims the right to establish his version of a good society where individual dissenters are to be suppressed by means of physical force."[44] "Make no mistake about the character of mystics. To undercut your consciousness has always been their only purpose throughout the ages—and power, the power to rule you by force, has always been their only lust."[45] " . . . the altruist-collectivist code . . . permits a man to suppose (or idly to daydream) that *he* can somehow guarantee . . . security to some men at the expense of others."[46]

THE ECONOMIC PREREQUISITES FOR OBJECTIVITY

Political freedom requires economic freedom. "Intellectual freedom cannot exist without political freedom; political freedom cannot exist without economic freedom; a free mind and free market are corollaries."[47] "The issue," writes political economist Ludwig von Mises, "is always the same; the government *or* the market. There is no third solution." "The choice," notes Barbara Branden, "is coercion—or voluntary trade; slavery—or freedom."[48] "Freedom is not a *sufficient* condition to assure man's proper fulfillment, but it is a *necessary* condition. And capitalism—laissez-faire capitalism—is the only system which provides that condition."[49]

Ultimately, then, Ayn Rand's philosophy itself is, to use a phrase appropriately applied to her novel *Atlas Shrugged,* "a moral defense of capitalism."[50] For Rand, capitalism is basically a moral issue, because " ... *capitalism is the only system based on an objective theory of values,*"[51] and "the free market represents the *social* application of an objective theory of values."[52] "Capitalism is the only system where able men are free to function and where progress is accompanied, not by forced privations, but by a constant rise in the general level of prosperity, of consumption and of enjoyment of life."[53]

Capitalism guarantees the right to disagree—a condition necessary for individual creativity. In a capitalistic society, all human relationships are voluntary and individuals "can deal with one another only in terms of and by means of reason, i.e., by means of discussion, persuasion and *contractual* agreement, by voluntary choice to mutual benefit."[54] "Capitalism recognizes that all good inheres only in individual men and that there is no moral reason why one man should be forced to accept, as the goal of his work and his life, the achievement of the good of another man."[55]

Capitalism and altruism are incompatible; "they are philosophical opposites; they cannot co-exist in the same man or in the same society."[56] Under capitalism, the positive goal of personal happiness is never subordinated to the negative end of self-denial. Concerned primarily with the individual as an individual and governed by a primary commitment to justice, "the *moral* justification of capitalism does not lie in the altruist claim that it represents the best way to achieve 'the common good.' It is true that capitalism does ... but this is merely a secondary consequence."[57]

TRADE AND JUSTICE

"The principle of *trade* is the only rational ethical principle for all human relationships, personal and social, private and public, spiritual and material. It is the principle of *justice.*"[58] "The man who hates and fears *laissez-faire* does not confess that what he resents is precisely the implacable justice of this system."[59] Under capitalism the value of man's labor is determined by "the moral meaning of the law of supply and demand" on a free market, "by the voluntary consent of those who are willing to trade to him their work or products in return."[60]

CAPITALISM

Capitalism—"an economic system in which the instruments of

production are owned by private individuals who operate them for their personal profit . . . and where goods and services are exchanged by free trade on a free market"—is the only economic system characterized by justice and honesty.[61] Justice demands "that you must judge all men as conscientiously as you judge inanimate objects . . . that every man must be judged for what he is and treated accordingly . . . "[62] Honesty resides in confronting the inexorable fact "that neither love nor fame nor cash is a value if obtained by fraud,"[63] that true value can never emerge from predicating one's own actions upon the stupidity and credulity of others. On the contrary, true honesty is dictated by the policy of rational selfishness. The honest man conscientiously refuses "to sacrifice the reality of his own existence to the deluded consciousness of others."[64]

Capitalism is the only system in which rewards are allocated in accordance with purely objective rational law. In a true capitalistic society, there are no slaves or masters, and happiness is no longer tied to guilt under a destructive code of self-sacrifice. Socialism, on the other hand, maintains that man's work and property belong to the group, that his interests are justifiably subordinated to the interests of society "and that society may dispose of him in any way it pleases for the sake of whatever it deems to be its own tribal, collective good."[65]

Under capitalism, rewards are allocated purely on the basis of merit, as this is determined by the objective value of the work performed. "The symbol of all relationships among rational men, the moral symbol of respect for human beings, is the trader . . . who earns what he gets and does not give or take the undeserved."[66]

PRIVATE PROPERTY

The right to hold and control property is basic to capitalism and therefore to economic freedom. Man is a material organism who experiences value (happiness) in his relationship with material objects. He is not a disembodied intellect who pursues purely conceptual ends. He finds value in his commerce with the real, objective world, through his power over and control of *things*. "Just as man can't exist without his body, so no rights can exist without the right to translate one's rights into reality—to think, to work and to keep the results—which means: the right of property."[67A]

Value is, then, always expressed in the guise of property relationships. *Human rights* are ultimately synonymous with *property rights.* As Rand indicates: " . . . there is no such dichotomy as 'human rights' versus 'property rights.' No human rights can exist without property rights . . . To deny property rights means to turn men into property owned by the state."[67]

Man is a material organism who expresses himself through material (property) relationships. By elevating so-called "human rights" over "property rights," we simply legitimize the attempt by the incompetent to victimize the productive efforts of the competent. "The doctrine that 'human rights' are superior to 'property rights' simply means that some human beings have the right to make property out of others."[68] " . . . if the producer does not own the result of his effort, he does not own his life. To deny property rights means to turn men into property owned by the state."[69]

Property rights are rooted in the law of cause and effect itself, for "all property and all forms of wealth are produced by man's mind and labor. As you cannot have effects without causes, so you cannot have wealth without its source: without intelligence."[70] In a similar sense, intelligence cannot be coerced to produce. "You cannot obtain the products of a mind except on the owner's terms, by trade and by volitional consent."[71]

Miss Rand favors voluntary taxation (i.e., payment for governmental services), *but not at this time.*[72] Such a program is, as she states, a goal for the distant future, "the last, *not* the first, reform to advocate."[73] It is not possible under present circumstances, and "what the advocates of a fully free society have to know, at present, is only the principle by which that goal can be achieved."[74]

In a totally free society, of course, all governmental services would be strictly voluntary. "Not only the post office, but streets, roads, and above all, schools, should all be privately owned and privately run . . . The government should be concerned only with those issues which involve the use of force."[75] Public services which are demonstrably necessary, such as those provided by the police, the military and the courts, would be paid for on a voluntary basis by individual citizens as they now pay for insurance.[76] Rand grants that "the question of how to implement the principle of voluntary government financing—how to determine the best means of applying it in practice—is a very conplex one."[77] She holds, however, that it is basically a theoretical problem which belongs to the philosophy of law. "The task of political philosophy is only to establish the nature of the principle and to demonstrate that it is practicable."[78] As she sees it, actual implementation would be premature at the present moment "since the principle will be practicable only in a *fully* free society, a society whose government has been constitutionally reduced to its own proper, basic functions."[79]

There are, as Miss Rand indicates, many possible methods of establishing and sustaining voluntary government financing. She mentions the use of a government lottery as one possibility.[80] She also suggests—although purely illustratively—taxing credit transactions so that a certain percentage of each transaction would be required as a condition for obtaining governmental insurance.[81] In all events, and as she indicates, it is in the best interests of the more competent men that they should pay for their own military and police protection, and their expenses would not be made significantly heavier by the marginal loss of financial support by the relatively unproductive members of society. In such cases, "free protection for the non-contributors represents an *indirect benefit* and is merely a marginal consequence of the contributor's own interests and expenses."[82]

THE TYRANNY OF STATISM

From the objectivist point of view, any sort of collectivism is bound to eventuate in statism and the establishment of governmental tyranny. Indeed, all types of statism—monarchism, socialism, fascism and Naziism—are equally "leftist" in their basic orientations and, as Barbara Branden suggests, "differ, not in basic principle or goal, but only in techniques of implementation."[83] As Rand indicates: "Socialism is merely democratic absolute monarchy—that is, a system of absolutism without a fixed head, open to seizure of power by all comers, by any ruthless climber, opportunist, adventurer, demagogue or thug."[84]

In socialism the means of production are owned by the state and are operated for the profit of all rather than for the private property of the producers. The state, not the free market, controls the production and distribution of all goods and services. Socialism regards individual good as an aspect of public good. The best interests of the individual are to be achieved through service to the public "which, in practical terms, means: by service to the State—which, in concrete terms, means: by service to the particular group of men in power at any given moment."[85]

One of the cardinal errors in dealing with socialism is to assume that it is possible to have a viable "mixed economy" which combines aspects of both capitalism and socialism in the same system, the so-called "private sector" of the economy being allowed to operate autonomously of the "public sector." In point of fact, of course, states Rand, "there can be no social system which is a mixture of Individualism and Collectivism. Either individual rights are recognized in a society, or they are not recognized. They cannot be half-recognized."[86]

The essence of capitalism is the separation of government and economics, the total liberation of trade and production from any kind of extrinsic political restraint. True capitalism is inevitably laissez-faire capitalism, "anything else is a *'mixed economy,'* that is: a mixture, in varying degrees, of freedom and controls, of voluntary choice and government compulsion, of individualism and collectivism."[87]

In a similar sense, it is absurd to talk about the distribution of a "social surplus" of goods which exists above and beyond that which is necessary to achieve some sort of hypothetical norm of material prosperity. "Social surplus" is a fiction. Wealth is invariably the product and possession of someone.[88]

A "mixed economy" necessarily and inexorably deteriorates into pure collectivistic statism in order to augment and bolster its own increasingly obvious inadequacies. The collectivist state becomes progressively more complex and ultimately comes to require a degree of expertise and knowledgability which far exceeds the average person's capacity for enlightened political choice.

All collectivistic systems are fundamentally self-fulfilling. They are designed to create precisely those symptoms of social pathology which are necessary to justify and sustain their own existence. Government interference in the free market inevitably entails greater and greater political intervention in the vain attempt to ameliorate the disastrous consequences of past meddling. This goes on "until all economic freedom has been legislated out of existence and socialism has replaced capitalism."[89]

At basis, then, the statist tyrannies of fascism and socialism are not the separate and distinct phenomena which they are so frequently assumed to be. Whatever *theoretical* distinctions may exist between the two, they are *operational* equivalents in the area of practice. "Under both systems, sacrifices are invoked as a magic, omnipotent solution in any crisis—and 'the public good' is the altar on which victims are immolated."[90] They are *in practice* identical. " . . . both came from the same collectivist-statist principle, both negate individual rights and subordinate the individual to the collective, both deliver the livelihood and the lives of the citizens into the power of an omnipotent government ... "[91] " ... socialism ... advocates 'the vesting of *ownership and control'* in the community as a whole, i.e., in the state; fascism leaves ownership in the hands of private individuals, but transfers *control* of the property to the government."[92]

The contemporary drift toward collectivism is not, on the whole, inspired by a sense of explicit ideological commitment. The political ideal of collectivism was largely destroyed by the second world war. Liberalism is no longer a moral crusade, it is now merely a routine adherence to the vague and sentimental metaphysics of group togetherness.

Even without an ideological base, though, the drift toward collectivism entails a corollary drift toward fascism—not the militant fascism of Europe in the twenties and thirties, however, for "ours is a tired, worn, cynical fascism, fascism by default, not like a flaming disaster, but more like the quiet collapse of a lethargic body slowly eaten by internal corruption."[93]

The end-result can only lie in the establishment of a new type of *de facto* fascism. Increasingly, we find ourselves "a random, mongrel mixture of socialistic schemes, communistic influence, fascist controls and shrinking remnants of capitalism still paying the costs of it all—the total of it rolling in the direction of a fascist state."[94]

A particularly significant subtype of socialism is that represented by the "guild socialism" which is practiced by such pressure groups as labor unions and professional organizations. This, states Rand, is one of the more dismal expressions of the statist orientations, for "if there is any one way to confess one's own mediocrity, it is the willingness to place one's work in the absolute power of a group, particularly a group of one's *professional colleagues.*"[95] By openly subordinating the able to the mediocre under the guise of vocational rules and regulations, guild socialism "represents an open embodiment of the basic motive of most statists ... the shackling of the men of superior ability down to the mean average of their profession."[96]

The "new fascism" which we are presently experiencing was largely consolidated during the years of the New Deal when various members of the administrative brain trust were infatuated with the economic reforms of Mussolini. Such schemes as the NRA and the AAA were, in the words of John T. Flynn (*The Roosevelt Myth*):

54

... a plan to take the whole industrial and agricultural life of the country under the wing of government, organize it into vast farm and industrial cartels, as they were called in Germany, corporatives as they were called in Italy, and operate business and farms under plans made and carried out under the supervision of the government.[97]

As Rand sees it, this tendency toward subgroup collectivism is particularly observable in an organized profession like college and university teaching where—to repeat an observation by Dr. Meng, the President of Hunter College in New York City, which Miss Rand quotes approvingly in *The Objectivist Newsletter*—"Yesterday's ivory tower has become today's foxhole. The leisure of the theory class is increasingly occupied in the organization of picket lines, teach-ins, think-ins, and stake-outs of one sort or another."[98]

It goes virtually without saying that Rand is unalterably opposed to guild socialism in labor and particularly where this is provided with formal governmental sanctions by means of so-called "right to work" laws.[99]

From the objectivist point of view, true democracy can occur only in the free marketplace where wealth "is achieved by a free, general, 'democratic' vote—by the sales and the purchases of every individual who takes part in the economic life of the country."[100]

There can be no appeal from the operation of the free market, for the free market is governed by the immutable and objective laws of reality itself.[101] Economic interventionism is always based upon the illusion that objective economic facts can be denied or manipulated. Political interference in economic affairs, states Nathaniel Branden, " ... is based on the belief that economic laws need not operate, that principles of cause and effect can be suspended, that everything in existence is 'flexible' and 'malleable,' except a bureaucrat's whim, which is omnipotent."[102]

Ultimately, all violations of economic law are implicit attempts to assert arbitrary power over the resistant laws of economic cause-and-effect. "Power, in a statist sense, means *arbitary* power. An *objective* law protects a country's freedom; only a *non-objective* law can give a statist the chance he seeks; a chance to impose *his* arbitrary will ... "[103]

The regulating mechanism in a truly capitalistic system is profit.

Profits are not, however, subjective. As Rand indicates, the stenographer who spends so much on cosmetics that she is incapable of paying for adequate medical treatment learns by her own errors to budget effectively; "she learns a better method of budgeting her income; the free market serves as her teacher: she has no way to penalize others for her mistakes."[104] If she is more prudent in the future, she will be able to afford whatever medical attention she requires. In so doing, she will "pay a part of the cost of scientific achievements, *when and as she needs them,*" but she will not be taxed "to support an entire hospital, a research laboratory or a space ship's journey to the moon."[105]

In his book *Planning for Freedom,* economist Ludwig von Mises makes the following statement in a passage which is quoted approvingly by objectivist Nathaniel Branden:

> Professor Harold Laski, the former chairman of the British Labor Party, determined the objective of planned direction of investment as "the use of the investor's savings will be in housing rather than in cinemas." It does not matter whether or not one agrees with the professor's personal view that better houses are more important than moving pictures. The fact is that consumers, by spending part of their money for admission to the movies, have made another choice. If the masses of Great Britain, the same people whose votes swept the Labor Party into power, were to stop patronizing the moving pictures and to spend more for comfortable homes and apartments, profit-seeking business would be forced to invest more in building homes and apartment houses, and less in the production of swanky pictures. What Professor Laski aimed at is to defy the wishes of the consumers and to substitute his own will for theirs. He wanted to do away with the democracy of the market and to establish the absolute rule of a production czar. He might pretend he is right from a "higher" point of view, and that as a superman he is called upon to impose his own set of values on the masses of inferior men, but then he should have been frank enough to say so plainly.[106]

Or, as von Mises indicates in still another of his works, *Planned Chaos:*

> If a man were to say: "I do not like the mayor elected by a majority vote; therefore I ask the government to replace him by

the man I prefer," one would hardly call him a democrat. But if the same claims are raised with regard to the market, most people are too dull to discover the dictatorial aspirations involved.[107]

Most of the charges which have been leveled against laissez-faire capitalism are not, properly speaking, charges against laissez-faire capitalism at all but, rather, against the abuses inherent within any sort of so-called "mixed economy." Unemployment, for example, is not the product of unhampered free enterprise. It is, rather " . . . *the inevitable result of forcing wage rates above their free market value.*"[108] In a similar respect, the Crash of '29 and the resultant depression of the '30's were not, as has so frequently been charged, the result of unchecked free enterprise at all. They were, rather, the result of precisely those sorts of governmental intervention which were repeatedly invoked to remedy the ills of the economy.

If, as Alan Greenspan suggests, the banking system and the variable availability of money act in pure capitalism as a fuse to prevent economic blowouts, the governmentally-imposed Federal Reserve System "put a penny in the fuse-box" giving rise to the economic explosion of 1929.[109] "Depressions are caused by *government intervention* into the economy, particularly by government manipulations of credit."[110] In a free economy based on the gold standard unjustified speculation of an uncontrolled sort is precluded because "the supply of money and credit needed to finance business ventures is determined by *objective* economic factors . . . the banking system that is the guardian of economic stability."[111] In laissez-faire capitalism, the private banking system is the cornerstone of economic stability. "The ultimate regulator of competition in a free economy is the capital market. So long as capital is free to flow, it will tend to seek those areas which offer the maximum rate of return."[112]

In point of fact, of course, and as Miss Rand indicates, "a system of pure, unregulated *laissez-faire* capitalism has never yet existed anywhere . . . America was the freest country on earth, but elements of statism were present in our economy from the start."[113] "Capitalism did not create poverty—it inherited it . . . the living conditions of the poor in the early years of capitalism were the first chance the poor had ever had to survive."[114]

Historian Robert Hessen, in his article "Child Labor and the Industrial Revolution," which is contained in *The Objectivist Newsletter* for April of 1962, goes on to attack the idea that children suffered in the "sweatshops" and coal mines during the British industrial revolution of the nineteenth century. As Hessen indicates, the introduction of the factory system into England in the eighteenth and nineteenth centuries "offered a livelihood, a means of survival, to tens of thousands of children who would not have lived to be youths in the pre-capitalistic eras."[115] "The proportion of those born in London dying before five years of age fell from 74.5% in 1730-49 to 31.8% in 1810-29 (Mabel C. Buer, *Health, Welfare and Population in the Early Days of the Industrial Revolution*, page 30.)[116] *Child labor was not ended by legislative fiat;* child labor ended when it became economically unnecessary for children to earn wages in order to survive—when the income of their parents became sufficient to support them."[117]

MONOPOLY

From the objectivist point of view, laissez-faire capitalism does not, contrary to popular opinion, inevitably lead to the concentration of wealth in the hands of the few or to the restriction of competition through the establishment of *coercive* momopolies.[118]

"A 'coercive monopoly'," states Greenspan, "is a business concern that can set its prices and production policies independent of the market, with immunity from competition, from the law of supply and demand . . . ."[119] Such a monopoly is able to restrict entry to competitors, is largely exempt from the normal pressures of competition, and is therefore free to earn artificially high profits.

In point of fact, such monopolies are entirely impossible in a free market.[120] No one, states Nathaniel Branden, "has been able to establish coercive monopoly by means of competition in a free market."[121] Every coercive monopoly that has ever existed *"was created and made possible only by an act of government . . .* by *legislative* actions which granted special privileges . . . to a man or a group of men, and forbade all others to enter that particular field."[122] "Without Government assistance," notes Greenspan, "it is impossible for a would-be monopolist to set and maintain his prices and production policies independent of the rest of the economy."[123] A free capital market guarantees that a monopolist whose profits are based on high prices instead of low costs will provoke competitors to invade his territory.

True monopoly, then, as the objectivists see it, "entails more than the *absence* of competition; it entails the *impossibility* of competition. That is a coercive monopoly's characteristic attribute—and is essential to any condemnation of such a monopoly."[124]

The only kind of monopoly which can exist under laissez-faire capitalism is a *non-coercive monopoly*. These are not really "monopolies" at all, because they are fully dependent upon the laws of supply and demand and exist solely on the basis of superior productive efficiency. They are therefore good. Indeed, "no one can morally claim the *right* to compete in a given field, if he cannot match the productive efficiency of those with whom he hopes to compete."[125] It is absurd to condemn a company for hampering competition by its superior enterprise, efficiency and foresight.[126]

In a similar sense, price wars and competitive bidding do not protect monopolies, for such economic coercion is simply implausible in a free market. As Branden indicates, a large, rich company cannot assume heavy losses in order to drive out competitiors (as by buying-out competitors or forcing them out of business by selling at a loss or slashing prices) then begin to charge exorbitant prices to recoup its losses, for this would stimulate new competitors to emerge and take advantage of the high profits to be had.[127] New competitors would invariably force prices down to market level, and the large companies would be forced to reset their prices at market level or court bankruptcy by engaging in incessant price wars. "It is a matter of historical fact no 'price war' has ever succeeded in establishing a monopoly or in maintaining prices *above* the market level, outside the law of supply and demand."[128]

Not even natural resources lend themselves to coercive monopolization in a free economy. Not even mining is immune from the dynamics which militate against the establishment of a viable coercive monopoly. Branden cites the example of International Nickel of Canada which produces more than two-thirds of the world's nickel yet prices as products *as though* it had a great many competitors by virtue of the fact that it does face competition with a variety of other metals and metal alloys. In other words, the free market is self-policing in this area. "The seldom recognized principle involved is this: no single product, commodity or material is or can be indispensable to an economy *regardless of price*. A commodity can be only relatively preferable to other commodities."[129]

Miss Rand is particularly incensed by "that legalized lynching or pogrom known as 'trust busting.' "[130] Indeed, the ultimate consequence of anti-trust is to penalize and discourage the able. "The Antitrust laws," she states, "were the classic example of a moral inversion prevalent in the history of capitalism."[131] Applied to all productive activity in general, they "would mean that none of us . . . should venture forward, or rise, or improve, because any form of personal progress . . . can discourage the kind of newcomers who haven't yet started, but who expect to start competing at the top."[132]

Implicit throughout the antitrust system, of course, is the traditional fear of unchecked power, the demand for safeguards, for countervailing authority, for "checks and balances."[133] The error throughout is that of assuming that free enterprise is *unchecked* to begin with, an error which is rooted in the failure to observe that it is bounded at all times by the objective laws of the marketplace which curtail abuses far faster and far more readily than the whims of governmental authority.[134]

MONEY AS VALUE

Wealth, symbolized by money, is objectified value. "The words 'to make money' hold the essence of human morality."[135] "Money is *made*—before it can be looted or mooched—made by the effort of every honest man, each to the extent of his ability. An honest man is one who knows that he can't consume more than he has produced."[136] "Money rests on the axiom that every man is the owner of his mind and his effort."[137]

Gold is objective value. It stands for productive wealth. Paper money is false wealth. "Whenever destroyers appear among men, they start by destroying money, for money is man's protection and the base of a moral existence. Destroyers seize gold and leave to its owners a counterfeit pile of paper."[138] Paper money signifies power. It is the creation of "legal looters." "Paper is a mortgage on wealth that does not exist. Backed by a dun aimed at those who are expected to produce it."[139] "Watch money. Money is the barometer of a society's virtue."[140]

THE INEXORABLE MORALITY OF PRODUCTIVE REASON

Money which is unearned or which is acquired dishonestly—i.e., through other means than through the application of productive reason—is a violation of the (moral) law of cause-and-effect and is not therefore true value. Such wealth symbolizes a thing (productive reason) which is not actually present and ultimately acts to destroy those who are not its legitimate producers. "There is only one class of men who receive moral condemnation: the men who demand any form of the unearned, in matter or in spirit . . . ."[141]

Money obtained by fraud is worthless. The man who seeks wealth by pandering to stupidity or vice is base. His wealth will be more than useless to him, it will be a source of suffering, "a reproach; not an achievement . . . a reminder of shame."[142]

Inherited wealth is only justified if it is gratuitous. Where the heir is unworthy, money is not a blessing but a curse. "Money is a living power that dies without its root. Money will not serve the mind that cannot match it."[143] "Only the man who does not need it is fit to inherit wealth . . . . If an heir is equal to his money, it serves him; if not, it destroys him."[144]

CREATIVITY

Creativity—productive reason—is always the act of an individual. There is no collective thought or collective brain.[145] The primary act of thinking is necessarily a solitary act. "No man can use his brain to think for another. All the functions of body and spirit are private. They cannot be shared or transferred."[146] "No work is ever done collectively, by a majority decision. Every creative job is achieved under the guidance of a single individual thought."[147] "This creative faculty cannot be given or received, shared or borrowed. It belongs to single, individual men. That which it creates is the property of the creator."[148] Both learning and the discovery of knowledge can be cooperative, but such cooperation entails the independent exercise of his rational faculty by every individual as an individual.[149] " . . . all learning is only the exchange of material. No man can give another the capacity to think."[150]

THE SUBJECTIVITY OF OBJECTIVITY

Truth and value are *objective phenomena*, but they can only be experienced *subjectively* (personally) by means of individual effort and on the basis of purely individual choice.[151A] Truth and value are ultimately the product of *self*-activity. Only the individual can choose to be rational and, hence, to seek objective happiness. "Nothing but a man's mind can perform that complex, delicate, crucial process of identification which is thinking. Nothing can direct the process but his own judgment. Nothing can direct his judgment but his moral integrity."[151]

In a similar sense, happiness is always and invariably personal. No one can *experience* value for anyone else, for happiness is the phenomenological consequence of an accurate perception of reality.

The neurotic is not only unhappy, he is cognitively in error. "A neurotic is a man who, when his desires clash with reality, considers reality expendable."[152] "Reason is an absolute that permits no compromise,"[153] and sanity "requires of man that he place no value above perception, which means: no value above consciousness, which means: no value above reality."[154]

SANITY AND SELFISHNESS

Self-love (selfishness) is the invariable basis for sanity. "If a man does not value himself, nothing can have value for him."[155] That man who is not ultimately concerned with his own self-gratification possesses no rational criterion for choosing among specific possibilities for action. The failure to attain a sufficient degree of self-love results in "a feeling of anxiety, insecurity, self-doubt, the sense of being unfit for reality, inadequate to existence. Anxiety is a psychological alarm-signal, warning of danger to the organism."[156]

"Selflessness" typically takes the form of a repression of the non-social self,[157] which Branden describes as a sort of implicit "social metaphysics." Such an orientation constitutes *the psychological syndrome that characterizes an individual who holds the consciousness of other men, not objective reality, as his ultimate psychoepistemological frame-of-reference.*[158]

OBJECTIVE EGOISM

Man is (and, therefore, should be) *objectively egoistic*—"rationally selfish"—because truth and value, while absolute and equally applicable to all, are always *experienced* privately. "Selfishness entails: (a) a hierarchy of values set by the standard of one's self-interest, and (b) the refusal to sacrifice a higher value to a lower one or to a nonvalue."[159] "Selfishness is, then, objective; "... feelings are not a criterion in ethics."[160] "The basic *social* principle of the Objectivist ethics is . . . that man must live for his own sake . . . that *the achievement of his own happiness is man's highest moral purpose.*"[161]

THE IMMORALITY OF ALTRUISM

Altruism is fundamentally evil, because it is a perversion of man's essential (psychological) nature as man. It is irrational and therefore doomed to failure. "Since there is no rational justification for the sacrifice of some men to others, there is no objective criterion by which such a sacrifice can be guided in practice."[162]

The ultimate value of life can only be life itself—i.e., individual happiness attained by means of productive reason—and not experience beyond life. "Man—every man—is an end in himself, not a means to the ends of others. *He is not a sacrificial animal.*"[163]

Altruism—which Rand defines as "the placing of others above self, of their interests above one's own"[164]—is invariably in error, because it is "a doctrine of moral cannibalism"[165] which advocates voluntary self-annihilation, a deliberate courting of self-curtailment and self-diminution.

According to Branden, it is contradictory to talk about selfishness "that includes or permits the possibility of knowingly acting against ones long-range happiness."[166] "Egoism," he continues, "holds that, morally, the beneficiary of an action should be the person who acts; altruism holds that, morally, the beneficiary of an action should be someone *other* than the person who acts."[167] "It is the *self* that altruism regards as evil: *selflessness* is its moral ideal. Thus, it is an *anti-self* ethics—this means: anti-man, anti-personal happiness, anti-individual rights."[168] "A viler evil than to murder a man, is to sell him suicide as an act of virtue."[169]

To Rand, the world is "perishing from selflessness,"[170] because it has sought to deny "the self-sufficiency of man's spirit."[171] The cardinal evil is "that of placing your prime concern within other men."[172] At basis, a self-sufficient ego is all that matters. "The man who does not value himself, cannot value anything or anyone."[173] "All that which proceeds from man's independent ego is good. All that which proceeds from man's dependence upon men is evil."[174] ". . . the word 'We' must never be spoken, save by one's choice and as a second thought. This word must never be placed first within man's soul, else it becomes a monster . . . ."[175]

The doctrine of psychological hedonism, the erroneous doctrine of "everyone is selfish,"[176] does not effectively refute the theory of rational selfishness. Such a theory, while it does not deny that men can consciously act against their own long-range happiness, holds that they are nevertheless acting "selfishly" in some more basic and pervasive sense of the term. The problem here is that "a definition of 'selfishness' that includes or permits the possibility of knowingly acting against one's long-range happiness, is a contradiction in terms."[177]

This is not to say that one may not become ego-identified with, or even undergo ostensible "sacrifices" for, those one loves. As Nathaniel Branden indicates, however, "If parents forego other purchases in order to provide for their children's necessities, their action is *not* a sacrifice, and they have no moral right to regard it as such."[178] Indeed, "concern for the welfare of those one loves is a rational part of one's selfish interests."[179] The mother who undergoes grave sacrifices for her child does not do so for *his* sake but, in a more basic sense, for *her own*.

Addressing herself to the traditional ethical dilemma of whether or not to risk one's life in attempting to save a drowning person, for example, Miss Rand takes the position that it would be immoral to risk one's life for a stranger unless the danger to one's own life were minimal. Indeed, "when the danger is great, it would be immoral to attempt it: only a lack of self-esteem could permit one to value one's life no higher than that of any random stranger."[180] "It is on the ground of that generalized good will and respect for the value of human life that one helps strangers in an emergency—*and only in an emergency.*"[181]

On the other hand, the objectivists are willing to sanction (and even, on occasion, to advocate) suicide or voluntary martyrdom in the defense of objectivist principles—i.e., in the cause of personal freedom. As Nathaniel Branden states: "It is in the name of the life proper to man that a rational person may be willing to die—not as treason to his own life, but as the only act of loyalty possible to him."[183]

PSYCHOLOGICAL MORALITY

Objectivist morality is, and as Nathaniel Branden maintains, a *psychological* morality, a morality which defines "the issue of good and evil in terms of the *actions of one's consciousness*—that is, in terms of the manner in which one *uses* one's consciousness."[184]

What Branden means, of course, is that, for Rand, morality is frequently equated with sanity. To be happy is to be moral; to be moral is to be rational; to be rational is to be sane. The sane person is ultimately that person who recognizes reality for what it is and who regulates his behavior with respect to objective (and, hence, psychological) necessity. To be sane is to have developed one's capacity for independent and productive rational action to the highest possible degree. *"Mental health is the capacity for unobstructed cognitive functioning—and the exercise of this capacity. Mental illness is the impairment of this capacity."*[185] *"Degrees of ability vary, but the basic principle remains the same: the degree of a man's independence, initiative and personal love for his work determines his talent as a worker and his worth as a man."*[186]

At basis, altruism always functions as "a suspension of one's consciousness," a "self-abdication"[187] which is experienced subjectively as a sense of alienation from the real world. Such alienation is not metaphysical, however. It is, rather, and as Miss Rand terms it, "psycho-epistemological."[188]

MORALITY AND SANITY

Immorality is always a type of insanity, a sort of neurosis. To be immoral/insane is always and inevitably to be alienated from the world as-it-is. To live in the erroneous dreamworld of altruism is to live through others and, hence, to live at "second-hand," alienated from one's real self. "When you suspend your faculty of independent judgment, you suspend consciousness. To stop consciousness is to stop life. Second-handers have no sense of reality."[189]

The traditional morality of self-sacrifice is both insidious and ultimately self-defeating, because it is based on an implicit denial of the true psychological nature of man. At basis, altruism is an impossible mode of response. Because it is impossible, it leads to anxiety and ultimately to alienation and to the insanity of subjectivism.

Altruism functions as an "anti-anxiety device" in which the individual is motivated primarily by the fear of facing reality. Instead of pursuing objective self-gratification, he establishes purely "defensive" values with the objective of protecting the integrity of a purely "pseudo-self-esteem."[190] As might be expected, however, such a misrepresentation is doomed to failure and eventually leads to a progressive downward spiral of circular frustration which is characterized by such profound psychological symptoms as fear, suggestibility, pessimism, subjectivistic thinking and profound feelings of practical impotence.[191] "To the extent that a man indulges in irrational, mind-subverting psychoepistemological policies, he sentences himself to a chronic anticipation of disaster."[192] "The neurotic's essential attribute, his chronic response to the universe, is uncertainty and fear . . . every neurotic is afraid. A cheerful neurotic . . . is a contradiction in terms."[193] Pathological anxiety is both a cause and effect of self-doubt. By subverting his already tenuous self-confidence it further encourages his tendencies toward subjectivity and irrationality. "The result is a pronounced tendency to lose the distinction between the subjective and the objective . . . so that consciousness *is given primacy over existence*—thus generating the cognitive distortions so characteristic of neurosis."[194] "A state of chronic dread is *not* man's natural condition . . . sin is not 'original,' it is *originated*. The problem of anxiety is psychological, not metaphysical."[195]

In the final analysis, it is not possible to trade truth and personal responsibility for unconditional love and belongingness. The result is both forseeable and inevitable—the individual passes into a neurotic state of objective intellectual disorientation which is characterized by "the absence of a firm, independent sense of *objective reality.*"[196] This frustration inevitably increases the individual's fearfulness, and this fear, in turn, further augments the individual's reliance upon altruistic self-delusion. "When a man's mind is trapped in a foggy labyrinth of the non-objective, that has no exits and no solutions," states Rand, "he will welcome any quasi-persuasive, semi-plausible argument."[197] " . . . the obliteration of reason obliterates the concept of reality, which obliterates the concept of achievement, which obliterates the concept of the distinction between *the earned* and *the unearned.*"[198]

Ultimately, then, and as Branden indicates, all true love is necessarily *conditional love*—love which is caused and deserved on the basis of actual behavior. The idea of *unconditional love* is always ultimately a symptom of mental pathology."[199] Altruism is never motivated by love—i.e., by the capacity for the positive evaluation of others based upon objective self-esteem. It is always motivated by its antithesis, hatred, which is the inevitable outgrowth of chronic fear and anxiety. The choice, then " . . . is not: selfishness or good will among men. The choice is: altruism or good will, benevolence, kindness, love and human brotherhood."[200] Altruism is motivated by "hatred of man, not the desire to help him—hatred of life, not the desire to further it—hatred of

66

the *successful state of life*—and an ultimate, apocalyptic evil: *hatred of the good for being the good.'*[201]

Egoism has traditionally been presented as if it were a sacrifice of others to self. Altruism as a sacrifice of self to others. The result has been to bind pleasure irrevocably to pain, value to sacrifice. Suffering became a precondition for virtue. "When it was added that man must find joy in self-immolation, the trap was closed. Man was forced to accept masochism as his ideal—under the threat that sadism was his only alternative."[202]

In a classic example of what semanticist Wendell Johnson once termed the "IFD" (idealism-frustration-demoralization) disease, then, altruism serves as an *ideal* which is admirably designed to guarantee failure as a guide for effective behavior. The failure of the altruistic ideal, in turn, engenders the *frustration* which is invariably created by feelings of guilt, shame and sin. A sequence of such failures inevitably leads to a chronic sense of frustration which, in turn, leads to an overwhelming sense of *demoralization*—a progressive diminution of self-respect, a growing sense of emotional estrangement from accepted goals and standards. As a result, the schism between theory and practice grows increasingly wider. With demoralization comes a heightened susceptibility to the ideas and standards of others. At a total loss for realistic goals—for goals that *work*—and, yet, at the same time, conditioned to the idea that value exists outside the self, in the well-being of others, the altruist finds himself increasingly more suggestible and therefore increasingly more conforming and more inclined to seek *self*-satisfaction in and through the lives and actions of others. In this way, the self-alienation of altruism progressively strangles self-respect and engenders the concomitant effects of conformity, suggestibility and self-hate. The end-product is a world of muted hostility and pervasive "other-direction."

There are, from Rand's point of view, two basic types of men: the individualists and the collectivists. "The man whose convictions, values and purposes are the product of his own mind—and the parasite who is molded and directed by other men."[203] According to Rand, the theme of *The Fountainhead* is "individualism versus collectivism, not in politics, but in man's soul."[204]

The true *individualist* is the goal of objectivism. An enlightened egoist who is committed to the course of productive reason, he is the "practical thinker" and the "philosophical business man."[205] He is a person who believes that "a human life is an end in itself" and that man possesses certain inalienable rights to life, liberty and the pursuit of happiness.[206] "He is in conflict with the world in every possible way—and at complete peace with himself."[207] He is the man who says, "I will not run anyone's life—nor let anyone run mine. I will not rule or be ruled. I will not be a master nor a slave."[208] "The creator lives for his work. He needs no other men. His primary goal is within himself. The parasite lives second-hand. He needs others. Others become his prime motive."[209]

The individualist's strong underlying sense of personal identity stems primarily from an integrated set of objective values which are the product of his fervent dedication to independent thinking.[210] Characterized by "metaphysical efficacy,"[211] his supreme devotion is to his own self-interest. He is honest and just, but he is also fervently committed to maintaining the social and economic conditions necessary for the fullest expression of objective individualism.

The *collectivist,* on the other hand, is that person who defines the good as a negation—for such a person "the good is the nongood for me."[212] The collectivist is fundamentally anyone whose behavior is determined and directed by his relationship with others. "The creator's concern is the conquest of nature. The parasites concern is the conquest of man."[213] "They have no self. They live within others. They live second-hand."[214] "They have no concern for facts, ideas, work. They're concerned only with people. They don't ask: 'Is this true?' "[215]

There are, in essence, two types of collectivists. These (to coin two terms which capture a distinction which is implicit within Rand's point of view) might be termed the *benevolent* and the *malevolent* collectivists.[216]

The *benevolent collectivist*—who is only ostensibly benevolent—is perhaps best represented by the idealistic Marxist who advocates "a society where all would be sacrificed to all."[217] This type of collectivist is motivated primarily by the well-being of others. There are two basic varieties of benevolent (or well-meaning) collectivists: (1) the supernaturalistic altruists, who use altruism as a means towards attaining otherworldly salvation, and (2) the naturalistic altruists (such as the idealistic Marxists) who regard the collective well-being of all as an end-in-itself.

Rand condones neither of these positions. For both, "thinking . . . is not a means of perceiving reality, it is a means of justifying their escape

68

from the necessity of rational perception."[218] In the case of the supernaturalistic altruists, and as Nathaniel Branden indicates: "The world will not be saved by that alleged defense of freedom . . . which consists of arguing that man should not be sacrificed to the State, he should sacrifice himself to God instead."[219A] " . . . God is non-man, heaven is non-earth, soul is non-body, virtue is non-profit, A is non-A, perception is non-sensory, knowledge is non-reason. Their definitions are not acts of defining, but of wiping out."[219]

The secular collectivist, unlike the religious type, is *directly* motivated by the well-being of others. Such a person does not create value, he sacrifices it; he makes of his life an offering. He lives at "second-hand" through others, sacrificing his own objective needs to their requirements. Such behavior is based on faith and not on reason, and the outgrowth of such behavior is a progressive loss of personal identity—a chronic and cumulative sense of meaninglessness, accompanied by a gnawing sense of guilt and anxiety.

The *malevolent collectivist* is, in effect, the altruist "gone sour." Like the altruist, his behavior is basically derived from his relationships with others. The difference resides primarily in the nature of these relationships, for, while the altruist equates value with the happiness of others, the malevolent collectivist is primarily concerned with the happiness of self *defined as a relationship to others.* Like the militant atheist, who is implicitly committed to the tacitly theistic goal of the active *non-being of God,* the true misanthropist *requires* his victims and finds pleasure only in the subjugation (and, hence, in the psychological negation) of others. In a sense, then, the true evil-doer is just as "collectivistic" as the altruist, for, like the altruist, he *requires others* in order to experience personal value. Attila (the man who rules by brute force), like the Witch Doctor (the man who rationalizes the use of brute force by means of pseudo-intellectualization—including the false prophet, the priest, and most philosophers) is, at basis, a collectivist.

MORAL ABSOLUTISM

There can be no compromise between good and evil. Relativism and agnosticism in the area of ethics are evasions of personal responsibility for moral action. "Just as, in epistemology, the cult of uncertainty is a revolt against reason—so, in ethics, the cult of moral grayness is a revolt against moral values. Both are a revolt against the absolutism of reality."[220]

69

Moral principles are beyond compromise. "The next time you are tempted to ask: 'Doesn't life require compromise?' translate that question into its actual meaning: 'Doesn't life require the surrender of that which is true and good to that which is false and evil?' "[221] "There can be no justification for choosing any part of that which one knows to be evil. In morality, 'black' is predominantly the result of attempting to pretend to oneself that one is merely 'gray.' "[222] "It is in such issues that the most rigorous precision of moral judgment is required to identify and evaluate the various aspects involved—which can be done only by unscrambling the mixed elements of 'black' and 'white' "[223] *"One must never fail to pronounce moral judgment."*[224] "There can be no meeting round, no middle, no compromise between *opposite principles.* There can be no such thing as 'moderation' in the realm of reason and of morality."[225] "The 'consensus' doctrine is an attempt to translate the brute facts of a mixed economy into an ideological—or anti-ideological—system and to provide them with a semblance of justification."[226]

REFERENCES—CHAPTER IV

1. Ayn Rand, "The Objectivist Ethics," in *The Virtue of Selfishness,* page 14.
2. *Ibid.,* page 23.
3. Rand, "The Ethics of Emergence," in *The Virtue of Selfishness,* page 74.
4. Nathaniel Branden, "Benevolence versus Altruism," *The Objectivist Newsletter,* I, 7 (July 1962), page 27.
5. Rand, "The Objectivist Ethics," *op. cit.,* page 29.
6. Rand, *Atlas Shrugged,* in *For the New Intellectual,* pp. 126-7.
7. Nathaniel Branden, "Intellectual Ammunition Department," *The Objectivist Newsletter,* I, 9 (September 1962), page 39.
8. Rand, "For the New Intellectual," in *For the New Intellectual,* page 18.
9. *Ibid.*
10. Rand, *Atlas Shrugged,* in *For the New Intellectual,* page 98.
11. Rand, "Collectivized Ethics," in *The Virtue of Selfishness,* page 80.
12. Rand, "Choose Your Issues," *The Objectivist Newsletter,* I, 1 (January 1962), page 1.
13. *Ibid.*
14. Rand, "Man's Rights," in *The Virtue of Selfishness,* page 93.
15. *Ibid.,* page 94.

16. Nathaniel Branden, "An Analysis of the Novels of Any Rand," in *Who is Ayn Rand?*, page 43.
17. *Ibid.*
18. Rand, "Man's Rights," in *The Virtue of Selfishness*, page 94.
19. *Ibid.*, page 96.
20. *Ibid.*, page 97.
21. *Ibid.*, pp. 102-103.
22. Rand, "Collectivized Rights," in *The Virtue of Selfishness*, page 102.
23. Rand, "Man's Rights," in *The Virtue of Selfishness*, page 93.
24. *Ibid.*
25. Rand, "Collectivized Ethics," in *the Virtue of Selfishness*, page 84.
26. Rand, *Conservatism: An Obituary* (New York: The Nathaniel Branden Institute, 1962), page 4.
27. Rand, "Intellectual Ammunition Department," *The Objectivist Newsletter*, IV, 2 (February 1965), page 8.
28. *Ibid.*
29. Robert Hessen, Review of the book *The Decline of American Liberalism* by Arthur A. Ekirch, Jr., *The Objectivist Newsletter*, I, 7, (July 1962), page 28.
30. Rand, *America's Persecuted Minority: Big Business*, (New York: The Nathaniel Branden Institute, 1962), page 4.
31. Rand, *Atlas Shrugged*, in *For the New Intellectual*, page 183.
32. Rand, *Textbook of Americanism* (New York: The Nathaniel Branden Institute, 1946), page 8.
33. Rand, *Atlas Shrugged*, in *For the New Intellectual*, page 183.
34. Rand, "The Objectivist Ethics," in *The Virtue of Selfishness*, page 32.
35. Rand, *Atlas Shrugged*, in For the New Intellectual, page 183.
36. Rand, "The Nature of Government," in *The Virtue of Selfishness*, page 112.
37. *Ibid.*, page 109.
38. *Ibid.*
39. Rand, *Textbook of Americanism*, page 7.
40   *Ibid.*
41. *Ibid.*
42. Nathaniel Branden, An Analysis of the Novels of Ayn Rand," in *Who is Ayn Rand?*, page 38.
43. Nathaniel Branden, "Intellectual Ammunition Department," *The Objectivist Newsletter*, II, 1 (January 1963), page 3.
44. Rand, "For the New Intellectual," in *For the New Intellectual*, page 57.
45. Rand, *Atlas Shrugged*, in *For the New Intellectual*, page 160.
46. Rand, "Collectivized Ethics," in *The Virtue of Selfishness*, page 81.
47. Rand, "For the New Intellectual," in *For the New Intellectual*, page 25.
48. Barbara Branden, Review of the book *Planned Chaos* by Ludwig von Mises, *The Objectivist Newsletter*, I, 1 (January 1962), page 2.
49. Nathaniel Branden, "Alienation," *The Objectivist Newsletter*, IV, 9 (September 1965), page 42.
50. Barbara Branden, "Who is Ayn Rand?," in *Who is Ayn Rand?*, page 187.

51.   Rand, "What is Capitalism? Part II," *The Objectivist Newsletter*, IV, 12 (December 1962), page 55.
52.   *Ibid.*, page 56.
53.   Rand, "Collectivized Ethics," in *The Virtue of Selfishness*, page 84.
54.   *Ibid.*
55.   Barbara Branden, *The Moral Antagonism of Capitalism and Socialism* (New York: The Nathaniel Branden Institute, 1959), pp. 3-4.
56.   Rand, "For the New Intellectual," in *For the New Intellectual*, page 54.
57.   Rand, "What is Capitalism? Part I," *The Objectivist Newsletter*, IV, 11 (November 1965), page 54.
58.   Rand, "The Objectivist Ethics," in *The Virtue of Selfishness*, page 31.
59.   Barbara Branden, Review of the book *Planned Chaos* by Ludwig von Mises, *The Objectivist Newsletter*, I, 1 (January 1962), page 2.
60.   Rand, "What is Capitalism? Part II," *The Objectivist Newsletterm*, IV, 12 (December 1965), page 59.
61.   Barbara Branden, *The Moral Antagonism of Capitalism and Socialism*, pp. 3-4. Miss Rand states that "capitalism is not the system of the past; it is the system of the future—if mankind is to have a future." (Rand, "The Objectivist Ethics," in *The Virtue of Selfishness*, page 33.)
62.   Rand, *Atlas Shrugged*, in *For the New Intellectual*, page 129.
63.   *Ibid.*
64.   *Ibid.*
65.   Rand, "For the New Intellectual," in *For the New Intellectual*, page 43.
66.   Rand, *Atlas Shrugged*, in *For the New Intellectual*, page 133.
67A. Rand, *Atlas Shrugged*, as quoted in *For the New Intellectual*, pages 182-3.
67.   Rand, "The Monument Builders," in *The Virtue of Selfishness*, page 91.
68.   Rand, *Atlas Shrugged*, in *For the New Intellectual*, pp.182-3.
69.   Rand, "The Monument Builders," *The Objectivist Newsletter*, I, 12, (December 1962), page 56.
70.   Rand, *Atlas Shrugged*, in *For the New Intellectual*, pp. 182-3.
71.   *Ibid.*
72.   Rand, *Playboy's Interview with Ayn Rand*, page 12.
73.   Rand, "Government Financing in a Free Society," in *The Virtue of Selfishness*, pp. 118-119.
74.   Rand, "Intellectual Ammunition Department," *The Objectivist Newsletter*, III, 2 (February 1964), page 7.
75.   Rand, *Playboy's Interview with Ayn Rand*, page 12.
76.   Rand, "Government Financing in a Free Society," in *The Virtue of Selfishness*, pp. 118-119.
77.   *Ibid.*, page 116.
78.   *Ibid.*
79.   *Ibid.*
80.   Rand, "Intellectual Ammunition Department," *The Objectivist Newsletter*, III, 2 (February 1964), page 7.
81.   *Ibid.*
82.   *Ibid.*, page 8.
83.   Barbara Branden, Review of the book *Planned Chaos* by Ludwig von Mises, *The Objectivist Newsletter*, I, 1 (January 1962), page 2.

84.   Rand, "The Monument Builders," *The Objectivist Newsletter*, I, 12 (December 1962), page 56.

85.   Barbara Branden, *The Moral Antagonism of Capitalism and Socialism* (New York: The Nathaniel Branden Institute, 159), page 4.

86.   Rand, *Textbook of Americanism*, page 8.

87.   Any Rand, *Intellectual Bankruptcy* (New York: The Nathaniel Branden Institute, 1961), page 7.

88.   Rand, "What is Capitalism? Part I," *The Objectivist Newsletter*, IV, 11 (November 1965), page 52.

89.   Barbara Branden, Review of the book *Planned Chaos* by Ludwig von Mises, *The Objectivist Newsletter*, I, 1 (January 1962), page 2.

90.   Rand, *The Fascist New Frontier*, page 5.

91.   Rand, "The New Fascism," *The Objectivist Newsletter*, IV, 5 (May 1965), page 19.

92.   *Ibid.*

93.   Rand, "The New Fascism," *The Objectivist Newsletter*, IV, 6 (June 1965), page 26.

94.   *Ibid.*, page 24.

95.   Rand, "The Cashing–in: The Student 'Rebellion'," *The Objectivist Newsletter*, IV, 9 (September 1965), page 44.

96.   Rand, "The New Fascism," *The Objectivist Newsletter*, IV, 6 (June 1965), page 26.

97.   Barbara Branden, Review of the book *The Roosevelt Myth* by John T. Flynn, *The Objectivist Newsletter*, I, 12 (December 1962), page 54.

98.   *New York Times*, June 18, 1965, as quoted in Rand, "The Cashing-in: The Student 'Rebellion'," *The Objectivist Newsletter*, IV, 9 (September 1965), page 44.

99.   Barbara Branden, "Intellectual Ammunition Department," *The Objectivist Newsletter*, II, 6 (June 1963), page 23.

100. Rand, *America's Persecuted Minority: Big Business*, page 5.

101. For a fuller description of these objective economic laws, Miss Rand recommends four works in particular. These are *Economics in One Lesson* by Henry Hazlitt, *The Anti-Capitalistic Mentality* by Ludwig von Mises, *Socialism* by Ludwig von Mises and *Capitalism the Creator* by Carl Snyder. (Rand, *America's Persecuted Minority: Big Business*, page 5.)

102. Nathaniel Branden, "Intellectual Ammunition Department," *The Objectivist Newsletter*, I, 8 (August 1962), page 33.

103. Rand, "Antitrust," *The Objectivist Newsletter*, I, 2 (February 1962), page 5.

104. Rand, "What is Capitalism? Part II," *The Objectivist Newsletter*, IV, 12 (December 1965), page 56.

105. *Ibid.*

106. Ludwig von Mises, *Planning for Freedom*, as quoted in the review by Nathaniel Branden, *The Objectivist Newsletter*, I, 9 (September 1962), page 38.

107. Ludwig von Mises, *Planned Chaos*, as quoted in the review by Barbara Branden, *The Objectivist Newsletter*, I, 1 (January 1962), Page 2.

108. Nathaniel Branden, "Intellectual Ammunition Department," *The Objectivist Newsletter*, II, 11 (November 1963), page 43.
109. Nathaniel Branden, "Intellectual Ammunition Department," *The Objectivist Newsletter*, I, 8 (August 1962), pp. 33-34.
110. Rand, *America's Persecuted Minority: Big Business*, page 6.
111. Nathaniel Branden, "Intellectual Ammunition Department," *The Objectivist Newsletter*, I, 8 (August 1962), page 33.
112. Alan Greenspan, *Antitrust*, (New York: The Nathaniel Branden Institute, 1962), page 6.
113. Rand, *America's Persecuted Minority: Big Business*, page 6.
114. Rand, *Faith and Force*, page 9.
115. Robert Hessen, "Child Labor and the Industrial Revolution," *The Objectivist Newsletter*, I, 4 (April 1962), page 14.
116. *Ibid.*
117. *Ibid.*, page 16.
118. Rand, *America's Persecuted Minority: Big Business*, page 6.
119. Alan Greenspan, *Antitrust*, (New York: The Nathaniel Branden Institute, 1962), page 6.
120. Nathaniel Branden, "Intellectual Ammunition Department," *The Objectivist Newsletter*, I, 6 (June 1962), page 23.
121. *Ibid.*
122. *Ibid.*
123. Greenspan, *Antitrust*, page 6.
124. Nathaniel Branden, "Intellectual Ammunition Department," *The Objectivist Newsletter*, I, 6 (June 1962), page 23. This is not true. It is the probability and practicality of effective competition, the practical impossibility of competing successfully, that makes an enterprise monopolistic and not the total impossibility of competing against it in the first place.
125. *Ibid.*
126. In this regard, Greenspan quotes a statment made by Judge Learned Hand in his indictment of ALCOA for monopolistic practices:
> It was not inevitable that ALCOA should always anticipate increases in demand for ingot and be prepared to supply them. Nothing compelled it to keep doubling and redoubling its capacity before others entered the field. It insists that it never excluded competitors; but we can think of no more effective exclusion than progressively to embrace each new opportunity as it opened, to face every newcomer with new capacity already geared into a great organization, having the advantage of experience, trade connections and the elite of personnel. (Judge Learned Hand, quoted by Alan Greenspan, *Antitrust*, page 8).

Actually, Judge Hand is quite correct. A massive corporate enterprise of this sort represents a sort of frozen and pre-focused intelligence. The mere fact that it already exists as a functional entity with a pre-established market and pre-formulated techniques gives it a tremendous advantage in meeting new competitors and, perhaps more importantly, in discouraging incipient competitors from entering the area altogether.

74

127. These comments are not entirely consistent with the observations which Miss Rand has made on the so-called "electrical conspiracy" case which occurred in February of 1961 and in which seven executives of some of America's leading electrical manufacturing firms were charged with, and subsequently convicted of, conspiring to fix prices in constraint of trade. According to Rand the charge leveled against the accused electrical equipment companies was that of making covert agreements in order to rig bids and fix the price of their products. *"But,"* notes Rand, *"without such agreements, the larger companies would have set their prices so low that the smaller ones would have been unable to match them and would have gone out of business, whereupon the larger companies would have faced prosecution, under the same Anti-Trust laws, for 'intent to monopolize.'"* (Rand, *America's Persecuted Monority: Big Business,* page 13.)

128. *Ibid.*

129. Nathaniel Branden, "Intellectual Ammunition Department," *The Objectivist Newsletter,* I, 6 (June 1962), page 24. This is nonsense, of course. What Branden states is, in effect, that a natural resource like oil cannot be monopolized because gasoline is only one way to power a car. Thus if the oil industry were to control all of the available oil resources, they would still not be able to establish a monopoly, because they would merely elicit competition from such competing fuel sources as electricity and atomic energy. This, of course, makes sense only if one is willing to buy Branden's peculiar definition of a "monopoly" as a *total* control over the market.

   In practice, of course, and as was mentioned earlier, effective monopolization requires only that competition prove sufficiently impractical. In the case of the oil industry, the disparity betweeen the cost of running a car on gasoline and running one on either electricity or atomic energy is, at this time, sufficiently dramatic to allow the oil industry to manipulate prices to a vast degree without incurring any real threat of competition from one of these competing types of power. For the oil industry to raise prices beyond reason—i.e., beyond the place where they would retain a competitive edge over other products—would, of course, be totally foolhardy and exceedingly unlikely. The fact that prices cannot be raised indefinitely, however, does not mean that monopolies on natural resources are not possible.

130. Rand, *America's Persecuted Minority: Big Business,* quoted in *The Objectivist Newsletter,* I, 1 (January 1962), page 2.

131. Rand, "Antitrust," *Objectivist Newsletter,* I, 2 (February 1962), page 5.

132. Rand, *America's Persecuted Minority: Big Business,* page 13. Rand objects to antitrust laws on a variety of grounds. In general, she holds they are ill-defined, unenforceable, uncompliable, unjudicable, inconsistent and contradictory. She also claims that they inhibit trade, encourage the arbitrary exercise of power by virtue of their ambiguity and are applied retroactively in such a manner as to intimidate legitimate enterprise and to violate due process of the laws. (Rand, "Choose Your Issues," *The Objectivist Newsletter,* I, 1 January 1962, page 1; Rand, *America's Persecuted Minority: Big Business,* page 9.)

75

133. Rand, *America's Persecuted Minority: Big Business,* page 9.
134. It is interesting to note that Miss Rand fails to look at big corporations as a type of big government. Miss Rand is all for checking public government but not the private governments of the giant corporations.
135. Rand, *Atlas Shrugged,* in *For the New Intellectual,* page 94.
136. *Ibid.,* page 89.
137. *Ibid.*
138. *Ibid.,* pp.93-4.
139. *Ibid.*
140. *Ibid.,* page 92.
141. Nathaniel Branden, "An Analysis of the Novels of Ayn Rand," in *Who is Ayn Rand?,* page 116.
142. Rand, *Atlas Shrugged,* in *For the New Intellectual,* page. 91.
143. *Ibid.,* pp.90-1.
144. *Ibid.*
145. Rand, *The Fountainhead,* in *For the New Intellectual,* pp. 78-9. Miss Rand is not entirely consistent in this point. In her essay, "For the New Intellectual," for example, she holds that, if you live in a true capitalist society, you receive "an incalculable bonus," because, "the material value of your work is determined not only by your effort, but by the effort of the best productive minds who exist in the world around you." (Rand, *Atlas Shrugged,* in *For the New Intellectual,* page 185.)

    How she reconciles this position with her dominant theme of purely autonomous individualism is difficult to say.
146. *Ibid.*
147. *Ibid.,* page 82.
148. *Ibid.,* page 79.
149. Rand, "What is Capitalism?, Part I," *The Objectivist Newsletter,* IV, 11 (November 1965), page 52.
150. Rand, *The Fountainhead,* in *For the New Intellectual,* page 79.
151A. The terms "objective" and subjective" are used as rough synonyms for "impersonal" and "personal." This approximates the way Miss Rand uses the terms throughout the bulk of her work. The fact that Rand makes the assumption that impersonal reality (truth) can be derived *by means of reason*—which is non-Aristotelian—has no significant effect on this basic distinction.
151. Rand, *Atlas Shrugged,* in *For the New Intellectual,* page 126.
152. Nathaniel Branden, "An Analysis of the Novels of Ayn Rand," in *Who Is Ayn Rand?,* page 64.
153. Rand, *Atlas Shrugged,* in *For the New Intellectual,* page 126.
154. Nathaniel Branden, "An Analysis of the Novels of Any Rand," in *Who Is Ayn Rand?* page 64.
155. Nathaniel Branden, "Benevolence versus Altruism," *The Objectivist Newsletter,* I, 7 (July 1962), page 27.
156. Nathaniel Branden, "Pseudo-Self-Esteem" *The Objectivist Newsletter,* III, 5 (May 1964), page 17.
157. Rand, "Psycho-Epistemology of Art," *The Objectivist Newsletter,* IV, 4 (April 1965), page 15.

158. Nathaniel Branden, "Social Metaphysics," *The Objectivist Newsletter,* I, 11 November 1962), page 50; Nathaniel Branden, "The Roots of Social Metaphysics," *The Objectivist,* IV, 10 (October 1967), page 6.

The "social metaphysics" orientation is not an all-or-nothing proposition. Branden, in his article "Social Metaphysics," indicates that these are not only subvarieties of social metaphysicians but that there is one type—the "ambivalent"—whose intellectual default is largely restricted to the extremely significant area of personal values. This person "notwithstanding a major psycho-epistemological surrender to the authority of others, has still preserved a significant degree of intellectual sovereignty." (Nathaniel Branden, "Rogues Gallery II," *The Objectivist Newsletter,* IV, 3, March 1965, page 12.) In this respect, he "retains a far greater measure of authentic independence than any other species of social metaphysician." (*Ibid.*)

159. Nathaniel Branden, "Isn't Everyone Selfish?" in *The Virtue of Selfishness,* page 58.
160. *Ibid.,* page 59.
161. Rand, "The Objectivist Ethics," in *The Virtue of Selfishness,* page 27.
162. Rand, "Check Your Premises," *The Objectivist Newsletter,* I, 9 (September 1962), page 38.
163. Nathaniel Branden, "An Analysis of the Novels of Ayn Rand," in *Who is Ayn Rand,* page 29.
164. Rand, "For the New Intellectual," in *For the New Intellectual,* page 36.
165. *Ibid.*
166. Nathaniel Branden, "Intellectual Ammunition Department," *The Objectivist Newsletter,* I, 9 (September 1962), page 30.
167. *Ibid.*
168. Nathaniel Branden, "Benevolence versus Altruism," *The Objectivist Newsletter,* I, 7 (July 1962), page 27.
169. Rand, *Atlas Shrugged,* in *For the New Intellectual,* page 96.
170. Rand, *The Fountainhead,* in *For the New Intellectual,* page 70.
171. *Ibid.*
172. *Ibid.,* pp. 70-1.
173. Rand, "The Objectivist Ethics," in *The Virtue of Selfishness,* page 32.
174. Rand, *The Fountainhead,* in *For the New Intellectual,* page 81.
175. Rand, *Anthem,* in *For the New Intellectual,* page 65.
176. Nathaniel Branden, "Isn't Everyone Selfish?" in *The Virtue of Selfishness,* page 60.
177. *Ibid.*
178. Nathaniel Branden, "Intellectual Ammunition Department," *The Objectivist Newsletter,* I, 12 (December 1962), page 55.
179. Rand, "The Ethics of Emergence," in *The Virtue of Selfishness,* pp. 44-5.
180. *Ibid.,* page 45.
181. *Ibid.,* page 47.
182. Nathaniel Branden, "Intellectual Ammunition Department," *The Objectivist Newsletter,* III, 4 (April 1964), page 15.
183. *Ibid.*

184. Nathaniel Branden, "An Analysis of the Novels of Ayn Rand," *op. cit.*, page 61.

185. Nathaniel Branden, "The Concept of Mental Health," *The Objectivist*, VI, 2 (September 1966), page 11.

186. Rand, *The Fountainhead*, in *For the New Intellectual*, pp. 81-2.

187. Nathaniel Branden, "Alienation," *The Objectivist Newsletter*, IV, 9 (September 1965), page 41.

188. The term "psycho-epistemological" was first introduced by Miss Rand in her book *For the New Intellectual*. (Nathaniel Branden, "Psycho-Epistemology," *The Objectivist Newsletter*, III, 10, October 1964, page 41.) She defines "psycho-epistemology" as the "the psychology of thinking," *(Ibid.)*, "the study of the mental operations that are possible to and that characterize man's cognitive behavior." *(Ibid.)* In the case of most non-objectivists, the individual's psycho-epistemology represents the psychopathology resulting from "how [he] chooses to use his consciousness. It is the product of man's revolt against thinking—which means: against reality." (Nathaniel Branden, "Alienation," *The Objectivist Newsletter*, IV, 9, September 1965, page 42.)

   While it is beyond the scope of this study, it should be noted that Branden has developed an entire system of psychotherapy which deals with the problem of how to solve psycho-epistemological mental disorders. Such therapy entails " . . . teaching the patient *a new way of thinking*, a new method of cognitive functioning, a new psycho-epistemology—building on the foundation of whatever elements of a rational psycho-epistemology the patient still possesses." (Nathaniel Branden, "Psycho-Epistemology," *The Objectivist Newsletter*, III, 11, November 1964, page 46.)

189. Rand, *The Fountainhead*, in *For the New Intellectual*, page 69.

190. Nathaniel Branden, "Pseudo-Self-Esteem," *The Objectivist Newsletter*, III, 6 (June 1964), page 22.

191. Nathaniel Branden, "Rogues Gallery I," *The Objectivist Newsletter*, IV, 2 (February 1965), page 5.

192. Nathaniel Branden, "The Nature of Anxiety II," *The Objectivist* V, 12 (December 1966), page 6.

193. Nathaniel Branden, "The Nature of Anxiety I," *The Objectivist*, V, 11 (November 1966), page 9.

194. Nathaniel Branden, "The Nature of Anxiety III," *The Objectivist*, I, 1 (January 1967), page 11.

195. Nathaniel Branden, "The Nature of Anxiety I," *op. cit.*, page 12.

196. *Ibid.*

197. Rand, "Check Your Premises," *The Objectivist Newsletter*, I, 9 (September 1962), page 40.

198. Rand, "The Cashing-In: The Student 'Rebellion,' " *The Objectivist Newsletter*, IV, 9 (September 1965), page 44.

199. Nathaniel Branden, "Alienation II," *The· Objectivist Newsletter*, IV, 8 (August 1965), pp. 35-6.

200. Robert Hessen, Review of the book *The Decline of American Liberalism* by Arthur A. Ekirch, *The Objectivist Newsletter*, I, 7 (July 1962), page 28.

201. Rand, "The Obliteration of Capitalism," *The Objectivist Newsletter*, IV, 10 (October 1965), page 50.
202 Rand, *The Fountainhead*, in *For the New Intellectual*, pp. 80-1.
203. Barbara Branden, "Who is Ayn Rand?" in *Who is Ayn Rand?*, pp. 154-5.
204. *Ibid.*, page 153.
205. Rand, "For the New Intellectual," in *For the New Intellectual*, page 52.
206. Barbara Branden, *The Moral Antagonism of Capitalism and Socialism*, page 5.
207. Barbara Branden, "Who is Ayn Rand?", op. cit., page 155.
208. Rand, *Textbook of Americanism*, page 6.
209. Rand, *The Fountainhead*, in *For the New Intellectual*, page 79.
210. Nathaniel Branden, "Alienation," *The Objectivist Newsletter*, IV, 9 (September 1965), page 41.
211. *Ibid.*
212. Rand, *Atlas Shrugged*, in *For the New Intellectual*, page 143.
213. Rand, *The Fountainhead*, in *For the New Intellectual*, p. 79.
214. *Ibid.*, page 68.
215. *Ibid.*, page 69.
216. Rand, "For the New Intellectual," *op. cit.*, pp.34-38.
217. *Ibid.*, page 19.
218. Nathaniel Branden, "An Analysis of the Novels of Ayn Rand," *op. cit.*, page 49.
219A. Rand, *Atlas Shrugged*, in *For the New Intellectual*, page 49.
219. *Ibid.*
220. Rand, "The Cult of Moral Grayness," in *The Virtue of Selfishness*, page 77.
221. Rand, "How Does One Lead a Rational Life in an Irrational Society?" in *The Virtue of Selfishness*, page 70. It is difficult to reconcile Miss Rand's total rejection of moral compromise, however, with the statement which she makes in her article entitled "Collectivized Rights" in which she states that, while there are no countries today that are fully free and unaffected by some degree of socialism, "there is a difference between a country that recognizes the principle of individual rights, but does not implement it fully in practice, and a country that denies and flouts it explicitly." (Rand, "Collectivized Rights," in *The Virtue of Selfishness*, page 105.)
222. Rand, "The Cult of Moral Grayness," in *The Virtue of Selfishness*, page 75.
223. *Ibid.*
224. Rand, "How Can One Lead a Rational Life in an Irrational Society?" in *The Virtue of Selfishness*, page 71.
225. Rand, "The New Fascism: Rule by Consensus." *The Objectivist Newsletter*, IV, 5 (May 1965), page 20.
226. *Ibid.*

PART TWO

OBJECTIVISM: A CRITICAL ANALYSIS

Chapter V

KNOWING AND THE KNOWN: AN ANALYSIS

Ayn Rand's philosophy is perhaps best described as a variety of traditional (essentialistic) realism. In common with all traditional philosophies, Miss Rand subscribes to certain absolute principles. She maintains that there is some sort of *a priori* meaning (Truth) which inheres within the world and that this meaning precedes and determines the basic nature of all human knowledge. She also adheres to the position that such ultimate knowledge is both *absolute,* in the sense of being unqualified by any sort of circumstantial considerations, and *objective,* in the sense that it is unmediated by any purely personal consideration, such as interests, needs or desires.[1A] As a realist, she maintains that, at the very least, an *operational dualism* exists between self and world.

The Problem of Philosophical Classification.

It is difficult to label Miss Rand's epistemological position in terms of the usual philosophical categories. No small part of this difficulty stems from her tendency to present caricatured definitions of rival positions and then to disdain any sort of identification with the implausible ideas which she has misrepresented. In her theory of knowledge, for example, Rand *seems* to be a "nominalist," but she avoids this classification by the simple expedient of presenting a quite loaded definition of "nominalism" and then disclaiming any sort of affiliation with it. Thus, according to Rand, the "nominalists" are those "who hold that all our ideas are only images of concretes, and that abstractions are merely 'names' which we give to *arbitrary* groupings of concretes on the basis of *vague resemblances" [my italics]*.[1]

Miss Rand is not entirely clear about the origins of objective knowledge. In some instances she seems to hold that ultimate truths and values, while objective, are experienced (and therefore derived) *subjectively.*[2] As she states at one point, "Man *is* the measure, epistemologically—*not* metaphysically. In regard to human knowledge,

83

man has to be the measure, since he has to bring all things into the realm of the humanly knowable."[3]

In still other places—and despite her insistence that truth is in no sense determined by choice or contingent upon emotional factors—she appears to hold that truth ultimately emerges by means of thought which is, in turn, conditioned upon individual moral integrity.[4]

The Basis of Knowledge

Miss Rand's emphasis on the absolute and objective nature of ultimate knowledge (Truth) gives rise to a number of perplexing problems when it comes to her theory of cognition. For one thing, and despite her explicit contempt for Platonism and the Platonic tradition, she is in many respects very close to Plato in her analysis of the knowledge process.

The Paths to Knowledge. At basis, most philosophers would agree that there are four possible sources of metaphysical knowledge (abstract philosophical truth).

1) Knowledge of underlying reality may be communicated directly and actively from a metaphysical source in the form of personal revelation.

2) Ultimate knowledge may be derived *from experience* through the process of abstraction (as it is in Aristotle's philosophy). Such knowledge is only indirectly *essential* (absolute), because it is necessarily contingent upon the abstractive process itself which is, in turn, a secondary manifestation of prior sense-perceptual experience. Such knowledge is, then, necessarily mediated by personal awareness.

3) Such knowledge may not be *acquired* at all but may preexist *within* the organism itself as inherent truth which is only subsequently recognized as corresponding to (or matching) the underlying nature of encountered reality.

4) Such knowledge may be derived pre-rationally on the basis of the earliest sort of motor-emotional behavior during the first months and years of childhood and may therefore only subsequently (if ever) be "rationalized" as explicit knowledge.

The Objectivist Dilemma

Since Miss Rand is opposed in principle to both supernaturalism (Point I) and non-rational (or instrumental) intuition (Point 4), we are necessarily left to decide whether she prefers (1) the Aristotelian "nominalism" which sees truth as an abstract description of *qualities within experience*—i.e., as knowledge derived from inference on the basis of activity—or (2) that sort of "realism" which sees truth as *an innate quality of consciousness* which corresponds to certain external events and which has the capacity to "recognize" its own concrete representations (by means of philosophical "reminiscence," or some sort of psychological "matching," as in Platonic theory).

Ironically, despite Miss Rand's enthusiasm for Aristotelianism, a thorough examination of her writings reveals that she is actually closer to the Platonic position with respect to the origins of knowledge. This is true for two reasons. First, she maintains, contrary to Aristotle, that natural truth—and all truth is "natural" for Miss Rand—is *discovered* and not *created*. The Aristotelian position is, of course, not that truth is *created* (in a purely subjective sense) but, rather, that it is *discovered* by an imaginative reconstruction (perceptual creation) of essential similarities which are observed to be present in all relevant instances. In other words, while Aristotle can scarcely be characterized as a simple solipsist, he does maintain (as do the Thomists) that even *essence* (Truth) must be construed indirectly through an examination of personal experience and is not directly accessible through some sort of mystical confrontation with "reality beyond appearance." In a sense, then, an Aristotelian "discovery" is simply a "creation," or inference, which corresponds to the facts in the sense that it is congruent with the actual phenomena which it purports to describe.

Miss Rand's account of the perception of essential truth as a process of identification is quite compatible with the Platonic point of view, for in Plato basic truth is innate and is not therefore relative to life-experience in any sense at all and can easily be utilized as a ready criterion for assessing any subsequent interpretation of reality. In this sense, for both Rand and Plato, truth (existence) is what corresponds to Truth (essence), what "matches" the image.

For Rand, a knowledge of ultimate reality exists, not merely *a posteriori,* relative to particular experience, but *a priori,* as a certitude which precedes and lays the foundation for knowing itself. Knowledge does not grow out of personal experience. Quite the opposite. Certain basic truths are self-evident, in the sense of being implicit within experience itself. They are neither chosen (which would be subjectivism) nor derived on the basis of contextual knowledge (which would be relativism). They are, rather, projected as a sort of paradigmatic vision of ultimate reality. All men recognize these truths, because a recognition of such truths is implicit in the nature of man as man. Man is not only *potentially* rational; he is rational *by definition:* he is the animal who is possessed of intuitive insight—an insight which can be suppressed but never successfully denied.

Miss Rand's concept of absolute and unvarying truth involves her in several difficulties. To begin with, she is faced with the difficulty of establishing a metaphysical base for her materialistic naturalism. In her attempt to combat mysticism, she ends up in a position where only two paths are available: (1) the way of solipsism and (2) the way of mysticism.

To espouse solipsism—i.e., the position that all knowledge is hypothetical, an outgrowth of personal awareness—is, of course, unthinkable. For Miss Rand even the highly qualified phenomenological solipsism of the pragmatist is anathema because of its contention that knowledge is derived, not from the world per se, but, indirectly, from one's *responses to* (and *experience of*) the world. In a similar sense, Miss Rand rejects all personal revelation from supernatural sources.

What she is left with is tautology—A is A. Direct and unmediated (objective) experience is the sole source of basic truth, and such truth is an unavoidable aspect of personal reality, a psychic microcosm of the objective macrocosm of ultimate reality. Man does not *learn* metaphysical truth in the usual sense of the word, for *learned truth* would always be *relative*—i.e., derivative upon the fallible byways of the variable knowledge process. Rather, an implicit (preconscious) recognition of truth *as truth* is one aspect of man's nature as man.

Since an awareness of ultimate reality (Truth) is implicit within man's nature as man, and, since (as Miss Rand also maintains) a conscious submission to the dictates of such knowledge is good, it naturally follows that any denial of Miss Rand's point of view falls into the general categories of deliberate untruth and/or willful evil.

What this adds up to, of course is a classic sort of self-fulfilling prophesy which can be outlined as follows:

1) Ultimate truth and value reside in X.
2) All men know that ultimate truth and value reside in X.
3) Therefore, to deny the reality of X is to be (willfully) untruthful and evil.

It is pointless to condone disagreement with such a position by pleading either ignorance or (except in the most radical cases) stupidity, for an intrinsic awareness of such knowledge is one of the determining characteristics of man as man. "X is thus and so" because "X is thus and so." To deny it is to be a willful liar. Not to know it is to be less than a man.

On the other hand, Miss Rand's implicit mysticism gives rise to grave problems with respect to still other aspects of her theory. For one thing, *if* all men are apodictically aware of the true nature of ultimate truth and value, how can any man choose *not to believe* that which he already *knows* to be true?

Again, there would seem to be two basic answers.

1) Men are evil because they fail to be rational, because, in short, they refuse to think and therefore to recognize the truth.

This answer is unacceptable because it is not compatible with Miss Rand's theory. If, in short, a true knowledge of ultimate reality is intrinsic within human experience as such and therefore exists prior to any particular sorts of experience, it must also precede all volitional rationality as well and is not therefore in any sense contingent on the exercise of self-conscious and willful reason.

2) Men are evil because they prefer some other course of action to the one which they know to be right.

This position is also untenable, for, if a person accords priority to one course of action over another, he cannot be said to "know"—i.e., to be implicitly convinced—that the first position is in fact preferable to begin with. Indeed, if he were convinced that the first course of action were *preferable*, he would not be *able*, given the choice, to choose anything else without being guilty of self-contradiction—without, in short, *being willing to do that which he does not want to do.*

It is, in short, absurd to speak of "non-volitional volitions." A man must always believe the truth as he comprehends it to be, because (speaking psychologically) the "truth" *is precisely what a person comprehends it to be.* A person must always do what he believes to be best in the light of whatever circumstances he perceives to exist, because to do otherwise would either (1) assume the possibility of unmotivated action (which would violate the law of cause-and-effect at the psychological level) or (2) assume the possibility of self-contradictory action by stating, in effect, that one may chose to do what one does not in fact choose to do.

From the objectivist point of view, knowledge of ultimate reality, as this exists prior to reason and prior to any particular sorts of knowledge, is not subjective. Indeed, it is not *personal* at all but *generic,* as essential and defining aspect of human nature as such—very much like the Kantian categories. By implication, then, Miss Rand posits something very much like the traditional Cartesian psycho-physical parallelism. There exist in the mind ideas which correspond to, but which are not merely interpretations arising from particular encounters with, the basic operational principles of reality itself. We recognize the truth—i.e., the true nature of reality—because our knowledge process is itself a sort of *reconnaissance* or secondary confrontation, with that which we already intuitively comprehend. Both ultimate reality and our knowledge of ultimate reality are, then, prior to, and independent of, particular (contextual) experiences in the world and serve as the objective basis for all purely contextual (relative) experience.

The Problem of Knowability.

The objectivists reject on principle the idea that ultimate truth is unknowable—i.e., that metaphysical knowledge *cannot be known*. They do this on the basis that "to claim that a thing is unknowable entails a logical contradiction."[5] As Branden states, "the idea of the 'unknowable' is indefensible,"[6] because the statement that something is unknown assumes a previous knowledge of precisely that which is denied, which would be self-contradictory. "The assertion that a thing is unknowable carries the necessary epistemological implication that the speaker is omniscient—that he has total knowledge of everything in the universe . . . ."[7]

Branden is extremely vulnerable here on several counts.

To begin with, he rejects the claims of "absolute unknowability" by asserting the contrary doctrine of "absolute knowability." In so doing, however, he leaves himself open to precisely those charges which he levels against the proponents of absolute epistemological limits.

Even those who would subscribe to Branden's contention that metaphysical truth is *totally knowable* must also grant that all of the objectivists' objections against those who claim absolute "unknowability" apply equally to those (like Branden) who claim absolute "knowability." In short, and following Branden's own processes of reasoning, four things should be noted with respect to this overall line of argument.

88

1) It is only possible to state that everything is knowable—i.e., intellectually comprehensible—if one knows everything to begin with. In other words, the only proof possible for the statement "Everything is knowable" is a prior knowledge of *all* those instances which are covered by such a sweeping generalization. In this sense, and as Branden so acutely observes with respect to the proposition of absolute *un*knowability, any claims for absolute knowability necessarily imply the epistemological omniscience of the speaker.

2) The only way in which it is possible to assert absolute knowability without being omniscient to begin with is to begin with mystical insight (or mystical intuition), innate knowledge or an act of faith. It is apparent, then, that Branden's only proof for his contentions about the absolute knowability of reality is his own absolute infallibility as a source of true knowledge, which is based upon a sense of implicit (and unverifiable) certitude.

3) He uses the term "knowable" in a very special way. For Branden something is "knowable" if it (1) exists (" . . . one already has knowledge of it . . . ") and (2) does so in terms of clearly definable attributes and dimensions (" . . . one would have to know enough about it to justify ones pronouncement . . . ") For something to be "known," in short, it is not enough that it be "perceived" *to be*. It must also be comprehended as a particular type of object or event complete with a specifiable *meaning*.

This is not, of course, the usual meaning of the term "knowable." For most people, it is quite possible to know that something exists without knowing what it is or what it means. It is, for example, quite possible to know *that* water freezes below certain temperatures without knowing how or *why* it does so. In such a case, one *recognizes* the fact without really *understanding* it at the causal, or explanatory, level.

For Branden, however, no such division is possible. As he conceives of knowability (at least, in the context of the quotations cited) "knowledge" always implies not only a *recognition* of a phenomenon but some degree of *comprehension* as well. He rejects the notion that it is possible to perceive a situation without comprehending it intellectually. This leads him to the quite indefensible conclusion that no one can make a pronouncement that anything is *unknowable* without being guilty of self-contradiction on the grounds that a thing must be *known* (i.e., comprehended) in the first place before it can *not be known*—i.e., actively *negated,* or *denied,* as an object of knowledge.

Taken at face value, this position is, of course, utter nonsense and terminates in two unavoidable conclusions.

a) All problems (or questions) are implicitly denials of solutions (or answers) which are already "known."

b) It is impossible *not to know* anything, because the act of not knowing implies a prior knowledge (comprehension) of that which is ostensibly "unknown."

4) He makes the error of assuming that assertions of absolute unknowability are unavoidably assertions of personal omniscience.

Again, this position is defensible only if one accepts Branden's extremely questionable definition of "knowledge." The scientist, however—to take perhaps the best counter to Branden's position—does not assert the *absolute* knowability or unknowability of anything. He merely states that such and such is true *if* it is verifiable in terms of pertinent evidence procured through the application of pre-determined techniques for observation and analysis. In other words, science, as Branden clearly senses, is basically pragmatic. As philosopher Jacob Bronowski states:

> This sequence is characteristic of science. It begins with a set of appearances. It organizes these into laws. And at the center of the laws it finds a knot, a point at which several laws cross: a symbol which gives unity to the laws themselves. Mass, time, magnetic moment, the unconscious: we have grown up with these symbolic concepts, so that we are startled to be told that man had once to create them for himself. He had indeed, and he has; for mass is not an intuition in the muscle, and time is not bought ready-made at the watchmaker's.
>
> And we test the concept, as we test the thing, by its implications. That is, when the concept has been built up from some experiences, we reason what behavior in other experiences should logically flow from it. If we find this behavior, we go on holding the concept as it is. If we do not find the behavior which the concept logically implies, then we must go back and correct it. In this way logic and experiment are locked together in the scientific method, in a constant to and fro in which each follows the other.[8]

When the scientist asserts that the existence of God is *not knowable* or that the freezing temperature of water *is knowable,* then, he does not mean what Branden means by "knowable." What he means is, in effect, that such and such is or is not knowable because the consequences of applying given techniques of observation and analysis do or do not confirm their knowability at some particular time and in the light of some particular set of circumstances (including the existing state of knowledge and technology).

Scientific statements about "knowability," then, are never absolute statements with respect to particular questions but merely derivative statements contingent upon prior assumptions about the truth and value of certain observational processes. For the scientist, all statements about the knowability of particular assertions are contingent upon prior epistemological assumptions about the nature of knowledge itself. The metaphysical basis of science can, then, be formulated as follows:

1) X is knowable (or not knowable) because
2) the evidence garnered from enquiries with respect to the nature and conditions of X support this conclusion when
3) this evidence has been gathered in conformity with established scientific procedures for investigation.

This does not mean, of course, that scientific statements about knowability are not ultimately derived from certain ontological (metaphysical) assumptions about the nature of truth. It does mean, however, that these assumptions differ from those of the objectivists in two basic respects:

a) In most instances, they are not *absolute* in the sense that they imply a total awareness of reality per se. The scientist merely states that certain types of knowledge are or are not possible in terms of established scientific techniques at any given instant. Certain facts about the physical topography of Mars were not, for example, until very recently "knowable" *in fact* because of technological limitations with respect to observation and analysis. Several centuries ago they were not even conceded to be "knowable" *in principle,* because modern developments in such widely varying fields as astrophysics, rocketry and photography made the collection of such knowledge virtually

91

inconceivable. If we go back several millennia, not only the answers to such questions but the questions themselves recede to the limbo of the "unknowable." In this sense, whole provinces of potential knowledge have evolved from the "unknowable" to the "knowable-in-principle" to the "knowable-in-fact."

b) Even the most "absolute" of scientific knowledge—the established principles of scientific observation and analysis—apply not to particular *facts* but to processes for *deriving* facts. In this sense, the "absolutes" of science are "procedural absolutes" which really describe a protocol for determining the objective dimensions of reality and which do not purport to describe particular answers or to delineate specific values. Ultimately, and as the philosopher of science Jacob Bronowski so acutely observes, science is merely a special way of solving problems. The problems posed, however, derive not from "science" but from human beings. The whole point of science is true knowledge, and the whole point of true knowledge—however rarefied this pursuit may occasionally become—is a greater mastery over the objective world which these truths purport to represent—a mastery ultimately motivated by humanistic (and hedonistic) ends.

Scientific knowledge does not represent a claim to omniscience precisely because it does not rest on *assertions about truth* but, rather, upon the *practical consequences*—which are ultimately measured in terms of individual emotional gratification (personal pleasure and happiness)—which grow out of the applications of such assertions in the attempt to solve practical problems. The assumptions of science are not based on faith. They are based on self-interest and confirmed by the emotional consequences of living in accordance with objective reality and objective reason.

The objectivists are wrong in asserting that there is a logical contradiction involved in holding that knowledge is "unknowable." When a scientist states that a thing is "unknowable" he means

1) that something exists which is imperfectly understood;

2) that this thing which exists is beyond verification in terms of established methods of scientific enquiry; and

3) that this thing may or may not become knowable—i.e., be confirmed as either existing or not-existing—as scientific procedures or

92

the application of such procedures become further perfected and progressively extended.

In a very fundamental sense, of course, what makes any aspect of scientific knowledge a "fact" is not just the particular manner in which it has been verified but also whether and to what extent such knowledge is capable of *being* verified. A singular fact—as, for example, the fact that I "love" apple pie—may be true in a subjective (or phenomenological) sense, but it can never be termed a *scientific fact* because no one but me can ever really experience and, hence, substantiate this "feeling" which I have. The problem is not one of reliability, for I may "feel" the same way whenever I eat apple pie. The problem is basically one of objective validity. Howsoever often I may testify to the fact, I cannot "prove" (i.e., scientifically-demonstrate) this emotional response in any "objective" sense.

In a very basic sense, of course, scientific "facts" are not *substantive facts* at all but *operational facts*. Contrary to popular opinion, the scientist as a scientist is not a "realist" at all in the traditional sense. The only "absolute" implicit in science is the purely procedural absolute of the scientific method itself. The scientist does not say that light travels at 186,000 miles per second *regardless* of evidence to that effect but precisely because there *is* the clearest evidence to this effect and because such a statement can be verified experimentally under certain stipulated and replicable conditions. For the scientist what is "assumed" in the sense of being beyond scientific verification is a certain process of enquiry. "Truth" is not "given"; it is always an inference arising out of this process.

A scientific fact is always and necessarily a fact which is verifiable by others, providing these others are competent and reliable observers who have addressed themselves to the same or similar problems under suitable conditions. Science is, then, basically and necessarily a dialogue between scientists, and a scientific fact is *objective,* not in the traditional sense of being "non-subjective," but in the sense of being "inter-subjective"—that is, supported by the evidence growing out of the independent research of many individuals dealing with the same problem in terms of the same general assumptions and procedures. As Abraham Kaplan states:

... the basic test for the objective is "do you see what I see?" To

93

be sure, it is only the subjectivity of the qualified observer that counts, and only observations made under appropriate conditions. The business of the logic of inquiry is just to formulate these qualifications and conditions. Values that have been sustained by inquiry, that is, objectively evaluated, are as public as any other matters of fact.[10]

The Fallacy of the Stolen Concept

One way in which objectivists attempt to justify their ontological assumptions is by invoking what they term the "fallacy of the stolen concept." This "fallacy," states Nathaniel Branden " . . . consists of *the act of using a concept while ignoring, contradicting or denying the validity of the concepts on which it logically and genetically depends.*"[11]

Branden illustrates this "fallacy" by citing Proudhon's well-known statement "All property is theft." If, states Branden, all property is "theft," the term "theft" itself loses its validity, because it possesses meaning in the first place only as a way of describing a particular type of "property" relationship. In this way, continues Branden, the concept "theft" is used unrightfully and is, in effect, "stolen" from the larger concept of "property," which it then illegitimately seeks to negate. One cannot, however, logically direct a term against one of the logical conditions which are required for its own meaning and coherency.[12]

In his review of Brand Blanshard's book *Reason and Analysis,* Branden approvingly quotes Professor Blanshard's contention that one cannot be illogical without entering into a series of self-contradictions. As Blanshard puts it:

> To deny the law [of contradiction] means to say that it is false *rather than* true, that its being false excludes its being true. But this is the very thing that is supposedly denied. One cannot deny the law of contradiction without presupposing its validity in the act of denying it.
>
> We accept the law and must accept it, because "nature has said it." If we hold that a thing cannot at once have a property and not have it, it is because we *see* that it cannot. The law of contradiction is at once the statement of a logical requirement and the statement of an ontological truth.[13]

What this position fails to indicate is the difference between *talking* about reality and *living it.* As Bertrand Russell indicates so well in his well-known theory of types, a *statement about statements* cannot be refuted within the purview of its own established context of assumptions. If, for example, I choose to be illogical, I cannot be accused of taking one of the two "logical" positions with respect to logic itself, for the simple reason that I have rejected logic altogether and have chosen to exist outside the framework of logical discourse. If I insist upon obeying the dictates of logic by giving lengthy logical reasons for why my illogical stance makes "better sense" than a logical one, I am, of course, implicitly violating my own professed beliefs and I become legitimately open to the charge of self-contradiction. If, on the other hand, I am sincere, and my stated rejection[13A] of the law of contradiction is the last *sensible* statement which I choose to make (since all normal discourse is based on logical assumptions), I cannot be accused of being self-contradictory because I abstain from all subsequent attempts to rationalize or defend my illogicality. In such a case, of course, my assertion that I reject the formal law of contradiction will be a terminal assertion. I have *now* quit playing the logic-game of true-false dichotomies altogether. In this sense, then, and contrary to Professor Blanshard's contentions, my statement does not mean that I reject the idea that the law of contradiction is *true.* Rather, I reject the idea that it is *meaningful*—i.e., relevant. My choice is to live without considering the idea at all, let us say, *intuitively* at a purely spontaneous (pre-verbal) level of response in something approximating Zen awareness.

But what of my behavior? Do I not implicitly contradict my illogicality by the effectiveness or ineffectiveness of my actions? Again, the answer is No. Adherence to the law of contradiction is no guarantee of effective behavior. It is even conceivable that I might become more effective on a practical level by returning to a purely pre-rational and unselfconscious mode of pure and unmediated behavioral response. Ineffective logic may be worse in certain circumstances than none at all. If I am lucky, I may, like the schizophrenic in certain Siberian tribes, be taken for a prophet or holy man and be elevated to a position of social eminence.

This is not to say that the law of contradiction is *not* both a logical requirement and, at the same time, a statement of ontological truth. It is, however, to say that to deny the law of contradiction may be to deny its meaningfulness (and therefore to deny it *either* truth *or* falsity) and not merely to affirm its contrary (by making a positive claim to its

95

falsity). It is also to suggest that it is entirely possible to deny logical assertions in this sense without being self-contradictory (in the verbal or intellectual sense), providing that subsequent assertions (or the lack thereof) are not inconsistent with such a denial. Finally, it is, to hold that it is entirely possible to deny the law of contradiction (as a principle regulating belief) without being condemned to behave in a self-contradictory way. It is entirely feasible that an individual may continue to behave "logically" (i.e., in conformity to objective requirements as these are construed by *others*) without, at the same time, feeling constrained to "rationalize" his behavior either to himself or to others by making his behavior conform to formal symbolic representations of its own implicit structure.

What makes the so-called "fallacy of the stolen concept" difficult to deal with is that, as in so many cases of objectivist reasoning, it is true in principle but misapplied in practice. Branden is quite correct in maintaining that it is invalid to contradict oneself in discourse by subverting ones own ulterior assumptions. Accepted rational procedures dictate that one should not make a statement in which the subject, either implicitly or explicitly, contradicts its own logical *opposite* or its own logical *contrary*. The statement "Goodness is non-goodness," for example, could be said to exemplify what Branden terms the "stolen concept" principle, because any concept ("goodness") implies and requires the reality of its opposite ("non-goodness") and, in fact, the negation of its opposite is an essential aspect of its definition. In a similar sense, the statement "Goodness is badness" is nonsensical because, again, a concept ("goodness") generally also implies the reality of its contrary ("badness"), a radically divergent state in which the same quality operates in a reverse direction. In such a case, and as is the case with logical opposites, the antonym becomes a distinctive aspect of the very definition of the term in question.

In a sense, then, the objectivists are simply talking about the law of contradiction. One cannot logically make a statement in which one contradicts oneself through the misuse of terms. Unfortunately, however, this is not *all* that the objectivists mean to convey, and this becomes quite apparent when we look at the actual applications of the so-called "fallacy." In practice, Branden is guilty of making three basic errors—one semantic, one empirical and one logical—in his use of the stolen concept principle.

His semantic error is apparent in the case of the Proudhon example—"All property is theft"—which has already been cited. He refutes Proudhon, not by invalidating his logic, but by misconstruing his statement. Taken quite literally, of course, Proudhon's statement is a logical absurdity which contradicts itself. The rub is, of course, and as virtually anyone who is even vaguely acquainted with Proudhon's anarchist theory is well aware, that Proudhon is simply making an elliptical statement based upon prior assumptions which are quite apparent (however factually dubious they may be) within the total context of his thought. He states "All property is theft." What he *means,* of course—and this is readily apparent in the context of his work—is "All *private property* is theft." His underlying assumption is that all property belongs by right to all of the people and is therefore *public property*—an assumption which is in no sense incompatible with his conclusion that any private ownership necessarily implies an unjust confiscation of public goods.

Still another instance where Branden is guilty of this kind of semantic legerdemain is in his refutation of the assertion "The laws of logic are arbitrary."[14] Again, strictly speaking, this is a nonsensical statement. But what—and, again, waiving the truth or falsity of the assertion in question—does a statement like this ordinarily *mean?* It does not typically mean that there are no laws of logic or that these laws, once construed, are arbitrary. It is, rather, in most cases, a statement which is quite logical within its own established frame of reference and in terms of its own assumptions. In most instances, it is simply part of a fabric of reasoning which runs roughly as follows:

1) Reality (life) has no transcendent meaning (order) or, if it has, this meaning is beyond comprehension.

2) Man creates meaning in the world through his own cognitive activity.

3) Man therefore creates the laws of logic.

4) Such laws, however, once created, are *not meaningless.* They are sustained by belief and are therefore *totally meaningful within the transcendentally meaningless (absurd) context* of the world-in-general.

This line of reasoning may not be *true*—most philosophers would object to it just as violently as do the objectivists—but it is not *illogical.* Granted the initial assumptions, the conclusions are in no sense incompatible with the more basic ideas involved.

A second error which Branden makes in applying the stolen-concept idea is a purely empirical one which has to do with his own initial premises. At still another point in his article "The Stolen Concept" Branden makes the following statement: "When neo-mystics declare that man can never know the facts of reality they are declaring that man is not conscious. If man cannot know the facts of reality, he cannot know *anything*– because there is nothing else to know."[15 A]

This statement is, to be charitable, questionable. Branden has the "right" to define his terms as he chooses. To say that man is not "conscious" unless he "knows the facts of reality" (i.e., objectivist Truth) is, however, to verge on empirical insanity. It contradicts not only the best evidence of modern science in the area of human behavior but Branden's own epistemological assumptions as well. To equate "consciousness" with "objectivism" is not only circular but, in being so, violates Branden's own cherished fallacy of the stolen concept. What he is saying is, in effect, "To be conscious is to know the truth." But what does this mean? If truth ("the facts of reality") is unavoidable and if there is nothing else to be known ("If man cannot know the facts of reality, he cannot know *anything* . . . ") two conclusions appear unavoidable.

1) There is no point in thinking about anything in particular (since truth is an automatic function of consciousness itself).
2) There is no possibility of error, since error would be the illogical perception of that which is non-factual and therefore non-existent.

In addition to this empirical error with respect to the nature of consciousness, Branden misconstrues the "neo-mystic" (pragmatic?) position by stating that, in effect, the only alternative to knowing *everything* (which seems to be Branden's position in the above instance) is to know *nothing*. "If [a person] cannot perceive existence, he cannot perceive *anything*–because there is nothing else to perceive. To know nothing and to perceive nothing is to be *unconscious.*"[15]

Again, this is simply tactical reasoning. The pragmatist does not, in rejecting theories of absolute knowledge, hold that man begins by knowing *nothing*. He states that man begins by *knowing* a great deal (factually) which he does not *understand.* In other words, he assimilates a great deal of knowledge and is conscious of this knowledge *before* he comprehends the *meaning* of such knowledge in terms of larger relational concepts—truths, values and so on.

Another instance where Branden plays essentially the same game of combining empirical and semantic errors in a fabric of ostensibly plausible reasoning is in the case of the epistemological function of faith with respect to assumptions, hypotheses and so on. "One of the most grotesque instances of the stolen concept fallacy," states Branden, "may be observed in the prevalent claim—made by neo-mystics and old-fashioned mystics alike—that the acceptance of reason rests ultimately on 'an act of faith.' "[16] In effect, of course, what Branden objects to is the assertion "Reason exists on faith." For Branden, this statement is untenable for two basic reasons:

1) Reason is objectively demonstrable on the basis of prior self-evident truths.

2) Faith is intrinsically opposed to reason. It is "the acceptance of ideas or allegations without sensory evidence or rational demonstration."[17]

There are three basic objections which can be leveled against Branden's line of reasoning in this instance. First, of course, by an act of persuasive definition, he has ruled out faith as totally implausible on a purely logical basis. To have faith is necessarily to be irrational. To most non-objectivists, however, "faith" is not "the acceptance of ideas or allegations without sensory evidence or rational demonstration."[18] It is, rather, the acceptance of ideas or allegations on the basis of empirical evidence and/or rational demonstrations which do not lend themselves to the usual procedures of scientific verification. This is not to say that there is no such thing as "irrational faith"—faith, for example, in the proposition that "two times two equals five" or that "the moon is made of green cheese." On the other hand, this is precisely why we ordinarily speak of *rational* and *irrational* faith in the first place.

Rational faith is merely an assumption (or hypothesis) which appears to be warranted on empirical and rational grounds. Even acts of rational faith differ in their degree of warrantability. To construct an artificial dichotomy between the God-term "reason"—which is always necessarily objective and therefore good—and the devil-term "faith"—which is always necessarily subjective and bad—solves absolutely nothing and merely paralyzes communication.

A second error which Branden makes is to violate his own injunctions against faith by (implicitly) invoking faith as the only plausible causal explanation for his underlying belief in reason. Reason, suggests Branden, is demonstrable on the basis of self-evident truth. Fine. But what do we mean by *self-evident?*

Since there cannot *logically* be a *logical reason for being logical*—for this would be circular reasoning—we are left in something of a quandary. What other possibilities are left? Mystical intuition, innate knowledge and revelation are all ostensibly ruled out. What about the *a posteriori* rationalization of prior pre-rational experience? Again, no, for this would be an implicit acceptance of emotivism, subjectivism and relativism. The only thing left is, of course, faith (belief which is beyond rational demonstration), and it *is* faith—whether the objectivists like it or not—which (necessarily) provides the basis for any kind of objective and self-evident truths.

To assert that we *know without knowing*, without having undergone any specifiable knowledge process, is absurd unless one is willing to subscribe to the practical equivalent of some doctrine of innate knowledge. One cannot *know rationally* unless one first knows *rationality*. One cannot know rationality *rationally* unless conceptual reason is an innate and prepotent category which pre-exists within the human mind itself. To accept reason without rational cause is to be reasonable on faith.

Faith and Reason. One thing which obfuscates the objectivist theory of knowledge is precisely the fact that the objectivists set up an extremely artificial and highly loaded dichotomy between *reason* and *faith.* "Reason," states Barbara Branden, "is the faculty that perceives, identifies and integrates the evidence of reality provided by man's senses. To base one's convictions on reason, is to base them on the facts of reality."[19] *Faith,* on the other hand, is "the acceptance of an idea without evidence or proof, or in spite of evidence to the contrary."[20]

Elsewhere, Nathaniel Branden makes essentially the same distinction and even goes on to add that " 'faith in reason' is a contradiction in terms."[21] " 'Faith' is a concept that possesses meaning only *in contradistinction* to reason. The concept of 'faith' cannot *antecede* reason, it cannot provide the grounds for the acceptance of reason—it is the revolt *against* reason."[22]

This is patent nonsense. There is no "contradiction in terms" in the concept of "faith in reason." Contrary to Branden's assertions, there is no reason why faith *cannot* antecede reason, and, except where theories of innate knowledge or mystical revelation are utilized, there is no

100

other way to ground reason except through faith. There are no "logical reasons for being logical."

In a similar sense, it is simply setting up a straw man to define "faith" as the acceptance of ideas or allegations without sensory evidence or rational demonstration and to say that it must always occur "in spite of evidence to the contrary" and in necessary contradistinction to reason.

Faith exists whenever there is belief in the absence of sufficient intellectual evidence to constitute proof. If, for example, I believe in my fellow-men, this is an act of faith. If I have hope for the future, this too is an act of faith. If I believe that it is better to be constantly rational and to seek the facts rather than to be impulsive and self-deluding, this is an act of faith as well.

The third major error which Branden makes in his application of the "stolen concept" idea is a purely *logical* one. This can be exemplified, once again, by returning to one—and perhaps the most significant—of Branden's own examples.

It is, contends Branden, nonsense to hold that reality is ultimately reducible to "process" or experience.[23] Any such proposition, continues Branden, overlooks the fact that the concept of "process" is stolen from the more encompassing concept of "entity." If there were not entities, "process"—as the active relationing of entities—would be implausible. Therefore the negation of the theory of absolute truth (as encompassed in the objectivist theory of absolute meanings which inhere within a world of concrete objects) in favor of a theory of relative process (and, more precisely, the pragmatic theory which holds that personal consciousness is the irreducible source of all knowledge) is a classic instance of an assertion which implicitly contradicts its own logical and linguistic antecedents.

Branden makes three errors in his line of reasoning.

To begin with, and from a purely logical point of view, Branden makes the indefensible error of falling into his own trap by "stealing" a concept. In short, and temporarily granting Branden's contentions that one can only speak of "process" when one has first identified the "things" which are in process, it soon becomes evident that it is equally true that one can only speak of *entities* in their relationship with and in contradistinction to other entities—i.e., in a context of *process.*

A cow, for example, is an object which can be *observed* to have certain characteristics and which *behaves* in a certain manner under

101

certain *conditions*. The fact that these observable features can be abstracted away from the total field of relationships in which they occur does not mean, however, that they do not describe actual uniformities within a pattern of more encompassing and continuing relationships. In a similar sense, to say that the concept (and truth) of, say, the formal law of contradiction in logic is a primary datum which can be asserted independent of the process of experiencing the kind of relationships which this concept represents is to assume that it has prior meaning in a world apart from that which is tangibly *real*.

Contrary to what Branden suggests, the term "entity" is *not* a logical prerequisite assumption for the use of the term "process." "Process" is the *larger* term which encompasses the term "entity." In effect—and to indulge in a vast oversimplification—the *opposite* and *contrary* of the term "entity" (being) are one and the same—the term nonentity (nothingness). "Process" refers to the active relationship between entities in terms of that which is (at least conceptually) regarded as not-being (i.e., the absence of particular entities). In effect, then, *"process" is active; "entity" is passive*—the conceptual presentation of a still-picture, or snapshot, of process.

All entities are partial representations of process, and process includes the abstract totality of all entities in their active and unceasing relationship one to another. The distinction, then, is basically *empirical* and not merely *formal*. *If* the knowledge of things is contingent upon the act of knowing and *if* the act of knowing grows out of an active relationship between the self and the world, knowledge of things is a product of the process of experience and, in fact, *things* are merely the labels which we attach to the constancies and continuities which inhere *within* our own experiences as these experiences are generalized to apply to other conditions which have not been personally encountered (and, indeed, to the world-in-general). If this is *not* so, we must assume that it is possible to have knowledge *directly*—i.e., without any mediating process of fallible personal awareness. But in this case, of course, we are right back to the paradox of "self-evident" knowledge or "faith without faith."

In essence, then, to say that reality is ultimately rooted in process is not "illogical" despite what Branden says. It merely rests upon a different theory of knowledge than that used by the objectivists—and one quite as logical (and far more empirical) than that of the objectivists. In addition, it rests upon the assumption (which again, is at least as plausible as the rival, static-truth theory of the objectivists) that the concept "entities" (a) is predicated upon the prior assumption of the *process* of knowing and (b) that the process assumption is both more coherent (in relationship to other warranted empirical assumptions) and more closely corresponding to the facts as scientifically-determined than that which begins with pre-formulated "meanings."

Paradoxically, the pragmatist is probably more firmly committed to the proposition that reality is logical than the objectivist. For Rand, the assertion that the world is logical is not a conclusion from experience but, rather, a self-evident precondition for experience itself. For the pragmatist, on the other hand, man has no certain awareness that the world is logical until the world inexorably impresses this fact upon him through behavior. In this sense, the pragmatist sees man's commitment to logic as the outgrowth of actual encounters with a world which is objectively logical. For Rand, man is logical by edict, as a condition for encountering the world in the first place.

Objectivism and Pragmatism. Perhaps the most interesting position which Branden attempts to refute by means of the "stolen concept" principle is the basic epistemological position of the pragmatist. This is particularly worth examining, because it presents virtually a textbook case of the objectivist method of dealing with rival theories. Through an exotic combination of misrepresentations, exceedingly dubious empirical assumptions and spurious reasoning, Branden weaves a position which is almost a classic case of intellectual legerdemain. To say that the principles of formal logic are merely probable, states Branden, is to be culpable of the same contradiction as that involved in other instances of the "stolen concept fallacy." The idea of the probable is not basic, because it takes on meaning only in relationship to that which is known and therefore certain. "Only when one knows something which is certain can one arrive at the idea of that which is not; and only logic can separate the latter from the former."[24]

When the pragmatist holds that man responds not to situations but to his responses to situations, to his perceptions or interpretations, he falls into the grievous error of forgetting that the very idea of perception or appearance is predicated upon a preconception of that which is real. "It is not rational to ask: *'Can* man achieve knowledge?—because the ability to ask the question presupposes a knowledge of man and of the nature of knowledge."[25]

Branden makes several errors in his analysis. To begin with, he factually misconstrues pragmatism to his own ends. As is customary, he establishes a thoroughly inflammable straw man.

The pragmatists do not state that the "hypothetical" (or probable) is primary. Quite the contrary, they hold that *experience* (personal awareness which grows out of behavior) is primary, that the child normally progresses through an era of naive realism (in which he normally mistakes his *ideas* of a thing for the *thing itself*) and that only gradually does he become capable of "hypothesizing–i.e., of holding beliefs tentatively and modifying these in terms of progressively more accurate and more complete information. From the pragmatic point of view, certain of these hypotheses–such as the laws of logic themselves–gradually become so fully and overwhelmingly verified that they become "truths"–i.e., operational absolutes which become (except in the rarest of instances) the automatic and unquestioning basis for virtually all future behavior.

A second misrepresentation is that which holds that the pragmatists "assert that man perceives, not objective reality, but only an illusion or mere appearance."[26] This is total nonsense. The pragmatic position is precisely that we *do* encounter reality and that this *process of encounter* is precisely what we mean by the *primary reality of experience.* To say, as Branden does, that the hypothetical–i.e., belief which is beyond certitude–*"acquires meaning* only in contradistinction to the known, the certain, the logically-established"[27] is to evade the entire question. For one thing, it is merely an untenable "proof by assertion" which lacks any sort of empirical verification. If we know certitude as a condition for recognizing non-certitude, where does certitude itself *come from?*

Again and again, the same question must be advanced. If our certainties do not derive from the clarification, testing and integration of our earliest uncertainties, *whence* do they come? In a similar sense, if we grant Branden's contention that logic requires a prior knowledge of certitude as a basis for comprehending illusion, does not the concept of "certitude" become equally reliant upon a prior conception of "illusion"? The answer is, of course, that the concepts of truth and falsity, reality and illusion, emerge concurrently as different aspects of the same process of concept-formation. In all instances, however, the larger concept is "experience" (knowledge), and certainty/uncertainty and truth/falsity are merely qualities of warrantability within such experience.

It is not true, as Branden charges, that the pragmatist evades "the question of how one acquires such a concept as 'illusion' or 'appearance.' "[28] The pragmatic position is, quite clearly, that all knowledge emerges out of experience which is, in turn, contingent on behavior. Questions of reality and unreality, truth and falsity, are initially *secondary* questions.

Whatever the very young child *believes* is *"truth"* for him, and his beliefs are radically contingent upon his own experiences. Whether a belief will become characterized as "reality" or "illusion" depends entirely upon the emotional consequences of acting upon such beliefs in the attempt to solve real problems and gratify real needs in the actual world of hard (if still largely indeterminate) facts. Since we all live in the same world and since we all suffer the same consequences from acting upon true and false assumptions, we all (barring insanity or the most extraordinarily abnormal conditions) arrive at substantially the same conclusions about the nature of "truth." Indeed, with increasing maturity and additional experience, we come to inhabit progressively similar worlds of personal truth—our "life-spaces" become increasingly less idiosyncratic and more generic.

Again, then, and contrary to Branden's assumptions, the pragmatist is not a Pyrrhonistic solipsist who believes that only personal reality exists and who doubts the possibility of attaining reliable knowledge of the nonsubjective world. He is *not* a solipsist precisely because the whole concept of *personal reality*—i.e., of a reality which is inviolate from practical encounters with the external world—is totally alien to the pragmatic temper. For the pragmatist, *experience is the primary reality. Experience,* however, is always and necessarily a process of interaction between self and non-self, and, since the self is initially merely an indeterminate predisposition toward effective (and therefore logical) experience, experience is always primarily conditioned (at least initially) by the determinative limits of the objective (factual) environment.

For the pragmatist, then, we *know* before we are capable of comprehending or evaluating *that which we know.* We start off with certitude which is largely error and work gradually toward a lesser number of progressively more accurate assumptions which are understood as necessarily tentative (and potentially fallible) generalizations from experience. Unlike the objectivist, the pragmatist does not start talking about the *known* and only subsequently talk about *knowing*. He starts with the truly radical questions concerning *how we know* and works toward a progressively clearer conception of that which can reliably be *known*.

For the pragmatist, logical principles are discovered within the processes of pre-verbal experience itself and are not a product of human imagination. Logic is more than a cognitive activity, it is rooted in factual being itself, reflecting, not simply a human predisposition toward ordered experience, but an order inherent within the process of personal experience in the world.

Even the traditional laws of logic are, in the final analysis, a product of pragmatic verification. We accept the law of contradiction because our experience affirms that it works better than any other assumptions in the appropriate circumstances. In a very basic sense then the laws of logic are psychological laws as well as formal principles. We are forced to be logical because it is our nature to seek pleasure through the medium of productive experience and because productive experience is predicated upon and provides the verification necessary for logical procedures. Effective behavior implies logical thought. And to think logically we must be willing to define terms which are sufficiently stable to be consistent with the requirements of discourse. If we are to talk intelligently, we must adhere to the law of identity, for we must continue to talk about the same thing in the same way for a sufficient period of time if we are to make sense at all.

The symbol is not, to be sure, that thing which it represents. Neither does it encompass all of the various possibilities inherent in the thing itself. Certainly no real object can be contained totally within a symbol. A map is not, as Korzybski indicates, an exact reproduction of that which it represents. If it were, it would no longer be a map. A symbol is necessarily an abstraction which represents only selected aspects of that which it signifies. By symbolizing, we abstract out precisely those elements which have the greatest relevance for us, which are most meaningful in terms of our needs and problems.

To grasp the "real meaning" of a thing—i.e., the meaning of this thing apart from its various instrumental significances—would not be to understand a thing apart from its relevance to particular situations but, rather, to grasp its potential relevance to every conceivable situation. In other words, human knowledge is always finite and contingent upon a particular body of experiences. On the other hand, it also functions *absolutely* in context. One cannot act *in doubt* or think without temporaily suspending any reservations which one may have about meaning. To "doubt" is not to reject partial meaning but to utilize partial meanings as the best device with which to approach partial problems. To grasp the total meaning of an idea is not to see it without perspective but to see it from many perspectives. In a very real sense, it may be true that it is indefensible to define "Aunt Mary" as an old woman wearing a red carnation, but this may be all I need to know if my sole concern is with picking her up in front of a bus station. It may well be true that this concept ignores other facts about Aunt Mary which are vastly more relevant in the long run—say, that she is 83, has a sparkling wit and is worth a million dollars. On the other hand, I am probably not *concerned* with Aunt Mary *in the long run* and, while I am quite willing to grant that she is doubtless *more complex* and, in certain respects, *different* than what I know of her, the fact remains that it would ultimately be *dysfunctional* for me to gather this sort of "useless" information for my particular purposes.

Research in the behavioral sciences has begun to cast an increasing shadow of doubt on the validity of the traditional distinction which has been made between self-evident (or analytic) and evident (or synthetic) truth. In line with contemporary evidence, it begins to appear increasingly apparent that the fundamental principles of deductive logic, while they may be "self-evident" in one sense, are not self-evident in the sense that they are either outside experience as such or comprise inherent (intrinsic) types of knowledge.[29] Instead, three conclusions would seem to be warranted with respect to the nature of *all* of the so-called self-evident (or analytic) truths.

1) These truths actually represent special sorts of synthetic (empirical) knowledge. All knowledge is contingent upon experience. The real distinction between *necessary truths* (such as the "self-evident" principles of logic and mathematics) and *contingent truths* (as, for example, the "truth" contained in a statement like "My dog is sick") resides not in the fact that *necessary truths* are known *prior to* experience while the latter type of statements are *contingent upon* experience but, rather, in the fact that the first are *totally contingent upon (and implied within) all experience while the second represents knowledge which is contingent upon only limited aspects of experience*. To put this in a somewhat different way, then, a *necessary truth* is one which could not conceivably be otherwise because it is an unavoidable aspect of conceivability itself. One cannot *imagine* a world in which something is both black and white at the same time because our

imaginations cannot exceed the limits of reason—we are limited to thinking within reason (factual relationships) and cannot speculate about reason itself. A *contingent truth* may be *otherwise,* precisely because it talks about *possibilities* and not, unlike logic itself, about *necessities.*

2) Analytic truths do not transcend phenomenal experience. They are *implicit within all phenomenal experience*—a substantially different thing. There are no specific referents for analytic truths, because analytic principles operate in every conceivable situation. In this sense, analytic truths provide the limits and define the context of experience itself. They are undemonstrable precisely because they provide the conditions necessary for all logical demonstrations and serve as the sole warrantable basis for all subsequent knowledge.

3) Analytic truths, while they comprise the implicit foundation for all cognition, are not themselves derived "cognitively." They are, rather, learned pre-verbally (intuitively) and grow out of behavior. The child is emotionally conditioned to respond to the world as it presents itself to him, directly and without symbolic or cognitive mediation. In this way, he learns to *respond* before he learns to *intellectualize about his responses.* In a very basic sense, then, the child learns to respond directly, organismically; he learns—psychologically, pragmatically—to act on the world. Only later does he learn to reflect upon his actions, to generalize on the perceived procedural regularities which have begun to appear within his own cognitive functioning. In other words, experience comes first and is regulated by psychological necessity. Cognition comes later and is largely an *a posteriori* rationalization (recognition) of psychological necessity.

In a basic sense, then, speech does not precede logic. Action precedes logic, and logic is a formalized statement about the psychological regularities implicit within effective action. Much of our learning is intuitive (preverbal) in this sense. We "learn" initially by behaving in a certain way. We subsequently "learn" about what we already *know;* we interpret (rationalize) the ruts that we have already worn into our lives.

In a basic sense, then, action is learned empirically, but it is learned directly and with none of the self-consciousness so characteristic of post-verbal learning. Logic is existentially-demonstrable; it is vindicated by and through practical experience itself. As philosopher John Hospers states with respect to values:

108

It's true that I can't validate a supreme norm in terms of any other ethical norms—to do so . . . is logically impossible. But although I cannot validate it—validation applies only to the subsidiary or derived principles—I *can* do something else; I can *vindicate* it. That is, the utilitarian principle is the apex of my moral system, and there is nothing above it in terms of which to validate it; but I can try to justify *my adoption of it*—and this justification is vindication. But remember, one doesn't vindicate propositions; one vindicates *actions* . . . . [30]

The pragmatist does not accept the position that, while logic may be *vindicated* through the practical consequences accruing to its utilization, it can never be *verified.* From the pragmatic point of view, *verification* is fundamentally a matter of *vindication,* and there is nothing more vindicable than the logical principles which underly all effective human behavior.

It is true that formal logic has a *prescriptive* function which makes it act as a self-confirming hypothesis. But logic is like the French revolutionary leader who had to run fast to overtake the mob he was "leading." It functions primarily to describe the psychological principles of cognition which inhere within effective experience itself. It is self-confirming only on a secondary basis. What makes it basically self-confirming is the inexorable organization of the objective world itself which underlies and conditions all thought.

A human being does not learn to be logical through learning logic any more than he learns to speak his native language by studying grammar. As in all things, the great preceptors are imitation and identification. The question is not whether it is possible to refute logical principles through experience, for, if logical principles do not in fact reflect the great consistencies which recur within experience itself, this would be tantamount to asking experience to negate itself. Experience confirms logic because logic derives from experience and is not *de novo.*

Ultimately, then, logic is beyond effective appeal because it is a primary and, hence, terminal proposition. The nature of logic is such that all truly basic ideas, pursued beyond a given point, deny themselves. To question the value of reason is, paradoxically, to ask for *reasons* to disbelieve. He who states that there is no truth states—again paradoxically—a truth. In either case, the end-result self-contradiction.

In a most fundamental sense, then, all ultimate truths are terminal propositions, and all terminal propositions are also true paradoxes—i.e., they are ultimately self-refuting if turned against themselves on the verbal level.

The Problem of Relative Knowledge

Ayn Rand's ideas about the nature of the knowledge process are clearly the most ambiguous aspect of her philosophy. This ambiguity arises in large part from the fact that, as has been indicated earlier, Miss Rand seems to vacillate between the two contradictory positions of experiential relativism and mystical intuitionism.

At many times, she takes the quite relativistic position that all belief is *a posteriori* and therefore contingent on human experience in the world. At least in one instance—in her discussion of concept-formation—she comes very close to adipting an *instrumental* concept of knowledge. She makes, for example, the following statement: "To grasp a concept is to grasp and, in part, to retrace the process by which it was formed. To retrace that process is to grasp at least *some* of the units which it subsumes . . . ."[31]

In her relativistic moods, Miss Rand categorically rejects the idea "that there's something above sense."[32] Don't say reason is evil—though some have gone so far and with astonishing success. Just say that reason is limited. That there is something above it."[33]

A close analysis of Miss Rand's writings reveals a wealth of similar sentiments. "The alleged shortcut to knowledge, which is faith, is only a short-circuit destroying the mind";[34] " . . . only a mystic would judge human beings by the standard of an impossible, automatic omniscience."[35]

In a similar sense, of course, her contention that " . . . man is the only living species who has to *perceive reality* " (my italics), who has to be conscious 'by choice,' " implies that truth and reason are neither self-evident nor apodictic—indeed, that man is "conscious through an act of violition and that his ultimate sense of reality is therefore always derived psychologically."[36]

The objectivist ostensibly rejects any doctrine of innate ideas.[37] There is, states Branden, no innate knowledge.[38] Values, as well as truths, emerge out of the life-process.[39]

In a similar sense, man is not born capable of reason. Reason—"the faculty that identifies and integrates the material provided by man's senses"[40] —is man's basic instrument of survival,[41] however, and is one of the earliest acquisitions of the maturing mind.

The first modality of reason to emerge is the sense-perceptual. These earliest perceptions—which are "groups[s] of sensations automatically retained and integrated by the brain of a living organism"—[42] provide the foundation for all subsequent cognition. As Rand indicates: "Percepts, not sensations, are the given, the self-evident. The knowledge of sensations as components of percepts is not direct, it is acquired by man much later: it is a scientific *conceptual* discovery."[43]

It is, then, percepts, and not sensations or concepts, which comprise the primary, or "self-evident," level of reality. Cognition begins with the "existents," or things, which are implicit within percepts.[44] These "implicit concept 'existents'" pass through three stages in the evolution of human cognitive development. Miss Rand terms these stages *"entity-identity-unit:"*[45] "The ability to regard entities as units is man's distinctive method of cognition. A unit is an existent regarded as a separate member of a group of two or more similar units."[46] The conceptual level of rationality is attained when the individual becomes capable of comprehending similarities in the relationship between two or more things on the basis of distinctive features which they hold in varying degrees.[47] Miss Rand defines a "concept" as "a mental integration of two or more perceptual concretes which are isolated by a process of abstraction and united by means of a specific definition."[48] "Every word we use (with the exception of proper names) is a symbol that denotes a concept, i.e., that stands for an unlimited number of concretes of a certain kind."[49]

Conceptual reason is man's defining characteristic as man. It is "that which is *essential* about him; it is the attribute which explains the greatest number of his own characteristics."[50]

Reason performs two basic functions: cognition and evaluation.[51] The cognitive process "consists of discovering what things *are*, of identifying their nature, their attributes and properties."[52] Evaluation, on the other hand, "consists of man discovering the relationship of things to himself, of identifying what is beneficial to him and what is harmful, what should be sought and what should be avoided."[53]

In her analysis of cognition, as in so much of Miss Rand's writing, she contaminates a high degree of psychological acuity with certain grave rational and empirical errors.

To begin with, while rejecting the position that man is born with

111

innate knowledge, the objectivists make a number of very peculiar statements. Man, states Nathaniel Branden, has certain inborn needs for food, shelter and so on, "but until his mind has recognized these needs, until he has chosen food, shelter and clothing as values and learned how they can be obtained, his body will not proceed to obtain them . . . . It does not have the power to pursue goals of its own volition, independent of man's consciousness, knowledge and values."[54]

This, of course, is a position that few reputable psychologists would countenance for a moment. The child learns—and, through learning, acquires knowledge, including both truths and values—precisely because he *is* impelled to act and because he learns (through a pre-rational process of motor-emotional conditioning) from the affective consequences of his own impulsive behavior. His body does not act "from instinct" it is true, but it does act continuously from the imperatives of precisely those incomprehensible biological drives which Branden concedes to exist.

To say that a child must become *self-consciously aware* of his implicit needs—that he must *choose* these needs—*before* he will proceed to seek their satisfaction is to reject the overwhelming and virtually indisputable evidence of contemporary pediatrics and child psychology.

Quite apart from such simple reflex actions as sucking and grasping, many of the infant's earliest actions are "structure-functions"—i.e., gross movements which are compelled by biological necessity and which are channeled through whatever bodily equipment is operational at any particular stage of physical development. The infant's "volition" is not *conceptual* (rational). Behavior precedes and provides the unavoidable basis for all experience and therefore for all subsequent knowledge. The earliest consciousness is not dependent upon knowledge and values. It is, rather, the essential basis from which knowledge and values are derived.

Does Branden seriously believe that the child crawls only after he has thought it over and come to a rational decision to do so? If so, by what pre-symbolic process of cognition does this decision occur since the emotions are not, by definition, "tools of cognition"? At still a later point in the same article, Branden notes that "just as [a person's] knowledge must be acquired, so his values must be chosen."[55] This is also untenable. The "acquisition of knowledge" and the "choice of values" are scarcely equivalent concepts. A number of serious questions immediately arise.

112

Why is knowledge "acquired" while values are "chosen"? Are not "values" a type of "knowledge" also?

How can one *choose* values except on the basis of *prior values?* If the earliest values are not "chosen" but "acquired" (as contemporary psychological evidence overwhelmingly affirms), how can the choice of subsequent values be anything but indirectly determined by fortuitous circumstances growing out of the earliest sort of motor-emotional conditioning?

How can knowledge be acquired except through *motivated behavior?* How can behavior, in turn, be *motivated* except on the basis of emotional/conative preconditions? Does not the acquisition of knowledge imply the existence of motivated behavior and therefore of implicit (unconscious) values?

If man behaves *before* he thinks—if he *experiences* the world before he *comprehends* it—is not his thought basically conditioned by the nature and extent of his *pre-rational experience?*

If perceptions do not emerge on an emotional (and incipiently conative) base, how *do* they emerge? What other plausible explanations for selective perception are there to account for concept-formation?

Still another objection which can be leveled against the objectivist theory of cognition stems from the fact that Rand erroneously defines a "percept" as "a group of sensations *automatically* (my italics) retained and integrated by the brain of a living organism."[58]

Again, this definition flies in the face of virtually all reputable psychological evidence. Still other questions invariably arise: If perception is *automatic,* how is it controlled? If man does not *select* his experiences on the basis of his problems, goals and values, why does he perceive one sort of meaning in the world and not another?

Branden seems to assume that the child is born, reflects upon his condition, chooses appropriate assumptions, formulates values which are consonant with such premises and then proceeds to act.

Branden subscribes to the theory that the infant's mind is initially a *tabula rasa.*[59AA] If it is a *tabula rasa*—and excepting the mystical *deus ex machina* of innate knowledge, revelation or mystical insight which are (at least, ostensibly) anathema to the objectivist—how do these percepts automatically congeal if one is unwilling to grant any sort of emotional channelization and if one is unwilling to make any assumptions about prerational knowledge which grows out of the spontaneous and non-volitional behavior during early childhood.

The fact is, of course, that the objectivists are faced with a severe dilemma in their attempt to formulate an objectivist theory of knowledge. To accept the established psychological explanations that cognition begins with infantile learning, which is basically a product of (prerational) motor-emotional conditioning based upon impulsive behavior governed by irrational (or, at least, non-rationalized) biological needs, would not only be to grant the totally unacceptable principle that "emotions are tools of cognition" but even to concede that the primary roots of all thought are grounded in the emotional antecedents of cognition which occur in the earliest months and years of life. To accept the idea that truth—i.e., conceptual knowledge (including both truths and values)—derives under the impetus of, and in unavoidable conjunction with, emotional behavior would be to subvert the entire cornerstone of the objectivist epistemology: absolute, impersonal truth.

Still another criticism that can be leveled against the objectivists' theory of cognition concerns their use of the term "reason." The major difficulty here is not so much that it is used as an omnibus term to describe everything from consciousness *per se* to the formal judgmental processes (although this is also true) but that they frequently fail to distinguish between (1) the way reason functions in the *formal relationing* of existing knowledge and (2) the way it functions in the *empirical derivation* of such knowledge. This is particularly apparent in various of Nathaniel Branden's statements which have already been cited. Reason, according to Branden, serves two primary purposes, cognition and evaluation.[59A] It "is the faculty that identifies and integrates the material provided by man's senses . . . . The process of cognition consists of discovering what things *are*, of identifying their nature, their attributes and properties."[59]

If Branden means here merely that reason includes perception (" . . . the process of discovering what things *are* . . . . "[60]) and also, on occasion, evaluation by means of rational analysis, he is not on particularly shaky ground. In a similar respect, if he means to convey the impression that one way to discover, verify and extend both factual and normative knowledge is by means of clear logical thinking, he is not open to serious criticism. If, on the other hand, he means (as he certainly seems to, when viewed in total context) that man *assimilates* knowledge—i.e., derives his initial and therefore formative awareness with respect to both truth and value—through a concerted application of formal logical procedures to a world as yet "untouched by human

114

hands," he is simply spinning lovely fancies which are totally unsupported by any reputable body of scientific evidence.

The Objectivist Epistemology

Ayn Rand's theory of knowledge—as well as the confusion latent within it—is perhaps best observed within the series of articles which comprise her "Introduction to Objectivist Epistemology."[61] Her position, as presented in these articles, can be summarized basically as follows.

Man is neither omniscient nor infallible, and he possesses no innate knowledge.[62] Knowledge is not " . . . a repository of closed, out-of-context omniscience."[63] All knowledge is derived *contextually,* from natural involvement in specific situations.[64] "All knowledge *is* processed knowledge—whether on the sensory, perceptual or conceptual level."[65] Concepts are "mental integrations of factual data computed by man . . . ."[66] Knowledge is always discovered, through personal experience in the world.[67] It is, therefore, *a posteriori.* "Man *cannot* know more than he has discovered—and he *may not* know less than the evidence indicates, if his concepts and definitions are to be objectively valid."[68]

Knowledge (or truth) is, then, always basically indirect and sensory.[69] What we know (i.e., our concepts) are always mental integrations or cognitive classifications of what we have experienced.[70] Knowledge is always relative to, and limited by, cognition,[71] which is the operation of human consciousness.

Consciousness as such, however, is *not relative.* It is an active process of relationship between objective givens within the real (factual) world.[72] Knowledge, then, while *relative to experience,* is not *subjective,* because it is indirectly dictated by a pattern of *objective relationships* which provide the basis for consciousness itself.[73] "The requirements of cognition control the formation of new concepts, and forbid arbitrary conceptual groupings."[74]

Knowledge, as represented by concepts or ideas, is not, then, "changelessly absolute."[75] It is determined through a context of particular relationships within the world. Our ideas grow out of our direct experiences within specific situations. Our definitions are, in turn, merely symbolic self-representations of concepts which have been abstracted or distilled from experience. Cognition (concept-formation) precedes communication.[76] At basis, concepts (ideas) are tools of

115

cognition and not tools of *communication.* "Cognition precedes communication."[77] A true definition describes a true concept and not vice versa.[78]

There are, at basis, two types of valid knowledge: (1) *knowledge determined contextually,* knowledge which is "contextually absolute" and (2) *axiomatic knowledge,* which is categorically true and beyond contextual demonstration.[79] The most objective knowledge consists of this latter, or axiomatic, knowledge.

Axiomatic truths are primary facts of reality which are implicit within all of the other facts.[80] They are the highest type of knowledge,[81] and they provide the basis for objectivity.[82] They may be *grasped conceptually,* but they are *experienced directly.* They are simply given—"they are what they are"[83]—and are therefore beyond proof.[84] They are in no sense contingent upon arbitrary choice. They are always recognized to be true, and they cannot be denied without self-contradiction (i.e., without invoking "the fallacy of the stolen concept").[85]

There are three basic axiomatic concepts (ideas). These are (1) "existence," (2) "identity"—which is a corollary of existence[86]—and (3) "consciousness."[87] None of these axiomatic concepts has any specifiable *content.*[88] They are merely tautological[89] hyperabstractions (meta-definitions) which describe the basic boundaries of experience itself. They simply explicate the passive knowledge implicit within every conceivable situation.[90]

Axiomatic concepts perform a significant role in emphasizing basic facts. Stated as formal axioms they invariably take the form of tautologies. "The concept 'existence' does not indicate what existents it subsumes: it merely underscores the primary fact that they *exist.'*[91 A] In a similar sense, the concept "identity" does not specify any particular meanings; "it merely underscores the primary fact that *they are what they are,'*[91 B] just as the concept "consciousness" functions to emphasize "the primary fact that one is *conscious.'*[91 C]

Unlike contextual absolutes, these axiomatic concepts are ultimate abstractions and therefore have no identifiable attributes which allow for further analysis or specification. They describe, not characteristics of things or situations, but *existents*—i.e., the underlying structure of reality itself. They are irreducible and, therefore, terminal concepts.[91] They possess no contraries and imply no alternatives. The axiomatic concept of "existence," for example, does not imply an illusory dimension of "nothingness."[92] The idea that it does is rooted in the "fallacy" (a variation of the "stolen concept fallacy"), which Rand terms "the *Reification of the Zero*" . . . [which] consists of regarding 'nothing' as a *thing*, as a special, different kind of *existent.*"[93]

"This fallacy breeds such symptoms as the notion that presence and absence, or being and non-being, are metaphysical forces of equal power, and that being is the absence of non-being."[94]

Axiomatic concepts are, then, the quintessential truths which provide the "epistemological guidelines,"[95] the objective criteria necessary to analyze and evaluate all other (contextual) concepts.[96] They act as the metaphysical basis for integrating all additional knowledge.[97]

Axiomatic truths are not, however, rooted in metaphysics. They are, rather, determined epistemologically.[98] "The radical difference between the Aristotelian view of concepts and the Objectivist view lies in the fact that Aristotle regarded 'essence' as metaphysical; Objectivism regards it as epistemological."[99] Since these axiomatic truths constitute the basis of objective knowledge and are both self-evident and beyond effective refutation, it stands to reason that all additional knowledge is essentially secondary and supplementary.

In a profound sense, there can be no new axiomatic truth, but only new derivative types of contextual knowledge within the existing metaphysical framework of established axiomatic certitude. Science, for example, is essentially a source of derivative knowledge and is not truly innovative in a radical sense.

"Philosophy is the foundation of science; epistemology is the foundation of philosophy. It is with a new approach to epistemology that the rebirth of philosophy has to begin."[101] "The highest responsibility of philosophers is to serve as the guardians and the integrators of human knowledge."[102]

It is not enough that axiomatic truths be known implicitly. They also require identification in conceptual form.[103] Man has an epistemological need to be both conscious and, at the same time, self-conscious of his own most fundamental beliefs; he requires an abstract philosophical statement of his own basic convictions in a form which makes provision for their rational verification.[104] "Objectivism tells you that you must not accept any idea or conviction unless you can demonstrate its truth by means of reason."[105]

Even non-axiomatic (contextual) concepts can be objective and therefore absolute.[106] Contextual concepts are not arbitrary but are controlled by the objective requirements of cognition in terms of purely objective (factual) circumstances.[107] Other things being equal, cognition is not subjective and is not guided by evaluation. Quite the contrary, it is cognition which lies at the basis of evaluation,[108] and this is true as a logical requirement for man's survival.[109]

"[Man's] survival requires that the evaluative function of consciousness be ruled by the cognitive function—i.e., that his values and goals be chosen in the full context of his rational knowledge and understanding."[110] In effective thinking, cognition determines evaluation, and evaluation, in turn, determines interests and goals. The opposite is always symptomatic of pathological thinking. "Reason" as such is not axiomatic (self-evident),[112] but "a complex, derivative concept."[113]

When a child comes to grasp the complicated idea "man," states Rand, the meaning contained within that idea has emerged out of particular perceptual data gathered from contact with various men. Gradually, the child begins to distinguish various significant characteristics or attitudes of men—"living," "moving," "conscious" and so on. As he becomes capable of distinguishing between various types of consciousness, he formulates the concept of "rational" behavior. In short, the idea of reason emerges from the progressive differentiation of experience.[114]

The axiomatic concept of "consciousness" has two fundamental attributes. These are "the *content* (or object) of awareness, and the *action* (or process) of consciousness in regard to that content."[115] "These two attributes are the fundamental Conceptual Common Denominator of all concepts pertaining to consciousness."[116]

A statement of non-axiomatic (contextual) knowledge always represents a symbolic condensation of personal experience. An objective (contextual) definition is a definition which is valid for all men and which was determined according to whatever relevant knowledge was available at that stage of man's development.[117] Such a statement is true (objective) if it meets two basic conditions: (1) If it covers relationships between known existents in terms of essential characteristics[118]—"essential characteristics being defined as characteristics which explain the largest number of other characteristics."[119] (2) If it does not contradict or evade other such known relationships.[120]

In other words, a statement of contextual truth is acceptable if it corresponds to the *facts* (the existents) and does not violate previously-established meanings (interpretations). A true statement

118

(definition) is, then, a statement which rests on a true idea (concept). A true idea (an objective concept) is, in turn, "determined according to the widest context of knowledge available to man on the subjects relevant to the units of a given concept."[121]

"Objective validity is determined by reference to the facts of reality."[122] "An objective definition, valid for all men, is one that designates the *essential* distinguishing characteristic(s) and genus of the existents subsumed under a given concept—according to all the relevant knowledge available at that stage of mankind's development."[123] Where disagreements exist, the final authority is "reality and the mind of every individual who judges the evidence by the *objective* method of judgment: logic."[124]

What all of this means is somewhat difficult to say. A rudimentary analysis, however, would seem to suggest the following interpretation of Miss Rand's epistemological position.

1) Knowledge is relative to personal experience.

2) Personal experience is, in turn, relative to a set of implicit and objective (axiomatic) facts.

3) A knowledge of these axiomatic facts is beyond evidential verification but is possessed by everyone.

4) There are, at basis, three axiomatic truths: "existence," "identity" and "consciousness." "Identity" is merely an aspect of "existence." "Existence" is, in turn, merely the objective (or *content)* dimension of "consciousness."

5) All men are objectively conscious by definition; therefore, to be a man is to know axiomatic truth.

6) Once a man knows axiomatic truth—which is an unavoidable aspect of living as a man—all other knowledge which is required (including moral knowledge) is demonstrable on a purely logical basis.

7) Man thinks logically. Concept-formation is basically a process of discovering new knowledge by logical demonstration on the basis of prior abstract concepts.[125A] Man is *psychologically logical.* All concepts, beyond the primary axiomatic concepts which are self-evident, are secondary and derivative. They can be analyzed and evaluated on the basis of axiomatic principles. In the process of cognitive development, the individual comprehends abstract concepts and derives concrete conclusions from a process of psychologically-directed deductive inference.

119

8) Since all men are both logical and apprehend the fundamental nature of objective reality, all men unavoidably know that which is true, and those who describe reality in varying terms are guilty of volitional error (which is both self-destructive and immoral in its consequences).

9) Since all men know essential (axiomatic) truth by necessity, and since all other truths are derivative and demonstrable on this basis, all contextual (non-axiomatic) truths are objective insofar as they do not contradict prior axiomatic beliefs and are fully compatible with previously-established "objective" conclusions. In short, the only criterion for validating existing knowledge is (1) acceptance of objective axiomatic truths and (2) agreement with prior knowledge which has, in turn, been substantiated in terms of prior axiomatic principles.

As is perhaps apparent, Miss Rand's epistemology is vulnerable to attack on at least seven counts.

1) She sets up an ostensibly objective epistemology, but she does so on a totally subjective and, ultimately, mystical basis. Her axiomatic concepts are, as she herself admits, beyond proof. They are merely true, because they are true.

2) She violates her own theory of axiomatic truth. She states that "all definitions are contextual."[125] She defines "axiomatic concepts" as true independent of any particular context and therefore beyond specification in terms of attributes or characteristics. She then proceeds to "define" the axiomatic concept of "consciousness" as possessing two attributes: content and action. She compounds this inconsistency by going on to suggest that all axiomatic concepts need to be identified in conceptual form. The question is, of course, if they cannot be defined in the first place, how can they be conceptualized in explicit form?

3) Related to this last point is Miss Rand's apparent confusion with respect to the relationship between concepts and communication. In a general sense, she is quite correct in holding that many concepts precede symbolic definitions. In a more specific sense, however, she seems to be guilty of making several errors. To begin with, she seems to overlook the fact that definitions (explicit concepts) also function as a type of knowledge in the development of subsequent concepts. In addition, she seems to be largely oblivious to the fact that cognition itself is largely a process of *internal communication* which is mediated by symbols and that the relationship between cognition and communication is largely reciprocal and interaffecting.

120

4) In a similar respect, Miss Rand appears to believe—in opposition to overwhelming scientific and psychological evidence to the contrary—that basic abstract concepts (such as "existence" and "consciousness") evolve prior to, and as a condition for, specific content knowledge. In contrast to Miss Rand's description of the learning process, evidence indicates that the earliest "axiomatic concepts," like all other concepts, are actually generalizations from quite specific types of contextual experience. The child's earliest behavior gives rise to his first experience which, in turn, provides the basis necessary for his first knowledge. The common elements inherent within his earliest pre-rational experiences provide the basis for his earliest generalizations and abstractions. The first deductive principles are, in short, the product, not of self-evident intuition, as Miss Rand seems to believe, but of pre-cognitive behavioral induction derived by means of motor-emotional conditioning in the earliest years.

5) Still another criticism which can be leveled against Miss Rand's epistemology is that it is basically both pre-scientific and anti-psychological. Miss Rand's epistemology (which is the basis for her psychological theories) is rooted in metaphysics. Children do not initially think by formal logic, following syllogistic patterns. In a similar sense, cognition does not guide evaluation. The opposite is true.

The reason Miss Rand feels obligated to ground her beliefs in metaphysics is that they do not make sense in terms of contemporary psychology. The child's first knowledge is not rational knowledge at all but emotional knowledge. Goal-seeking precedes evaluation, and evaluation precedes significant cognition. Miss Rand's distrust of emotion is founded on precisely the same sort of confusion between the *relative* and the *subjective* that she so acutely detects in others. What she fails to perceive is that emotional experience is also conditioned and directed by objective encounters with factual reality and is, therefore, as likely to culminate in objective reason as experience which is grounded in mystical types of self-evident truth.

6) Another objection which can be directed at Miss Rand's theory of knowledge is that it rests on a whole series of "hidden axioms." Contrary to what Miss Rand says, it is not possible, on purely logical grounds, to derive a coherent philosophy of life out of one or two infinitely abstract metaphysical assumptions. It is also necessary to elaborate a far more involved agenda of more specific beliefs. Miss Rand talks about "objective reality." Implicit in her concept of objective reality, however, is a world where men obtain value only from the

acquisition of, or control over, material objects; where all men are free and morally responsible regardless of circumstantial considerations; where children learn logically by psychological necessity; and where only laissez-faire capitalism "makes sense." These are the tacit dimensions of Miss Rand's fervent commitment to self-evident abstract principles. Applied to the real world, these are the "facts" as Rand sees them.

7) Finally, of course, Miss Rand's prescription for the verification of contextual knowledge is totally circular and self-confirming. Do not, she says, believe anything that violates your own basic assumptions or which undercuts whatever you already believe on the basis of these assumptions—*providing* that your assumptions agree with mine. If we agree, you are objective. If, on the other hand, you have any ridiculous notions about environmental determinism, altruistic love, etc., you are not being "objective," because these things simply are not "true." *"Nature, to be apprehended, must be obeyed."*[126]

Logic and Truth.

Still another difficulty in Miss Rand's philosophy is associated with her attempt to define the specific nature and content of ultimate reality. In a very general sense, Miss Rand holds that such reality is limited to the formal principles of pure logic—identification, contradiction, excluded-middle and so on.

The difficulty with this sort of definition is, as Miss Rand no doubt perceives, twofold: (1) it provides an excellent *context* for discourse but very little descriptive *content*, and (2) it is scarcely an insight which is designed to provoke a significant degree of either interest or controversy.

The basic laws of formal logic are purely relational principles which are considered to inhere within all experience. There are, in essence, three basic laws, two deductive—the laws of *identity* and *contradiction*—and one inductive—the law of *cause-and-effect*.

The deductive principle of *identity* states that any given idea is, *for rational purposes*, only that idea and not something else. In purely logical terms it may be stated in the form "A is A." In order to be "thought about" a thing can represent neither totality (which is indefinable) nor a state of indefinite flux (which is also indefinable.) It must necessarily be some*thing*—however abstract—in contrast to other available objects or events: it must be conceptually distinguishable in a sufficiently stable sense to retain this identity throughout the course of rational analysis.

The deductive principle of *contradiction* states that no idea can have both one identity (A) and its contrary (non-A) at the same time. It is based on the common sense principle that any concept takes its meaning not only from that content which it includes but also from that which it excludes and that, just as, in the principle of identity a thing must be some*thing* as compared with other things, so also, in the principle of contradiction, it cannot at any given moment, be both the presence of one thing and also its absence without cancelling itself out altogether.

A deductive principle which is sometimes taken as the third basic proposition of traditional deductive logic is the principle of *excluded middle*. This principle, which states, in effect, that something cannot be both A *and* non-A, is, however, so clearly implied by the more basic principles of identity and contradiction that it scarcely warrants separate statement and consideration. In other words, if everything must be some*thing* and no thing can be its contrary as well, it simply stands to reason that nothing *can* be both one thing and the negative of that thing concurrently.

In a very basic sense, of course, the foregoing deductive principles assume a certain ontological primacy over the inductive principle of cause-and-effect, because this principle possesses meaning only in terms of certain sense-empirical phenomena which must already possess some sort of perceptual (and at least implicity *deductive*) identity. In other words, inductive inquiry is necessarily a way of investigating things which already possess some sort of structural organization with respect to identity and contradiction. As Hospers indicates, induction is founded upon the (deductive) principle of the uniformity of nature.

> —If the question is still asked, "How are we going to prove the Principle of Uniformity of Nature which is required to establish our inductions?" the answer is of course that we cannot. It cannot be proved by means of itself, and it cannot be *proved* without itself . . . to prove (deductively) a conclusion involving the future we must have a proposition involving the future in the premises. In other words—as in the case of the principles of logic—we cannot give a *logical* justification for the Principle of Uniformity of Nature; we cannot give a logical basis for the very

123

principle which is itself the logical basis for the deduction of laws.[127]

In a very basic sense, then, it can be said that inductive logic reinforces the terminal assumptions of deductive logic through the simple fact that it is implicitly *founded* upon such assumptions. In a fundamental sense, and with induction as with deduction, the *basic principles of logic* are not *logical principles;* they are undemonstrable in the sense that any logical *"truth"* would necessarily be circular in nature. Again, to quote Hospers

—We can't prove the principles of logic by means of themselves—that would be circular. But we can justify the rules or principles of logic by saying that discourse would be impossible without them and that any attempt to deny them presupposes them in the very denial. Similarly, we can justify inductive procedure by saying that, although the existence of an order of nature continuing into the future cannot be demonstrated or even shown to be inductively probable because the very laws of probability are based on the assumption of such an order, we can say that *if* there is an order of nature, then the inductive methods of science will disclose that order. Thus induction as a pragmatic justification, that is, we have vindicated our use of it.[128]

The inductive principle of *cause-and-effect* states that, within any given situation, every action is determined by some other prior action or actions. (It does not, however, and contrary to much belief, assert that everything has a "cause" in the sense, for example, that Being—that is, "situationality" itself or even the causality principle as such—must necessarily be "caused." This line of reasoning is ultimately paradoxical—terminating in the fruitless search for the cause of the cause of the cause ad infinitum. It is also, ultimately, contingent upon the definition of Being as an "effect," which is argumentative to say the least.)

In a basic sense, there are three types of rational knowledge:

1) The most fundamental sort of rational knowledge consists of the

two basic deductive principles of identity and contradiction. These are frequently held to be intuitive "analytical" truths.

2) The second basic realm of rational knowledge consists of the various sorts of inductive generalizations. There are, in essence, three types of rational-inductive knowledge: (a) the basic and universal principle of inductive logic *(cause-and-effect);* (b) the basic inductive procedures for ascertaining the nature of truth within certain areas of activity (for example, scientific problem-solving procedures); and (c) the more general inductive conclusions with respect to the nature of particular aspects of the available sense-empirical environment (for example, "All whales are mammals" or "$E=mc^2$").

3) Finally, the realm of *demonstrable truth* consists of that knowledge which is capable of being derived on the basis of inductive assumptions which have been subsequently subjected to deductive analysis. If, for example, I know that "All dogs are animals," I also know (or, at least, I am incipiently aware of the fact) that, by logical necessity—i.e., demonstratively—dogs cannot also be either "vegetable" or "mineral."

The two basic deductive principles of identity and contradiction have traditionally been viewed as "self-evident" (or analytic) truths, while most inductive, as well as the vast bulk of "mixed" (or demonstrable) knowledge, has been looked upon as essentially evidential (synthetic).

Contrary to Miss Rand's assumptions, the traditional principle of identity does not state *how* a given object or event should be identified (defined). It simply indicates that, in order to reason logically about anything, (1) this thing must be defined in some way; (2) this definition must, in some significant sense, set this object or event apart (and, hence, make it distinguishable from other objects or events); and (3) this thing must retain this *same* meaning throughout the sequence of any particular rational discourse. As Aristotle states in his *Metaphysics:*

> If it be said that "man" has an infinite number of meanings, obviously there can be no discourse; for not to have one meaning is to have no meaning, and if words have no meaning there is an end of discourse with others, and even, strictly speaking, with

oneself; because it is impossible to think of anything if we do not think of one thing.[129]

It is very important, states Susanne Langer, to bear in mind that "once a variable is given a meaning, it keeps it throughout the whole assertion; but it must also be remembered that *in another assertion it may have another meaning.*"[130] What the principle of identity does *not* mean is precisely what Miss Rand so often suggests: i.e., (1) that a thing cannot be defined variously in different situations or for different purposes; (2) that a thing cannot alter its meaning over a period of time; (3) that a thing is just one thing and nothing else.

In other words, what the principle of identity means is really quite simple: If anything is going to mean anything it has to have a meaning which is sufficiently constant to be represented throughout a particular sequence of thought. *One thing* should stand for just *one idea* at *one time.*

In a very basic sense, of course, identity is a precondition for any sort of effective thought. We cannot think *about* a thing unless that thing has been *defined*—unless it has assumed some sort of stable and predictable identity as apart from other things present or possible. The very act of communicating with others is based on the assumption—if frequently fallacious—of an identity of meaning, i.e., that we mean the same thing by the same terms and do not change the semantic ground rules during the course of a conversation.

Stated in a somewhat different way, then, the traditional laws of logic do not state how we shall *define* our terms. They merely determine how we shall *use* them. They state that it is only possible to talk about anything in *one way*—i.e., with respect to one possible meaning—at any given time. Some statements may be both true and false depending upon how and where they are used. On the other hand, any statement—if properly defined and provided it is applied within an appropriate situation—is necessarily *either* true *or* false with respect to any given problem. If, for example, I say that "Men are larger than women," I may be right or wrong relative to a number of different considerations. If I mean all men are *larger* in sheer bulk than all women, I am clearly wrong. If I mean "larger" in the sense of possessing common features to a more exaggerated degree, I am, again, clearly wrong, since, in our culture, women tend to have longer hair and longer fingernails than men. If, on the other hand, I mean, as I probably would, that men are *on the average* heavier and taller than women, I

126

would, at least in our own culture, be correct. My problem is basically one of completely specifying what my real meaning is and in what situations this meaning applies.

The traditional laws of logic do not, then, preclude a very real sort of empirical ambiguity. They simply indicate that some specific meaning should be determined and retained within any stable pattern of discourse.

The question is, then, not legitimately one of whether definitions say everything about those things to which they refer. If they said everything, they would not be *definitions* at all, but, rather, literal *descriptions*. What makes any definition useful in the first place is that it pertains only to those aspects of a thing which are relevant within a particular situation. In a general sense, the greater the inclusiveness of a term the less its utility as a symbol and the less the corresponding psychic economy accruing to its use.

Aristotle does not mean that a *term* is a *thing*. What he does mean is, in effect, that a term, once defined in a certain way—once taken to represent a certain thing—must continue to be defined in that way within a given universe of discourse. If, for example, I choose to define the term "bird" in a particular manner and then proceed to make certain assertions about birds and their behavior based upon such a concept, it is going to be extremely difficult to follow either the meaning or the validity of my statements if I insist on modifying my initial idea of what it is that I mean when I use the term "bird." It is, in short, Aristotle's contention that, at any given time and with reference to any given situation, it is wise to use just one meaning for any particular term. The traditional law of identity in logic does not pertain to *what* a term shall mean or whether such a term shall be indefinitely available for redefinition. It is concerned fundamentally with *validity of reasoning* and not with *truth* in the assumptive sense.

As philosopher John Herman Randall indicates in his excellent study of Aristotle's philosophy, "logic" in the true Aristotelian sense refers basically to the art of discourse, the use of language,[131] and "we can be said to 'know' a thing only when we can state in precise language what that thing is, and why it is as it is."[132]

> Aristotle presents the syllogism as an implication, not as an inference. It takes the form: *if* A and B, *then,* "necessarily" C; not the form: A and B *are,* "therefore" C *is* [my italics] . . . . Aristotle defines a proposition . . . as "a statement affirming or denying something of something." Its elements he calls

127

"terms" . . . the "limits" or "boundaries" . . . of the statement. He avoids all psychological or metaphysical overtones, all words like "notion," "concept," in their Greek equivalents.[133]

This is not to say that Aristotle was not concerned with the question of empirical truth. On the other hand, and as Randall indicates, Aristotle developed and used one set of terms appropriate to *talking* and another appropriate to *living*. The first comprises the logical concepts featured in what Randall terms "Aristotle's Platonic side, his concern with an intelligible structure 'separated in thought, *logos,*' "[134] and are prominent throughout the *Analytics* and the *Organon*. The second are best illustrated in the *De Anima*.[135] "The *Analytics* are concerned with talking, or dialectic, and with good talking or demonstration. The *De Anima* is concerned primarily with living and knowing."[136]

Randall's overall conclusion, which is convincingly documented, is that Aristotle is both a functionalist and an operationalist. "Aristotelianism" he states:

> means a functional realism, a philosophy of process. Aristotle is the major functionalist in the Western tradition. The structures found are always those of determinate processes, of functioning in determinate contexts: Aristotle is clearly a contextualist.[137]

Accordingly, Aristotle is not a system but "a spirit, a method, an intellectual technique."[138]

> He [Aristotle] treats knowing as a function of the human organism responding to its environment, as a way of dealing with its world, a way of functioning in a context. He treats it as a natural process: there is no gulf between "mind" and the rest of nature. Mind is an intelligible interaction between a knowing organism and a knowable world. There is no problem of "How knowledge is possible, and why it isn't." For Aristotle, "knowing" is not a problem to be solved, but a natural process to be described and analyzed.[139]

From the Aristotelian point of view, then, it is not a question of whether *A is A* outside of any particular context of inquiry, it is simply a question of whether it is wise—on the quite pragmatic basis of encouraging effective thought and communication—to change the ground rules by shifting the meaning of terms once the game is in progress. It is, of course, up to each individual to decide whether he wants to start a new game.

In a very basic sense, of course, it can be said that the very fact that Aristotle felt the necessity of framing the law of identity implies a recognition of the law of non-identity as well. Clearly, the implication behind Aristotle's reasoning is that the term is not the "thing," that the term can represent various "things," that definitions are malleable and that—for this very reason—terms must continue to represent only what they purport to represent with respect to any given problem at the risk of destroying all coherence whatsoever.

In a similar respect, the traditional law of contradiction in logic states that nothing can be both A and non-A at the same time. This last phrase, "at the same time," is of basic importance. Aristotle does not state that a man cannot be both "good" and "bad." What he says is that, with respect to a particular situation—that is, relative to given information—a particular individual at a given moment may act in such a way as to be described as either "good" or "bad." Indeed, "goodness" may be a relative concept. Being more "good" than "bad" *on balance* may be the criterion for being characterized as "good" in a particular situation to begin with. The fact is, however, that a human being is psychologically put together in such a way that he is capable of comprehending only one meaning (one aspect or definition) of any given situation at any given instant. If he is to perceive a situation at all, he must necessarily perceive it partially by breaking it up into its constituent aspects and then responding to one selected aspect of its "meaning" at a time. He may then utilize this meaning as a proposition for purposes of reasoning.

The law of excluded-middle, similarly, does not state that something cannot be both good and bad, A and non-A; it simply states that since thought operates dialectically through a tension of rival propositions, it is necessary in an operational sense to work on the *assumption* that something is either A or non-A at any particular moment. In other words, the way to discover if something is A, non-A or both, is to look for A or non-A, or for one and then for the other, and subsequently decide. If, for example, you want to know if John tells the truth, you must necessarily know what the "truth" (and, by implication, what a "lie") *is* in this particular situation and look for either one or the other. Indeed, through a progressive process of

129

inquiry, you may come to the conclusion that John tells the truth and lies in approximately equal proportions. This does not disrupt the idea of excluded middle—indeed, John may now be described as one who either tells *both* truth and lies or only truth *or* lies—because it stands to reason that, relative to any given instance, John must still be either lying or telling the truth or (in which case the question would be irrelevant) doing neither.

In the final analysis, then, Aristotelian logic does not hold that any statement of truth—for example, "This stove is hot"—necessarily *is* what it represents or even that it is necessarily *all* that *can* or *should* be said about what it represents. What the three great logical principles of identity, excluded middle and contradiction intend to convey is, quite simply, that *for purposes of valid reasoning,* the truth underlying a statement must be assumed to be nothing more nor less than what it is *represented to be.* In a very basic sense, then, these laws are not statements of *truth* at all. They do not purport to indicate any substantive correspondence between a particular concept and some particular state of affairs in the external world. The law of identity does not, for example, state that the symbol "dog" must necessarily stand for some particular type of object which exists in the world. It simply says that, if you are to talk intelligently about any object through the medium of any symbol, it is necessary to be internally coherent by retaining some stable identification of what you are talking about. The question then is not whether you are using the term "dog" correctly but, rather, whether you are using the term reliably, with continuous reference to the same underlying idea.

Identity and Objectivism

The basis of Miss Rand's objectivism is the law of identity. It is also, interestingly enough, the weakest link in her line of reasoning.

Despite Miss Rand's professed respect for Aristotle, she is radically non-Aristotelian in her definition of "identity." Thus, where Aristotle conceives of identity as a purely formal (logical) principle designed to ensure effective communication, Miss Rand's law of identity has three distinct dimensions:

1) It is in the traditional Aristotelian sense, a logical principle governing the use of terms in rational discourse: i.e., *in context of discourse* a term shall have but one meaning, and this meaning shall remain constant.

2) Miss Rand, unlike Aristotle, uses the law of identity not only as a

rational principle in the validation of knowledge but also as an empirical principle to be used in determining the nature of truth. Thus, when Miss Rand states that "A is A" she may mean that, in any particular situation the term "A" should be used, in the traditional Aristotelian sense, in reference to the situation "A" and to nothing else. Far more frequently, however, she means, not this, but, rather, that *in any situation and at all times* there exists a situation "A"—i.e., a factual state of affairs—which should be represented by the statement "A."

This is perhaps best clarified by an example. If I make the statement "John is a bad boy," I may mean various things. Logically, however, if I wish to validate my assertion, it is incumbent upon me to define my terms—and particularly, of course, the key term "bad"—in such a way that, by establishing my total line of reasoning, I can prove that John's "badness" is rationally entailed by what I mean by the term "bad" as it relates to my description of John's behavior. I might, for example, state:

1) A *bad* boy is one who is *heedless of others.*
2) *John* is *heedless of others.*
3) Therefore, *John* is a *bad* boy.

The reasoning here is valid and easy to follow because, I have retained the same definition of the term "bad" throughout the argument. This is *not* always, however, the case. For example, I might say

1) A *bad* boy is one who is *heedless of others.*
2) *John* is *heedless of others.*
3) But *John* is NOT a *bad* boy *because I like him.*

In this instance, of course, I have been inconsistent, because I have not retained a constant meaning (or identity) of the key term "bad." In the last statement, I have implicitly altered my concept of what constitutes a "bad boy" by including my own subjective response as a new defining characteristic. I have violated the formal (Aristotelian) law of identity.

If I use the law of identity as an empirical principle, however, I arrive at a somewhat different situation, for I am no longer concerned with *logic*—i.e., the relationship of statements—but with *truth*—the factual basis of statements as such. Thus, the statement "John is a bad boy," used as an empirical statement of identity means, essentially,

"My statement 'John is a bad boy' corresponds to a factual state of affairs in which John *is* a bad boy."

The prime example of an empirical statement of identity used by Miss Rand is her basic precept "Existence exists." "This," states Rand " . . . is a way of translating into the form of a proposition, and thus into the form of an axiom, the primary fact which is existence."[140] In one sense, of course, this is a good example of a pseudo-proposition—a statement which *appears* meaningful but *is not*.

From a purely semantic point of view, the statement "Existence exists" is characterized by two basic defects:

1) The term "existence" refers to *everything* and therefore to *nothing*. It lacks any sort of specific and identifiable *relational* meaning with respect to anything in particular.

2) The term "exists" is simply the predicate form of the subject "existence." Assumedly; the term "existence" is intended to mean the sum total of that which *is*. It is tautological to say "That which is *is*" however, since the predicate is contained within the subject.[141]

Perhaps the gravest error which Miss Rand makes is that of confusing a knowledge *of* things with a knowledge *about* them. There is, as philosopher Susanne Langer indicates, a decided difference between the *specification* of meaning with respect to particular terms (ie, describing the *content* of the term) and the formal laws by which meanings are interrelated. Logic, as Langer so aptly points out, is concerned entirely with *concepts* and not with *conceptions*.[142] Logic relates to the formal context of discourse and not to the specific values attached to the particular terms involved. Logic, unlike natural science, is principally concerned with the discovery of abstract forms—with ultimate abstraction—and not with general formulae for concrete facts.[143] As Langer indicates:

> The consideration of a form, which several analogous things may have in common, apart from any contents, or "concrete integuments," is called *abstraction*. If we speak of *the* major scale apart from any particular key, we are treating it as an abstracted form.[144]

Interpretation is the reverse of abstraction; the process of abstraction begins with a real thing and derives from it the bare form, or concept, whereas the process of interpretation begins with an empty concept and seeks some real thing which embodies it.[145]

The laws of formal logic are *propositional forms* — i.e., general statements about the way in which knowledge occurs independent of identifiable referents—and not empirical *propositions* in the usual sense.[146] Again, and as Langer states, "The bridge that connects all the various meanings of form—from geometric form to the form of ritual or etiquette—is the notion of *structure.*"[147]

> ... form is not another constituent, but is the way the constituents are put together .... We might understand all the separate words of a sentence without understanding the sentence: if a sentence is long and complicated, this is apt to happen. In such a case we have knowledge of the constituents, but not of the form. We may also have knowledge of the form without having knowledge of the constituents.[148]

At basis, then, the laws of logic are simply extended analogies which, like all analogies, recognize a common form, or principle, to be operating in different things. It is only by analogy that one can represent one thing by another which does not resemble it.

> Whenever we draw a diagram, say the ground-plan of a house, or a street-plan to show the location of its site, or a map, or an isographic chart, or a "curve" representing the fluctuations of the stockmarket, we are drawing a "logical picture" of something. A "logical picture" differs from an ordinary picture in that it need not look the least bit like its object. Its relation to the object is not that of a *copy,* but of analogy.[149]

Grammar, then, is simply "the logical form of our language, which copies as closely as possible the logical form of our thought."[150] In a similar sense, mathematics demonstrates the logical form of measurement by demonstrating the relationships which are possible between quantities.[151]

In all fairness to Miss Rand, it is clear that she is doing more than playing tautological games with the verb "to be." When she states "Existence exists," she actually appears to have three things in mind.

a) We all intuitively share the same view of life, and this view is adequately conveyed by the common-sense term "existence."

b) At basis, life, as we all intuitively comprehend it to be, *is* Truth (ultimate reality). The statement "Water is wet" is, for example, a common-sense self-evident statement about reality at the operational level of abstraction where all flesh and blood people actually "live." The statement "Water is energy" is less *meaningful* (although equally true), because it is a technical description of water at an abstract and somewhat unreal level of analysis which lacks practical relevance for most people in their everyday lives.

c) The proper focus for thought and behavior is in the middle-range of abstraction, in the sphere of common-sense intuitive objects, events and relationships. It is dysfunctional and even erroneous to push reason and analysis beyong the realm of practical material operations. Thought which has no visible application to some significant area of practical action is merely mystical self-engrossment, a sort of intellectual masturbation. The proper figure-ground relationship is always one in which practice directs theory in the area of real (practical) relationships.

In a sense, of course, this position implies a sort of tacit anti-intellectualism. Thought is good, but *excessive* thought is bad. There is a level of predefined meanings—values, truths, assumptions—which exist at the practical common-sense level of awareness and which are legitimately exempt from any subsequent sort of regressive analysis.

It is evil to doubt "truths" which are already self-evident. Knowledge is not only inherent to man's nature, it is also imperative to his realization as a man to comprehend and to assent to such knowledge. In areas of self-evident awareness, dissent is not only inhumane but evil as well and should not be condoned.

3) Finally, Miss Rand uses the law of identity as a normative principle. "Existence exists" not only as a self-evident truth and not merely on a purely rational basis, but also as a predefined standard for the regulation of personal conduct. The good life is invariably the rational life—i.e., the life which adheres *prescriptively* to the dictates of self-evident truth (as defined by empirical identity) and the dictates of self-evident reason (as defined by logical identity).

For Rand, there are three basic categories of self-evident truths:

134

1) the self-evident truths of formal logic (reality-as-process)—the procedural laws of traditional logic, such as identity and contradiction;

2) the self-evident empirical truths (reality-as-content)—the various empirical manifestations of the law of identity, such as free will; and

3) the self-evident moral truths (reality-as-value)—the axiological manifestations of the law of identity, such as the principle of enlightened egoism.

Miss Rand runs into a number of purely logical problems throughout her discussion of the knowledge process. As an essentialist, she subscribes to the position that ultimate truth is in no sense dependent on value—that our initial encounter with the world is intellectual and not emotional. This could only culminate in the position that we possess inherent truth, for, to say otherwise, would be to hold that truth is relative to personal knowledge acquired through either personal experience (which would be an indirect affirmation of the relativistic position) or through supernatural intervention (which would entail an active metaphysical realm of experience beyond the world as such). Since Miss Rand finds both of these positions unacceptable, she is necessarily faced with a decision between two possibilities.

1) A knowledge of metaphysical truth, while confirming the existence of a rational world, is prerational in origin and constitutes a type of (inborn) awareness.

2) A knowledge of metaphysical truth is a product of pure (non-instrumental) rational thought which is unmediated by any sort of conative/emotional considerations.

It is difficult to say with any surety which of these positions Miss Rand adheres to, but all indications are that the first is the best expression of her ideas for two reasons:

1) She propounds no consistent theory of pure (non-instrumental) cognition.

2) If she were to posit such a process of pure cognition, unmediated by volition, she would, in effect, be subscribing to a type of gratuitous, or uncaused, action, which would be an implicit violation of her own professed adherence to the logical principle of cause-and-effect. She would, in effect, be subscribing to the idea of "irrational" (unmotivated or uncaused) behavior.

135

Still another factor which complicates Miss Rand's concept of knowing and the known is the fact that many of her self-evident "truths," which are established by means of (tautological) empirical-identity are not simply "facts"—such as the logical principle of identity or the empirical law of cause-and-effect—but, rather, "meanings" which purport to be objective.[152]

This leads to complications for several reasons. To begin with, a "fact" is essentially a simple truth—a metaphorical assertion of pure, or descriptive, *relational* (logical) identity. A good example of a fact is provided by the basic *logical* law of identity as originally formulated by Aristotle: No valid inferences can be drawn from a statement of fact unless the meanings attached to the various terms within this statement are held constant throughout the process of deduction. Such a formal statement differs from a tautological statement of empirical identity such as "Existence exists" in various respects.

For one thing, all tautological statements—e.g., "All dogs are animals" or "Two times two equals four"—are essentially empirical statements. They are not *proofs* but *assertions.* This can be seen by looking at a typical tautological statement like "Water is wet." In the statement "Water is wet" we have a subject ("water") which is linked by a cupola verb, "is," to one of its own defining characteristics ("wetness"). In essence, then, we have three elements:

1) An implied statement of truth: There is something called "water" which is recognizable in terms of certain unvarying characteristics or qualities.
2) The term "is" which is a form of the linking verb "to be" used to specify *identity* or, more specifically, an *aspect* of identity.
3) A restatement of the original statement in terms of one of its constituent qualities (wetness).

At basis, then, there are four things to note about a tautological statement like "Water is wet."

1) The subject ("water") is meaningful only because it has already been either explicitly or implicitly defined.
2) Since it has been *defined,* it obviously *exists* in some sense. It is, in short, either a real thing or the imaginative recombination of qualities inherent within real things.
3) The statement "Water is wet" is therefore *true* only if the quality

136

indicated is recognized to be one of the qualities already implied by the subject (water).

In short, if a person knows what the essential qualities of water *are,* he must also know (1) that water exists (which eliminates the necessity of "is") and (2) that "wetness," along with colorlessness and fluidity, is an essential characteristic of water in contrast to such accidental qualities as shape, volume, and so on.

4) This being so, it follows that the statement "Water is wet" is tautological only (1) if it is *true* and (2) if the nature of water is understood prior to the time that the statement is made.

The statement "Water is lighter than air" is not true and cannot therefore be tautological because it is non-factual.

If a person is being told about water who has *never encountered water,* the statement is *not* tautological, because he does not know the qualities of water and is therefore receiving new information which in fact enables him to define the term in the first place. Once he comes to comprehend the term "water" in terms of its essential existential qualities, the same statement will, however, *become* tautological.

All tautological statements are not meaningless, then, for, while the predicate ("is wet") does not provide any information which is not contained in the subject ("water"), it may function in two other ways.

1) It may focus attention on one essential quality ("wetness") as apart from other qualities (such as colorlessness) and, in this sense, it may actually serve as a subdefinition of the more encompassing term and may not be simply a redundant reassertion of the subject.

2) By identifying merely one of the essential qualities of the phenomenon in question, it may act to define (and, in certain cases, to redefine) the manner in which the subject-term is being used.

In essence, then, a tautology is basically a definition in which the predicate functions as a partial paraphrase of the subject, either clarifying the use of the subject or designating some special aspect of the subject for special attention. In this sense, Miss Rand is guilty of using a meaningless tautology—"Existence exists"—in order to convey the non-tautological idea that life is precisely what traditional common-sense says it is and nothing more:

137

Causality and Identity

With respect to the principle of causality too Miss Rand is wrong in several respects. To begin with, and as indicated earlier, she fails to recognize the difference between *empirical* logic and *formal* logic and, in fact, gets the two inutterably confused.

The laws of identity, excluded-middle and contradiction are, as Miss Rand so acutely observes, different statements of the same principle. The law of identity in formal logic states that, if legitimate rational inferences are to be drawn, the meaning of a term cannot be altered in the course of the reasoning process without also altering the rational relationships involved and therefore invalidating the conclusions derived. In effect, then, "A is A," and it stands to reason that (in any particular universe of discourse) "A cannot be non-A" (contradiction) and "A cannot be both A and non-A" (excluded middle). Rand is, in this sense, quite correct in holding that the principles of contradiction and excluded-middle are merely logical derivatives of the basic law of identity.

She is, however, in grievous error in maintaining that the law of causality is merely "the law of identity applied to action." In this instance, she makes a very basic mistake. She fails to recognize the fact that the law of causality, unlike the law of identity and its logical corollaries is a law of *empirical* logic and not a law of *formal* (relational) logic. As such, it differs from the law of identity in two significant respects:

a) It purports to describe the relationship of actual entities and not the relationship of statements; and

b) It provides the necessary empirical context which underlies all purely formal logic and, without which, identity itself would be meaningless.

Miss Rand, in holding that causality is entailed by identity fails to see two very significant facts.

First, identity itself is implicitly a statement of causality. In the statement "A is A" the subject is not "A" at all but, rather, the ostensible verb *is*. In short, what the statement "A is A" actually asserts might be rephrased to hold "Reality (isness)—i.e., the total dynamic *relationship* of actual entities one to another—*causes* (and therefore sustains) the conditions termed "A." The statement "A is A," then, is

138

actually an elliptical and somewhat misleading statement of causation: "Being *causes* A."

At basis, then, formal logic (and the law of identity) does not commence with itself—and is not therefore self-evident—but, rather, grows out of empirical logic (which is, in turn, founded on the law of causality). Identity is ultimately founded on the assumption of causality, and all logical inference is merely a chain of causal entailment commencing with the assumption of causality itself. In this sense, the laws of contradiction and excluded-middle could not be corollaries of the law of identity if they were not *caused* by it.

Formal logic merely describes the protocol for discussing real objects and events in such a way that our statements reflect the inexorable causal factuality of the real world. A is A and not non-A, a tree is a tree and not a house, not because we cannot *assert* otherwise but because, beneath our assertions, there is a real world made up of dynamic and interrelated forces which create and sustain certain conditions rather than others. In a sense, it is the inexorable working of causality in a world in which the nature and variety of possible causes is *finite* which gives rise to a world of constant identity in which prediction (by means of causal implication) is possible. Thus, we live in a world in which there are objects called "trees." These objects are the product of a total field of forces which interact in such a way as to yield an abiding phenomenon which has identifiable characteristics and not others. "A tree is a tree," then, precisely because the total configuration of forces available entails a sequence of controlled relationships which we experience as such an object.

Ultimately, then, *causality* is a controlled sequence of non-volitional action.

Still another difficulty stems from Miss Rand's contention that the nature of an action (including its moral nature) is caused and determined by "the nature of the entities which act."[153] Thus to follow the argument inherent within her own line of reasoning

1) Practical reason, when applied to real problems, causes profit (which *is* "objective value").

2) Profit is therefore the *effect* of its true causes: right reason and true knowledge (which combine to yield what might be termed "productive reason").

3) Therefore, productive reason causes profit and conversely, *any*

"profit" arising under different conditions is, by ontological necessity, not "profit" at all but, rather, "counterfeit" profit which does not possess real (objective) value at all.[154]

As is quite clear, Miss Rand makes three basic assumptions here.

1) Value is objectively represented by profit (i.e., wealth derived through the application of practical reason). Material profit is the outward sign of inward grace.

Miss Rand is, of course, entirely consistent with her own position in equating money (wealth) with value. She is a materialist, and her basic position is that value can only lie in the direction of direct need-gratification or in the enhanced capacity for such gratification brought about through the power conferred by wealth.

2) Profit *invariably* accrues to productive reason.

3) Any "profit" which does not grow out of the application of productive reason is not real profit but merely counterfeit profit which is incapable of producing true value.

This position can be attacked on at least four basic grounds.

1) She assumes, in the face of much evidence to the contrary, that productive reason *invariably* causes profit (value). Even the most enlightened reason, however, does not function in a vacuum, and success can scarcely be said to be totally dependent on purely volitional (rational) factors.

2) Value may be rooted in objective relationships, but it is nevertheless a *subjective experience.*

Objective prosperity does not guarantee value, because value is the subjective *response to* objective conditions and does not reside in the conditions themselves. The mere fact that Miss Rand finds it necessary to prescribe wealth as value indicates that other values—religious, esthetic, altruistic, et cetera—are both possible and, on occasion, functional. In short, if wealth is a self-evident value, it need not be prescribed, because it would be prepotent (operational) by definition. If it is not, however, it cannot be established as such by dictum or by definition.

3) Value is mediated in man through consciousness. Value is not found in objects but in *experienced relationships to objects*—which is a substantially different kettle of fish. It is precisely because man has the

capacity to formulate nonmaterial values that his capacity to experience value is (1) extended and (2) liberated from the purely material (objective) conditions required by lower animals who lack the capacity for symbolic (non-material) experience.

4) Miss Rand is guilty of "persuasive definition."

She uses the concepts of wealth and profit *normatively* to encompass only the outgrowth of productive reason. In addition, she holds that all other wealth—e.g., inheritances, winnings derived from gambling, and so on—are incapable of producing "real value." She justifies this position by asserting that the moral (normative) nature of an act is always determined by its derivative conditions. Thus, since a rational act is good, it leads (by irrefutable definition) to good consequences (profit). Since an irrational act is bad, it can only lead to bad consequences (non-profit). Such a position is, of course, true by definition—it functions as a self-fulfilling prophesy at a purely intellectual (ideological) level.

What this adds up to is, of course, a sort of secular dogma of original sin:

1) All rational acts are good; all irrational acts are bad.

2) All acts are either rational or irrational and therefore good or bad. No act is either cognitively or morally "mixed."

3) "The nature of an action is caused and determined by the nature of the entities that act: a thing cannot act in contradiction to its nature."[155]

4) A man who is not entirely good is bad.

5) A bad man cannot perform a good act. (This would violate the law of contradiction as well as the law of excluded-middle.)

6) Therefore, a bad man is condemned to be bad without hope of redemption. Similarly, a good man is inevitably the source of good actions which, in turn, cause more good actions and so *ad infinitum*.

For Rand, then, what makes an act *good* or *bad* is not so much its *effects* as its *etiology*. An act which is non-rational, irrational or ill-motivated is bad *regardless of its consequences* because—since like begets like in the moral sphere—its consequences cannot be "good" *by definition*. It does not avail me to fall sudden heir to an unearned fortune, for such wealth is not earned. It is not derived from "productive reason" and cannot therefore eventuate in true profit and real value. Indeed, for it to do so would be "irrational," a violation of identity-causality at the moral level—an implicit denial of the entire objectivist ethic.

FOOTNOTES (CHAPTER V)

1A. Obviously, Miss Rand's position is not that all men, descriptively, *possess* such knowledge in the sense that they concur with her assumptions, but, rather, that, prescriptively, they *should* possess such knowledge (1) because it is true and (2) because they are in error by virtue of the fact that they deny such truth in the first place. She further holds that knowledge is determined by reason, not emotion, and that even the choice to be reasonable is necessarily predicated upon some sort of objective knowledge which is a necessary basis even for subsequent error. These beliefs are examined in detail in the the following pages. Rand is quite willing to allow for relative knowledge, and she goes to great lengths to accommodate her epistemology to various kinds of psychological conditions pertaining to perception and such, but none of these qualifications apply to her basic principles, her "axiomatic concepts" of existence, identity, and consciousness, or to their logical corollaries, and it is precisely these that provide the metaphysical context which makes the vast corpus of her after-the-fact epistemological subtleties rather beside the point.

1. Rand. "Introduction to Objectivist Epistemology, I," *The Objectivist*, V, 7 (July 1966), p.2.
2. See Chapter V, pp. 110-112.
3. Rand. "Introducing Objectivist Epistemology, I," *The Objectivist*, V, 7 (July 1966), p. 5.
5. Nathaniel Branden. "Intellectual Ammunition Department," *The Objectivist Newsletter*, II, 1, (January 1963), p. 3.
6. *Ibid.*
7. *Ibid.*
8. Jacob Bronowski. *Science and Human Values* (New York: Harper and Brothers, 1956), pp. 46-7.
10. Abraham Kaplan. *The New World of Philosophy*. (New York: Random House, 1961), p. 49.
11. Nathaniel Branden. "The Stolen Concept," *The Objectivist Newsletter*, II, 1 (January 1963), p. 4.
12. Susanne Langer. *An Introduction to Symbolic Logic.* (New York: Dover, 1953), p. 324 ff.
13. Brand Blanshard. Review of Blanshard's book *Reason and Analysis* by Nathaniel Branden, *The Objectivist Newsletter*, II, 2 (February 1963), p. 7.
13A. I assume that a "rejection" can constitute an "unwillingness" to believe which is not founded upon logical reasoning and which is not therefore a contrary sort of "logical" choice.

14. Nathaniel Branden. "The Stolen Concept," *The Objectivist Newsletter*, II, 1
15A. *Ibid.*
15. *Ibid.*
16. *Ibid.*, p. 4.
17. *Ibid.*
18. *Ibid.*
19. Barbara Branden. "Intellectual Ammunition Department," *The Objectivist Newsletter*, III, 1, (March 1962)p. 11.
20. *Ibid.*
21. Nathaniel Branden. "The Stolen Concept," *op cit.*, p.4.
22. *Ibid.*
23. *Ibid.*
24. *Ibid.*, p. 2.
25. Ibid., pp. 2 and 4.
26. *Ibid.*
27. *Ibid.*
28. *Ibid.*
29. In his series of articles entitled "The Analytic-Synthetic Dichotomy," objectivist philosopher Leonard Peikoff takes the position that "There is no distinction between the 'logically' and the 'empirically' possible (or impossible)." (Leonard Peikoff, "The Analytic-Synthetic Dichotomy," "*The Objectivist*, VI, 9 (September 1967), p. 12.) According to Peikoff, "Man's knowledge is not acquired by logic apart from experience or by experience apart from logic, but *by the application of logic to experience.* All truths are the product of a logical identification of the facts of experience." (*Ibid.*, VI, 8 (August 1967), p. 11.) This sounds marvelous but, in or out of context, I haven't the foggiest clue as to what it means. Granted that logic is an aspect of experience and all experience is inherently logical (casual), precisely how does one derive basic empirical assumptions (including assumptions about the laws of logic themselves) by applying logic to experience?
30. John Hospers, *Human Conduct: An Introduction to the Problems of Ethics.* (New York: Harcourt, Brace and World, 1961), p. 584.
31. Rand, "Introduction to Objectivist Epistemology: II," *The Objectivist*, V, 8 (August 1966(, pp. 6-7.)
32. Rand, *The Fountainhead*, in *For the New Intellectual*, p. 74.
33. *Ibid.*
34. Nathaniel Branden, "Mental Health Versus Mysticism and Self-Sacrifice," *The Virtue of Selfishness*, pp. 37-8.
35. Rand, *Atlas Shrugged*, in *For the New Intellectual*, p. 179.
36. Rand, "For the New Intellectual," *op. cit.*, p. 15. Italics mine.
37. Nathaniel Branden, "Intellectual Ammunition Department," *The Objectivist Newsletter*, I, 10 (October 1962), p. 44.
38. *Ibid.*, p. 43.
39. *Ibid.*
40. Nathaniel Branden, "Emotions and Values," *The Objectivist*, V, 5 (May 1966), p. 1.

41. Nathaniel Branden, "Social Metaphysics," *The Objectivist Newsletter,* I, 11 (November 1962, p. 47.)
42. Rand, "Introduction to Objectivist Epistemology," *The Objectivist,* V, 7 (July 1966), p. 3.
43. *Ibid.*
44. Rand, "Introduction to Objectivist Epistemology, II," *The Objectivist,* V, 8 (August 1966), p. 1.
45. *Ibid.*
46. *Ibid.*
47. *Ibid.*
48. Rand, "The Psychoepistemology of Art," *The Objectivist Newsletter,* IV, 4 (April 1965), p. 15.
49. Rand, "Introduction to Objectivist Epistemology, I," *op. cit.,* p. 6.
50. Nathaniel Branden, "Emotions and Values," *op. cit.,* p. 1.
51. *Ibid.*
52. *Ibid.*
53. *Ibid.*
54. Nathaniel Branden, "Intellectual Ammunition Department," *The Objectivist Newsletter,* I, 10, (October 1962), p. 43.
55. *Ibid.*
56. *Ibid.*
57. *Ibid.*
58. Rand, "Introduction to Objectivist Epistemology, I," *op. cit.,* p. 3.
59AA. Nathaniel Branden, "Intellectual Ammunition Department," *The Objectivist Newsletter,* I, 10, (October 1962), p. 43.
59A. Nathaniel Branden, "Emotions and Values," *op. cit.,* p. 1.
59. *Ibid.*
60. *Ibid.*
61. Rand, "Introduction to Objectivist Epistemology," *The Objectivist,* V, 7 (July 1966) through VI, 2 (February 1967).
62. *Ibid.,* Part IV, p. 7; Part VIII, p. 5; Rand, "Playboy's Interview with Ayn Rand," p. 8.
63. Rand, "Introduction to Objectivist Epistemology," Part VII, p. 6.
64. *Ibid.,* Part VII, p. 2.
65. *Ibid.,* Part VIII, p. 7.
66. *Ibid.,* Part V, p. 6.
67. *Ibid.,* Part IV, p. 6.
68. *Ibid.*
69. *Ibid.*
70. *Ibid.*
71. *Ibid.,* Part VIII, p. 7; Part IV, p. 6.
72. *Ibid.,* Part VIII, p. 7; Part III, p. 1.
73. *Ibid.,* Part VIII, p. 7; Part V, p. 6.
74. *Ibid.,* Part VIII, p. 2.
75. *Ibid.,* Part VI, p. 2.
76. *Ibid.,* Part VII, p. 7.
77. *Ibid.*
78. *Ibid.*

79. *Ibid.*, Part VII, p. 2; Part VI, pp. 2-3.
80. *Ibid.*, Part VII, p. 2;
81. *Ibid.*, Part VIII, p. 2.
82. *Ibid.*, Part VII, p. 2; Part VI, pp. 2-3.
83. *Ibid.*, Part VI, p. 5.
84. *Ibid.*, Part VII, p. 2.
85. *Ibid.*, Part VI, p. 3.
86. *Ibid.*, pp. 2-3.
87. *Ibid.*, Part VII, p. 2.
88. *Ibid.*, Part VI, p. 3.
89. *Ibid.*, p. 4.
90. *Ibid.*, p. 3.
91A. *Ibid.*, p. 5.
91B. *Ibid.*
91C. *Ibid.*
91. *Ibid.*
92. *Ibid.*, pp. 5-6.
93. *Ibid.*,
94. *Ibid.*
95. *Ibid.*, Part VII, p. 2.
96. *Ibid.*, Part VIII, pp. 7-8.
97. *Ibid.*, Part V, p. 5.
98. *Ibid.*
99. *Ibid.*, Part VI, p. 2.
100. *Ibid.*, Part VII, p. 11.
101. *Ibid.*, p. 10.
102. *Ibid.*, Part VI, p. 6.
103. *Ibid.*, Part VI, pp. 2-3.
104. *Ibid.*, Part V, p.4.
105. Rand, *"Playboy's* Interview with Ayn Rand," p.9.
106. Rand, "Introduction to Objectivist Epistemology," Part VI, p. 2.
107. *Ibid.*, Part VIII, p. 2.
108. Nathaniel Branden, "The Concept of Mental Health," *The Objectivist,* VI, 2, (February 1967), p. 10.
109. *Ibid.*
110. *Ibid.*
111. Rand, "Introduction to Objectivist Epistemology," Part VII, p. 5; Part V, p. 3.
112. *Ibid.*, Part VI, p.6.
113. *Ibid.*
114. *Ibid.*, Part VII, p. 5.
115. *Ibid.*, Part IV, p. 1.
116. *Ibid.*, Part III, p. 2.
117. *Ibid.*, Part VI, p. 2.
118. *Ibid.*
119. *Ibid.*, Part V, pp. 1-2.
120. *Ibid.*, Part VI, p. 2; Part IV, p. 7.
121. *Ibid.*, Part IV, p. 6.

122. *Ibid.*
123. *Ibid.*
124. *Ibid.*
125A. *Ibid.*, Part VII, p. 5; Part V, p. 3.
125. *Ibid.*, p. 4.
126. *Ibid.*, Part VIII, p. 8.
127. John Hospers, *An Introduction to Philosophical Analysis* (Englewood Cliffs, New Jersey; Prentice-Hall 1953), p 176.
128. Hospers, *Human Conduct,* p. 586.
129. Aristotle, *Metaphysics,* in John Herman Randall, Jr., *Aristotle* (New York: Columbia University Press 1960), p. 116.
130. Susanne Langer, *An Introduction to Symbolic Logic.* (New York: Dover, 1953). p. 87.
131. John Herman Randall, *Aristotle* (New York: Columbia University Press, 1960), p.6.
132. *Ibid.*, p. 7.
133. *Ibid.,* pp. 48-9.
134. *Ibid.*, p. 294.
135. *Ibid.*, pp. 59-60
136. *Ibid.*, p. 61.
137. *Ibid.*, p. 299.
138. *Ibid.*, p. 245.
139. *Ibid.*, p. 105
140. Rand, "Introduction to Objectivist Epistemology, I," *op. cit.,* p. 2.
141. Much of the confusion which arises from Miss Rand's remarks about the law of identity stems from the fact that she seems to be largely oblivious to the vast ambiguity involved in virtually any philosophical discussion which centers about the term "to be" which is conducted without any clear definition of meaning. This is well-exemplified by Susanne Langer in her excellent book on logic (*An Introduction to Symbolic Logic.* New York: Dover, 1953) in which she discusses at great length the various ambiguities which are inherent in using "existence" as a verb. "Consider," she states " . . . the following propositions:
>   (1)   The rose is red.
>   (2)   Rome is greater than Athens.
>   (3)   Barbarossa is Frederick I.
>   (4)   Barbarossa is a legendary hero.
>   (5)   To sleep is to dream.
>   (6)   God is.

In each of these sentences we find the verb "is." But each sentence expresses a differently constructed proposition:
>   (1)   ascribes a *property* to a term; in
>   (2)   "is" has logically only an auxiliary value of *asserting* the dyadic relation, "greater than"; in
>   (3)   "is" expresses *identity;* in
>   (4)   It indicates *membership in a class* (the class of legendary heroes); in

146

(5)   *entailment* (sleeping *entails* dreaming); in

(6)   *existence*. (Susanne Langer, *An Introduction to Symbolic Logic*, p. 56).

The way in which symbolic logic can be used to clarify these distinctions and to minimize the usual confusion occupies a significant part of Miss Langer's book.

142.   Langer, *op. cit.*, p. 79.

143.   *Ibid.*, p. 17.

144.   *Ibid.*, p. 33.

145.   *Ibid.*, p. 38.

146.   The distinction between a *proposition* and a *propositional form* entails a technical discussion which goes beyond the requirements of this study. In essence, however, the distinction is well covered by Miss Langer in her book *Introduction to Symbolic Logic*. As she states, the sentence: "I knew you would not do it," is a genuine propositional form; as long as no values are assigned to the pronouns, it is neither true nor false. Even if we assign a value to one or two of the three pronouns, the expression as a whole keeps its variable character; only when *all* its terms are fixed it acquires truth-value, i.e., becomes a proposition. Thus, we may say:

(1)   I knew you would not do it.

(2)   I, George, knew you would not do it.

(3)   I, George, knew you, John, would not do it.

(4)   I, George, knew you, John, would not cheat at cards.

Only (4) is a proposition; all others are propositional forms with different numbers variables, i.e., in different stages of *formalization*. (Langer—*op. cit.*, p. 91) " . . . the thing to remember is that *as soon as we replace a single term in a proposition by a variable, we have a propositional form* which has many values as there are values for that variable; and *the more elements we "formalize," the greater becomes the range of the entire propositional form."* (Ibid., p. 93)

147.   *Ibid.*, p. 24.

148.   Bertrand Russell, quoted in Langer, *op. cit.*, p. 32.

149.   Langer, *op. cit.*, p. 29.

150.   *Ibid.*, p. 31.

151.   *Ibid.*, p. 40.

152.   A "meaning" differs from a "fact" in several basic respects. For one thing, of course, a meaning is more complex than a fact. It is a configuration, or relationing, of facts—an interpretation of facts. If a fact is basically a metaphorical statement of identity, a meaning is essentially an analogical pattern of relationships. In addition, a meaning is always a solution to a problem, an answer to a question. In this sense, a meaning is always implicitly instrumental.

153.   Cf. Chapter II, p. 28-9; chapter IV, pp. 60-61.

154.   Cf. Chapter IV, pp. 60-61.

155.   Cf. Chapter II, p. 28-9.

CHAPTER VI

VALUES AND THE NATURE OF MAN: AN ANALYSIS

The objectivist ethics is necessarily rooted in metaphysics. "To prescribe what a man ought to do, one must first know *what* he is and *where* he is—i.e., what is his nature (including his means of cognition) and the nature of the universe in which he acts."[1]

Contrary to the *intrinsic* and *subjectivist* theories of value, notes Rand, values neither inhere within things and actions as such nor do they derive from arbitrary emotional whim. They are, rather objectively discoverable within the province of reason itself.[2] The good is *"an aspect of reality in relation to man."*[3] It is *"an evaluation* of the facts of reality by man's consciousness according to a rational standard of value. (Rational, in this context, means: derived from the facts of reality and validated by a process of reason.)"[4]

According to Rand a system of rational and objective (absolute) ethics is possible on the basis of certain predetermined and self-evident truths which pertain to the basic nature of reality. In this sense, her ethics is simply a logical outgrowth of her previously-established system of metaphysics, and there should not, as Miss Rand points out, be any conflict between rational men when it comes to ethical questions.

From the objectivist point of view, all values, on a psychological level, are rooted in material (sense-perceptual) being. In a very general sense, then, life itself is the ultimate value and the basis for all subsequent valuation. All life-experience is necessarily an outgrowth of that continuous transitive relationship between the physical organism and its physical environment which is termed "behavior." Man is rational only within a practical—an activistic—context. He is, at basis, a "rational-doer."

The Nature of Value

From the objectivist point of view, a "value" is "a concept pertaining to a relation—the relation of some aspect of reality to man (or to some other living entity.)"[5] "A 'value' is that which one acts to

148

gain and/or keep. It is that which one regards as conducive to ones welfare. A value is the object of an action."[6]

It is through values that the individual directs his actions.[7] "Values constitute man's basic motivational tie to reality."[8]

Pleasure and Happiness

Value resides only within natural experience. Not all natural experience is valuable, however. At basis, value corresponds to that particular quality (or kind) of experience we term "pleasure." As Branden indicates: " . . . the value of pleasure and the dis-value of pain, as well as the value of efficacy and the dis-value of helplessness. remain the psychological base of the phenomenon of valuation."[9]

Pleasure is intrinsically gratifying to man and occurs as a normal by-product of effective action. It is therefore a self-evident (innate) value which precedes any sort of logical demonstration. All men seek pleasure, and this is the motive which underlies all more specific types of self-realization. All pleasure is invariably a personal (i.e., subjectively-*apprehended*) response derived from gaining or keeping a value.[10]

While *pleasure-experience* (i.e., the phenomenon of pleasure *per se)* is *psychological* (and, therefore, *personal*), the *conditions* necessary to *experience* pleasure (i.e., *the context of pleasure*) are *ontological,* in the sense that they are grounded in the objective requirements necessary for acting effectively in the real world. Reason and emotion are never objectively antagonistic,[11] and "the particular species of pain which is the feeling of alienation announces to a man that he is existing in a psychological state improper to him—*that his relationship to reality is wrong.*"[12]

There are, by logical implication, two kinds of pleasure-experience:

1) *True pleasure* (pleasure which generates happiness) is experienced as a "sense of noncontradictory joy," and it is invariably manifested as "a desire to celebrate . . . control over reality."[13] Such pleasure always grows out of behavior which is consistent with the objective demands of the real world and is therefore congruent with other personal values. True pleasure elicits no sense of guilt and logically entails no penalizing consequences.[14]

2) *False Pleasure* is, on the other hand, invariably tainted with ambivalence and expresses itself as a desire to escape from reality.[15]

149

Such pleasure is invariably inconsistent with the objective requirements of the situation as it exists and is also incongruent with a person's true (objective) values and ultimately acts to engender a disproportionate number of negative (displeasurable) consequences. It ultimately elicits unhappiness.

The actual experience of pleasure (pleasure *per se*) can serve as neither the goal nor the standard for actual behavior. In line with the well-known hedonistic paradox, then, *true pleasure* can serve as the *implicit* goal of behavior but never as its *standard,* because true pleasure is always the emotional by-product (consequence) of effective behavior and never its *cause.*

True pleasure is, then, never autistic or based on "mindless self-indulgence."[16] It is invariably a concomitant of effective behavior—i.e., of practice which is based upon *true (objective) theory.*

Productive Reason

Effective behavior is, in turn, caused by productive reason—i.e., rational thought directed to the solution of objective (real) problems. The value of reason is, in turn, predicated upon two underlying facts.

1) The world itself is "rational" in two basic respects: It is characterized by objective *truth*—both *empirical* (e.g., "All truth is apprehensible by reason") and *formal* ("A is A")—and objective *value* (e.g., "Pleasure is intrinsically good").

2) Man is essentially rational; he possesses the potentiality for discovering true (objective) knowledge.

Productive reason is demonstrably good, then, because it is the sole means of obtaining true pleasure (which yields happiness). It therefore constitutes the ultimate *practical* value in life, because it is the only reliable *means* to obtain the true *end* of personal happiness.

* * *

It is interesting to note how close to theology, Miss Rand gets at this point. She employs, as has been mentioned earlier, an omnibus definition of *ultimate reality* which encompasses not only the principles of formal logic, but also certain basic ideas about the basic empirical *content* of truth and value. She then proceeds to define "man" as that aspect of objective Being who has the unique capacity to "reason about reason"—i.e., to grasp the fundamental bases of objective truth—and goes on to suggest that only by doing so will he be able to control and thereby obtain true value through the satisfaction of his needs.

In a sense, then, she holds that man is that *aspect* of material Being who has the capacity to comprehend—and, thereby to transcend—the particular by means of abstract reflection. She holds, however, that this reflection should not be performed *esthetically*—i.e., as an end-in-itself—but, rather, as a means of seeking *control over* material circumstances.

In a sense, of course, this is paradoxical. If reason leads a person to perceive a fabric of inviolable truth which he can in no sense alter, why should he subsequently seek to exercise power over that which he comprehends to be objectively necessary and therefore fundamentally inviolable to change?

* * *

The Origin of Values

Man, state the objectivists, possesses no innate values.[17] His values are always an expression of his conceptual consciousness,[18] "of the thinking he has done or failed to do."[19] Both values and emotions are the outgrowth of prior intellectual conclusions, the consequence of acting on the basis of given ideological premises.[20]

As Branden indicates: "Differences in men's basic values reflect differences in their basic premises, in their fundamental views of themselves, of other men, of existence . . . . "[21] In a similar sense "an emotional response is always the reflection and product of an estimate—and an estimate is the product of a person's values, *as the person understands them to apply to a given situation.* "[22]

Men are always entirely free in their selection of values. They are not biologically programmed to make only right choices; no determinative internal or external forces compel them to arrive at the objectively correct decisions.[23]

The relationship which exists between philosophical principles and value-choices is not ordinarily conscious and direct. Rather " . . . it is *implicit* in man's evaluations reflecting earlier conclusions which are, in effect, 'filed' in his subconscious."[24]

The earliest values are invariably acquired through the experience of pleasure, which grows out of a sense of efficacy in dealing with problems.[25] Indeed, "the value of a sense of efficacy *as such* is introspectively experienced by man as a primary."[26]

Pleasure, on the other hand, is an emotional response. It is not therefore a psychological first principle and cannot be used as a criterion for the verification of values. To use it as such is to indulge in circular reasoning, for, since all emotional responses are effects of prior value judgments, such responses would invariably act to confirm their own implicit intellectual assumptions. As objectivist philosopher Leonard Peikoff states, objectivism rejects all varieties of hedonism because "in practice, men have no way of obeying the tenets of hedonism, except by taking *their already formed feelings*—their desires and aversions, their loves and fears—as *the given* . . . . "[27]

Values and the Sense of Life

From the point of view of the individual's psychological development, then, the earliest choices and value-judgments invariably *precede* the formulation of intellectual principles. The earliest life-values are the product of an implicit worldview which emerges when the child "establishes a habitual pattern[that] becomes his automatic response to the world around him."[28]

This implicit metaphysic Miss Rand terms "the sense of life."[29] It is "a pre-conceptual equivalent of metaphysics."[30] " . . . the emotional form in which a person experiences his deepest view of existence and his own relationship to existence."[31] As she states: "What began as a series of single, discrete conclusions (or evasions) about his own particular problems, becomes a generalized feeling about existence, an implicit *metaphysics* with the compelling motivational power of a constant, basic emotion . . . . "[32]

"A sense of life represents man's early value-integrations, which remain in an extremely fluid, plastic, easily amendable state, while a man gathers knowledge to reach full *conceptual* control and thus to *drive* his inner mechanism."[33]

Regardless of its particular content or its relationship to objective reality, "a sense of life always retains a profoundly personal quality; it reflects a man's deepest values; it is experienced by him as a sense of his own identity."[34] "Introspectively, one's own sense of life is experienced as an absolute and an irreducible primary—as that which one never questions, because *the thought of questioning it never arises.*"[35]

This formative "sense of life" is the cumulative product of a child's earliest choices.[36] It originates through a process of *subconscious emotional generalization*. It is, as Miss Rand indicates, a "process of *emotional* abstraction: it consists of classifying things *according to the emotions they invoke*—i.e., of tying together, by association or connotation, all those things which have the power to make an individual experience the same (or a similar) emotion."[37] "Even though such emotional abstractions grow into a metaphysical view of man, their origin lies in an individual's view of *himself* and of his *own* relationship to existence."[38]

The sense of life is particularly important in Miss Rand's esthetic theory. It is, she asserts, "the source of art, the psychological mechanism which enables man to create a realm such as art."[39] As she suggests: "Art is a selective re-creation of reality according to an artist's metaphysical value-judgments. It is the integrator and concretizer of man's metaphysical abstractions. It is the voice of his sense of life."[40]

Still another area closely related to the sense of life is sexual love, for "more than any other relationship, romantic love involves the objectification of one's *self-value.*"[41] Sex is, in the best sense of the term, "the highest form of selfishness."[42] "In sex, more than any other activity, man experiences the fact of being *an end in himself* and a feeling that the purpose of life is happiness."[43] "It is with a person's sense of life that one falls in love . . . . It is not a matter of professed convictions (though these are not irrelevant); it is a matter of much more profound, conscious *and subconscious* harmony."[44]

Art and the Esthetic Experience

"Art," states Rand, "is a selective re-creation of reality according to an artist's metaphysical value-judgments."[45] As such, it is inextricably involved with questions of moral value and, indeed, functions as "the indispensable medium for the communication of a moral ideal."[46]

On the other hand, and Miss Rand is quick to indicate, the "primary focus" of art is not *ethical,* but *metaphysical.*[47] Moral values are the *consequences* and not the *causal determinants* of art, and art is not a substitute for philosophy.[48]

The basic goal of the artist is not to educate or to prescribe specific types of behavior. "Art is not the 'handmaiden' of morality," states Rand. In a similar sense, *"art is not the means to any didactic end,"*[49] and it *"is not* the means of *literal transcription.'*[50] Instead, states Rand, the proper role of the artist is that of "model-builder"[51] "The basic purpose of art is *not* to teach, but to *show*—to hold up to a man a concretized image of his nature and his place in the universe."[52]

True art emerges from man's conceptual mind, from his capacity for abstract reasoning.[53] The artist requires an ethical theory and "without a conceptual theory of ethics, an artist would not be able successfully

153

to concretize an image of the ideal."[54] *Esthetic ideas* differ from *cognitive ideas*—which are determined by the criterion of what is *essential*—and *normative ideas*—which are determined by the criterion of what is *good.* "Esthetic abstractions are formed by the criterion of: What is important?"[55] In most cases, however, the conceptual basis for esthetic activity is not founded on a conscious and systematized theory but, rather, derives from the pre-cognitive "sense of life" which provides the artist with "the integrated sum of his metaphysical abstractions."[56] "Art concretizes [these implicit metaphysical assumptions] and allows him to perceive—to *experience*—their immediate reality."[57]

Art, then, is a sort of spontaneous short-hand metaphysics. By synthesizing concrete objects and events with the realm of objective truth, the artist embodies abstraction and, in so doing, reaffirms and concretizes objective principles of truth and value. Through the esthetic act, objective reality is reborn in symbolic form and communicated to others. For the artist the process of artistic communication is primarily a matter of deductively objectifying abstractions; for the artist's public it is primarily a matter of inductively abstracting the concrete by means of esthetic response.[58] The significance of art lies in its "psycho-epistemological" function of particularizing abstract truth.[59] "Out of the countless mumber of concretes . . . an artist isolates the things which he regards as metaphysically essential and integrates them into a single new concrete that represents an embodied abstraction."[60] "Art is a concretization of metaphysics. *Art brings man's concepts to the perceptual level of his consciousness and allows him to grasp them directly, as if they were percepts.'*[61]

Miss Rand's esthetic principles are perhaps best observed in her observations with respect to literature. Many readers of *The Fountainhead,* she comments, have used the character Howard Roark as a way of resolving difficult moral problems. "They asked themselves: 'What would Roark do in this situation?' And, faster than their mind could identify the proper application of all the complex principles involved, the image of Roark gave them the answer."[62]

The appraisal, or evaluation, of art should be quite objective and, properly, has nothing to do with "liking" or "not liking" the work in question. According to Miss Rand, the act of *objective evaluation* entails two processes: (1) identifying the theme of the work (i.e., the abstract meaning of the work *per se*) and (2) evaluating the (technical) means by which such a meaning has been conveyed.[63]

A man's taste and discrimination in matters of art are a primary expression of his own psycho-epistemological state of health. As Rand suggests, "A man's treason to his art values is not the primary cause of his neurosis (it is a contributory cause), but it becomes one of its most revealing symptoms."[64]

In a similar respect, "style" expresses "a 'psycho-epistemological sense of life,' i.e., an expression of that level of mental functioning on which the artist feels most at home."[65] Style is always a deeply personal matter. "To the artist, it is an expression, to the reader or viewer a confirmation, of his own consciousness—which means: of his efficacy—which means: of his self-esteem (or pseudo-self-esteem)."[66]

It should be noted that Miss Rand, like most ideologues, is not terribly enthusiastic about the sort of disengaged perspective which is so frequently reflected in those who demonstrate a "sense of humor." "Humor" comments Rand "is not an unconditional virtue; its moral character depends on its object. To laugh at the contemptible, is a virtue; to laugh at the good, is a hideous vice. Too often, humor is used as the camouflage of moral cowardice."[67]

She is particularly incensed by philosophical humor—i.e., the sort of humor expressed by the man who does not take his own intellectual commitments seriously enough, the sort of man who is capable of looking at his own absolutes relatively. She is, in this respect, particularly contemptuous of a philosopher like Bertrand Russell who, when asked if he would be willing to die for his beliefs, is reputed to have said, "Of course not. After all, I may be wrong."[68]

Miss Rand's criticism of humor is not restricted to the more philosophical areas, however. She is also offended by the "camp" treatment of heroic themes which occur in the various media and particularly by the mock-heroic treatment afforded to the character of Napoleon Solo, the hero protagonist of television's spy series *The Man from Uncle*, by actor Robert Vaughn. "Mr. Vaughn," complains Rand, "giggles, chortles, snickers, leers and sneers without any discernible reason, but with an air of bored, supercilious amusement, throughout an entire show, no matter what action is involved."[69]

These esthetic principles of objectivism can be observed in virtually any work of art, for all art reflects its own characteristic psycho-epistemological orientation. In the case of painting, for example, " . . . a man whose normal mental state is . . . full focus, will [ordinarily] create and respond to a style that projects sharp outlines,

155

cleanliness, purpose, and intransigent commitments to full awareness and clear-cut identity . . . ."[70]

Perhaps the antithesis of such esthetic sanity is provided by the non-representational or, as Miss Rand terms it, the "Rorschach" school of painting " . . . consisting of blobs, swirls, and smears which are and aren't, which are anything you might want them to be provided you stare at them long enough, keeping your eyes and mind out of focus."[71]

The "moral sense of life" is important, not only in creating art, but also in responding to it. The objectivist esthetics is perhaps best exemplified in romantic art and, as Rand points out, perhaps the clearest evidence of psycho-epistemological disturbances is provided by an individual's attitude toward such romanticism.[72] With respect to the usual classifications of literature, Miss Rand describes herself as a "romantic realist." Thus, and as she indicates with respect to her own literary responses, "[Victor] Hugo gives me the feeling of entering a cathedral . . . Spillane gives me the feeling of hearing a military band in a public park—Tolstoy gives me the feeling of an unsanitary back yard which I do not care to enter."[73]

In the case of literature, the objectivist esthetics are most easily observed in the romantic novel of the nineteenth century, which is perhaps best exemplified in the works of Victor Hugo, a writer who Miss Rand describes as "the greatest novelist in world literature."[74]

The romantic novel is the product of two forces that were particularly influential in the last century, reason and capitalism. It grows out "of the Aristotelian influence which, in the nineteenth century, gave man the confident power to choose his own goals—and of the politico-economic system that left him free to achieve them."[75] "The Romantic writers," comments Rand, " . . . regarded [man] as a product of his own value-choices . . . they did not record the choices men *had* made, but projected the choices men *ought* to make."[76] " . . . read the stories of O. Henry or listen to the music of Viennese operattas . . . then ask yourself: which psycho-epistemology is appropriate to man, which is consonant with the facts of reality and with man's nature?"[77]

Romanticism in contrast to naturalism, centers on the recognition that man possesses "the faculty of volition."[78 A] One goal of romantic art is to envision the ideal man.[78] "It offers a concrete, directly perceivable answer to the very abstract question which a child senses, but cannot yet conceptualize: What kind of person is moral and what kind of life does he lead?"[79] "Romantic art is the fuel and the spark plug of a man's soul; its task is to set a soul on fire . . . . The task of providing that fire with a motor and a direction belongs to philosophy."[80]

The romantic portrayal of moral ideals is not merely a *means,* however. It is ultimately an *end-in-itself.*[81] Art is ultimately *non-social;* it "belongs to a non-socializable aspect of reality, which is universal (i.e. applicable to all men) but non-collective: to the basic nature of man's consciousness."[82]

In a sense, of course, it is precisely the fact that art is intrinsically *non-collective* which explains its current neglect,[83] for art is always the moral "barometer of a culture."[84] "It reflects the sum of a society's deepest philosophical values: not its professed notions and slogans, but its actual view of man and of existence."[85]

The state of art in contemporary Western civilization is an eloquent expression of an acute contemporary moral deterioration. "It reflects precisely that fear, guilt and pity (a pity which is characteristically self-pity) with which our society is presently afflicted."[86]

This decline in esthetic sensibility is particularly apparent in the case of contemporary literature where the last vestiges of the once flourishing romantic fiction are to be found today primarily in the detective thrillers of a Mickey Spillane and the spy adventures of an Ian Fleming. The significant thing about both of these writers is precisely that they "both offer the cardinal element of Romantic fiction. Mike Hammer and James Bond are *heroes.*"[87] The end-result is that Spillane's best passages are literarily superior to the work of most of today's so-called 'serious' writers."[88] "Mickey Spillane is a moral absolutist. His characterizations are excellent and drawn in black-and-white; there are no slippery half-tones, no cowardly evasions, no cynicism—and no forgiveness; there are no doubts about the evil of evil."[89] "Thrillers are a simplified, elementary version of Romantic literature . . . taking certain fundamental values for granted, they are concerned with only one aspect of a moral being's existence: the battle of good against evil in terms of purposeful action . . . . "[90]

In the formative years of childhood, romantic art serves as the basic source of a truly objective moral commitment and is the basis for a rational "sense of life."[91] In later childhood and adolescence it serves as a symbolic reaffirmation and reinforcement of such a commitment and may even provide the sole remaining source of such experience.[92]

157

Free Will and the Choice to Think

According to Branden, man is characterized by inalienable free will. This free will guarantees that man is potentially capable of acting independent of external controls, "that man is capable of making choices which are *first causes* within his consciousness, i.e., not necessitated by an antecedent factor."[93]

This free will resides fundamentally in man's original *meta-choice* to think or not to think. "The act of thinking is man's primary act of choice."[94] "In the choice to focus or not to focus, to think or not to think, to activate the conceptual level of his consciousness or to suspend it—and in this choice alone—is man psychologically free."[95] "Objectivism locates man's free will in a single action of his consciousness, in a single basic choice: to focus his mind or to suspend it; to think or not to think."[96]

The majority of men are not capable of living truly intellectual lives. Non-creative and group-oriented, "they don't sustain their thinking consistently, as a way of life, and . . . their abstract range is limited."[97] "To what extent they are stunted by the anti-rational influences of our cultural traditions, is hard to say; what is known, however, is that the majority of men use only a small part of their potential intellectual capacity."[98]

On the other hand, Rand is clearly contemptuous of the collectivistic concept of man which "is based on a view of man as a congenital incompetent, a helpless, mindless creature who must be fooled and ruled by a special elite with some unspecified claim to superior wisdom and a lust for power."[99] She is also firmly opposed to the traditional view of the old-fashioned "conservatives" who advocate freedom, not as an inalienable right, but rather as a necessary safeguard against man's "natural" tendency to abuse power.[100]

"Thinking," states Rand, "is an activity that must be initiated, sustained and directed by man's volitional, self-generated effort."[101] As such, it must be distinguished from all categories of choice.[102] The choice to think "is man's basic freedom of choice. This choice—given the context of his knowledge and of the existential possibilities confronting him—controls all of man's other choices, and it directs the course of his actions."[103] "Reason does not work automatically . . . . At any hour and issue of your life, you are free to think or to evade that effort."[104]

The choice to think is not an emotional choice which emerges out of behavior. It is determined neither by a *desire for reason* nor by *reason itself* (for this would merely entail a backward analytic regress in order to explain the causal determinants of these factors in turn). The only other possible explanations—revelation and mystical intuition—are, of course, rejected on purely objectivist grounds.

The *choice to think* is essentially a choice to focus one's mind, a choice to seek a volitional expansion of awareness. To enquire about such a choice is "to ask: 'what *made* one man choose to focus and another to evade?' The choice to think and the process of focusing his mind are an indivisible action, of which man is the causal agent."[105]

The basic choice to think or not to think entails three basic subdecisions—"three fundamental cognitive alternatives."[106]—with respect to intellectual operations. These are (1) the choice to initiate and sustain a clear intellectual focus, the individual's choice of "seeking to bring his understanding to an optimal level of precision—and clarity,"[107] (2) the choice to differentiate clearly between *knowledge* and *feelings;* and (3) the choice to employ active and independent critical analysis in solving problems.[108]

The choice to think refers, then, not merely to simple awareness but, rather, to "the *human* form of consciousness"—*conceptual* awareness."[109] Not only the choice to focus the mind but also the end sought—rational *awareness*—is a *primary* value.[110] As Nathaniel Branden indicates: "The decision to focus one's mind (to value awareness and make it one's goal) or not to focus, is the basic choice that cannot be reduced further. In this issue, man is a *prime mover.*"[111]

Knowledge begins, not with *behavior,* but with *uncaused awareness.* The first choice, rooted in primary awareness, is necessarily the choice, not of particular *content,* but of the *operation* of reason itself.[112] "*What* a man thinks about, depends on his values, interests and context . . . but whether or not, in a given situation, he chooses to think at all, is an issue of his free will."[113]

Simple sense-perceptual awareness is not volitional, however, but automatic.[114] Only *thought*—i.e., conceptual awareness—is contingent upon choice. Man alone has "*the power to regulate the action of his own consciousness.*"[115] " . . . the exercise of his rational faculty, unlike an animal's use of his senses, is not automatic . . . the decision to think is not biologically 'programmed' in man . . . *to think is an act of choice.*"[116]

Perception as such yields not the *truth about reality* but merely the *facts about the environment.* Ultimately, however, *reality* is not merely

159

a collection of circumstantial *facts*. It is, rather, a *meaning* derived from such facts by means of a conscious and rational application of mind. At basis, then, knowledge is determined not by *perception* but by *cognition*. "Reason is your faculty of perceiving reality."[117]

Man is essentially a self-programmer.[118] The choice to think is "a psychologically irreducible natural fact"[119] which is "uncaused" by any chain of antecedent forces.[120] It is "a primary, a *first cause* in consciousness"[121] which is not in any significant sense dependent upon subjective or situational factors. "The choice to think and the process of focusing his mind are an indivisible action, of which man is the causal agent . . . . Neither motives nor desires nor context are causal imperatives with regard to this choice."[122]

Phrased somewhat differently, then, the objectivists contend, not that the choice to think is "uncaused," but, rather, that it is "caused" (determined) precisely by man's nature as man. In other words, and as Nathaniel Branden maintains: "This freedom of choice is not a negation of causality, but a category of it, a category that pertains to man. A process of thought is not causeless, it is caused by man."[123]

At basis, the choice to think is not "uncaused" but, instead, *caused (entailed) by the law of identity itself*. It is precisely man's nature *qua* man which obligates him to be free. Indeed, "freedom" is precisely one of the essential "qualities" of man which defines his potentialities for action. "The actions possible to an entity are determined by its nature: What a thing can *do* depends on what it *is* . . . actions *consistent* with their natures are possible to entities, but *contradictions* are not."[124]

At basis, man is *determined* to be *beyond determination*. His freedom is "uncaused" in the usual sense of the word precisely because it is rooted in his *identity as man* and because any limitation upon such freedom would logically contradict this nature. In this way, and as Branden indicates, Hume's classical arguments against causality are easily disposed of. One cannot *prove causality causally* precisely because causality is ultimately contingent upon identity. According to Branden, we can only understand why things in a given situation were as they are by understanding the properties of the things involved, and any explanation in terms of prior actions always presupposes such an understanding.

> . . . if one states that the *action* of a wastebasket catching fire was *caused* by the *action* of a lighted match being thrown into it, this constitutes a satisfactory causal explanation only if one

160

understands the *nature* of paper and of lighted matches; a description of the action sequence, in the absence of such knowledge, would explain nothing.[125]

Naturally, then, the objectivists take strong exception to the doctrines of the psychological determinists. As Branden indicates:

> Psychological determinism denies the existence of any element of freedom or volition in man's consciousness. It holds that every action, desire and thought of man is determined by forces beyond his control. It holds that, in relation to his actions, decisions, values and conclusions, man is ultimately and essentially *passive;* that man is merely a *reactor* to internal and external pressures; that those pressures determine the course of man's actions and the content of his convictions just as physical forces determine the cause of every particle of dust in the universe. It holds that, in any given situation or moment, only one "choice" is psychologically possible to man, the inevitable result of all the antecedent determining forces impinging on him, just as only one action is possible to the speck of dust; that man has no *actual* power of choice, no *actual* freedom or self-responsibility. Man, according to his view, has no more actual volition than a stone; he is merely confronted with more complex alternatives and is manipulated by more complex forces.[126]

> That which a man does, declare the advocates of determinism, he *had* to do—that which he believes, he had to believe—if he focuses his mind, he *had* to—if he evades the effort of focusing, he *had* to—if he is guided solely by reason, he *had* to be—if he is ruled instead by feeling or whim, he *had* to be—*he couldn't help it.* But if this were true, no *knowledge* would be possible to man. No theory could claim greater plausibility than any other—including the theory of psychological determinism.[127]

In line with this, Branden also rejects the traditional Thomistic conception of free will which is founded upon the assumption that man has an innate predisposition to think—an internalized causal drive to be self-determining. For Branden, this is merely a form of covert determinism in which man is coerced into freedom by means of psychological imperatives which act in the guise of determinative "tendencies." For the objectivist, on the other hand, "the *capacity* of conceptual functioning is *innate;* but the *exercise* of this capacity is *volitional.*"[128] The Thomistic tradition, states Brended, is not actually a theory of free will at all. The real problem "is not *which* forces compel man's choices, but *whether* man's choices are compelled. If the primary functions of man's consciousness, the act of thinking, is not in man's control, then man is not a self-responsible being."[129]

The objectivist rejects all deterministic explanations of cognition at the primary level. Man's freedom to think is limited neither by causal predispositions nor by environmental conditions. Rather, it is a unique human capacity to *originate* the process of abstract thought gratuitously—*for no reason whatsoever.* Again, and as Branden notes: "Man's greatest distinction from all other living species is the capacity to originate an action of his consciousness—the capacity to originate a process of abstract thought."[130]

For the objectivist, then, the choice to think is essentially a normative commitment—the choice of a rational life which is "reason-guided and reason-motivated."[131] "To be in focus is to set one's mind to the purpose of *active cognitive integration.*"[132] For the focused mind, action is grounded causally in philosophical principles. Such a person, states Branden, "has learned to make rationality 'second-nature' ... his psychological state must be maintained *volitionally;* he retains the power to betray it. Each new issue he encounters, he still must *choose* to think."[133]

The choice to focus or not to focus is never totally divorced from the "level of awareness" which one has attained. Instead, and as Branden indicates, the choice to focus "refers to the degree of *active cognitive integration.*"[135] This is "reflected in (a) the clarity or vagueness of the mind's contents, (b) the degree to which the mind's activity involves abstractions or is concrete-bound, (c) the degree to which the relevant wider context is present or absent in the process of thinking."[136]

One is not faced with a simple alternative between a state of *literal unconsciousness* and one of *literal consciousness,* then. It is, rather, a significant shift in the *degree* of awareness—a shift which is characterized by the movement to a higher level of consciousness which is characterized by "directed cognitive integration."[137] The person who has made the "choice to think" has the ability to ground his behavior in intellectual principles, and he has accepted responsibility for the conduct of his own life.

The choice to think is always a *rational* and not an *emotional* choice.

162

As Nathaniel Branden comments: "Neither motives nor desires nor context are causal imperatives with regard to this choice. They are not irrelevant to a man's thinking or evasion, but ... by themselves, they do not and cannot constitute a causal explanation."[138] "A man characteristically can differentiate between *knowledge* and feelings, letting his judgment always be directed by his intellect, not his emotions .... "[139]

From the objectivist point of view, an *emotion* " ... is the psychosomatic form in which man experiences his estimate of the relationship of things to himself. An emotion is a *value*-response. It is the automatic psychological result of a man's value-judgment."[140] " ..: the content of man's emotions is the product of his rational faculties; his emotions are a derivative and a consequence, which ... cannot be understood without reference to the conceptual power of his consciousness."[141]

Contrary to popular opinion, emotions do not determine values. They are invariably the product of cognitive appraisals. "The relationship of value-judgments to emotions is that of *cause* to *effect* .... It is the automatic psychological result (involving both mental and somatic features) of a super-rapid, subconscious appraisal."[142]

On the other hand, emotions tend to be experienced prior to conscious evaluation. Again, and as Branden indicates: "The form in which these lightning-like appraisals [i.e., value-judgments] initially present themselves to man's conscious mind is his *emotions.* "[143] The chain of events can be properly described, then, as "from perception to evaluation to emotional response. On the level of immediate awareness ... the sequence is: from perception to emotion. A person may or may not be consciously aware of the intervening value-judgment."[144]

At basis, emotions are merely unexplicated ideas. "Reason and emotion are not antagonists; what may seem like a struggle between them is only a struggle between two opposing ideas, one of which is not conscious and manifests itself only in the form of a feeling."[145]

For the objectivist, then, man is absolutely *free* to choose *necessity*, to opt for the objective and logical requirements of life itself. The individual must make this "choice" gratuitously, however—without any sort of pre-existing proclivities and in the absence of any sort of prior logical and empirical knowledge. If he makes the wrong choice, he is immoral and must justly suffer the behavioral consequence of his own epistemological sins. If he chooses correctly, he is precipitated into a state of psycho-epistemological grace which invariably yields the maximum degree of moral and material satisfaction.

Repression and the
Unconscious

The objectivists do not reject the concepts of *repression* and the *subconscious mind.* "The 'sub-conscious'," states Nathaniel Branden, "is the sum of mental contents and processes that are outside of or below conscious awareness."[146] It functions "as a store of past knowledge, observations and conclusions . . . and it operates, *in effect,* as an electronic computer, performing super-rapid integrations of sensory and ideational material."[147]

Repression acts as a volitional screening-out of objective reality and is therefore regarded as the most significant factor militating toward a sense of psychological alienation. It is the automatic shutting-out of certain subjectively-discomforting types of mental content from conscious awareness. It is an *"automatized avoidance reaction,* whereby a man's focal awareness is involuntarily pulled away from any 'forbidden' material emerging from less conscious levels of his mind or from his subconscious."[148] As such, it "entails an automatized standing-order exactly opposite to the one involved in creative thinking: an order *forbidding* integration."[149] Reality-avoidance practices such as rationalization and repression act to subvert cognition. They are "the prime instigators of psychological disorders."[150]

Repression, however, is fundamentally a *cognitive* and not an *emotional* device. " . . . it is not emotions as such that are repressed . . . . What is blocked or repressed, in the case of emotions, is either evaluations that would lead to emotions or identifications involving one's emotions."[151] "Evasion is willful disintegration . . . setting the cognitive function in reverse and reducing the contents of one's mind to disconnected, unintegrated fragments that are forbidden to confront one another."[152]

Freedom and Circumstances. It is possible for a person to be reared under circumstances which make the establishment of a firm and rational cognitive structure exceedingly difficult.[153] In his article "The Objectivist Theory of Volition," Branden takes the position that it is entirely possible for a child to be subjected to such brutalizing conditions during the earliest phases of life "that it would be impossible for him to develop normally, impossible to establish any kind of firm base of knowledge on which to build."[154A] Such a child, Branden concedes, might be psychologically-crippled or even mentally-retarded as a result of such circumstances. "But this would represent the *destruction*, not the 'conditioning,' of a child's mind; it is scarcely the pattern of the overwhelming majority of mankind; and this is *not* what is meant by those who claim that man is the product of his background."[154] "On every day of this boy's life," writes Branden

> and at every crucial turning-point the possibility of thinking above his actions were open to him. The evidence on which to base a change in his policy was available to him. He evaded it. He chose not to think. If, at every turning-point, he had thought carefully and consciously, and had simply reached the wrong conclusions, he would be more justified in crying that he could not help it. But it does not help the bewildered, conscientious thinkers who fill reform schools and who murder one another on street corners—through an error in logic.
>
> If one wishes to understand what destroyed the boy, the key lies, not in his environment, but in the fact that he let himself be moved, guided and motivated by his feelings, that he tried to substitute his feelings for his mind. There was nothing to prevent him from thinking, except that he did not feel like it.
>
> To the extent that a man defaults on his responsibility of thinking, he *is*, in significant measure, "the product of his environment." But such is not the nature of man. It is an instance of pathology.[155]

* * *

Without going into a detailed analysis of this particular example, it is perhaps evident that Branden is guilty of making three very dubious assumptions. The first of these is the assumption that the *destruction* of the child's mind does not represent the "conditioning" of it. Branden does not explain *why* this is true. What he *seems* to mean is that there is ultimately no such thing as "bad knowledge." There is, instead, merely (1) *objectivist truth* and (2) *insanity*. By equating error (i.e., any lack of agreement with objectivist principles) with neurosis on the basis of his own "psycho-epistemological" theory, Branden manages the rather neat trick of relegating all those who disagree with him to the status of the irrational.

Actually, and apart from specifics, Branden concedes a very

important point here—i.e., that it is possible for a person to be subjected to childhood conditions which would make it virtually impossible for him to develop productive rationality. If this is true, the objectivist ethic surrenders its claim to infallibility, and the moral stance of the objectivist position is effectively undermined.

The other two points which Branden makes—that such pathological conditions are exceedingly rare and that this sort of thing is not what is meant by those who claim that man is determined by his background—are simply not true, as any unbiased survey of the appropriate evidence will attest. Indeed, this is precisely what contemporary experts in the appropriate areas of study *do* mean when they talk about environmental determinism, and the prevalence of precisely such conditions as Branden describes is easily documented.

To say that a child who has been reared under the conditions which Branden describes is always free to ask "Why?"—to question, to analyze and, ultimately, to reformulate his beliefs—is an absurdly simple answer to an extremely complicated problem. Ultimately, of course, it is precisely the possibility of asking such questions, performing such analyses and of arriving at such self-induced changes which are in doubt to begin with in such cases as these.

On what basis does the slum child question his beliefs if not in terms of his own environmentally-debased intellectual perspective? In many cases, of course, such "negative" values are highly appropriate within his own slum environment. The roles of criminal, dope pusher and prostitute are not dysfunctional or unproductive orientations in many diseased environments. Why should the Negro thief who is acculturated to living in a predominantly criminal, lower-class, Negro ghetto reject the criminal way of life? Wouldn't this entail precisely the sort of "self-sacrifice" which Branden decries? Even granted an objective insight into his own conditions, might not a continued career of crime be a justifiable compromise with the realities of an otherwise sick society?

How is the successful criminal in a marginal sub-culture which places a premium on crime to *know* that he is "unproductive" and "unhappy?" Since we cannot rely on his "neurotic" altruistic conscience, on what basis shall we anticipate a desire for change? Why should the Negro delinquent seek or (having sought) take to heart an awareness that middle-class white citizens *in their world* do not approve the sort of "negative adjustment" which he has made? Indeed, in view of his typically anti-white value-orientation, wouldn't this merely increase the satisfaction which he already derives from his criminal revolt against established white morality and even further strengthen his predisposition toward "antisocial" practices?

To say that reason and a broader viewpoint should induce such things is merely to beg the question, for it is precisely reason and a broader viewpoint which are generally lacking to begin with. It is the absence of a rational commitment, rational techniques and the inclination to indulge in rational speculation that makes the application of such intellectual proceedures of self-therapy so exceedingly unlikely. It is, in other words, precisely the cultural conditioning that has created the problem, and it is the existence of the problem which, in turn, precludes an appeal to the usual sort of voluntaristic "bootstrap" solutions.

It is not, after all, merely *ability* but *inclination* as well which is forged in the matrix of social conditions. If the Negro slum child had "at every turning point . . . thought carefully and consciously, and had simply reached the wrong conclusion,"[156] he would not, in all likelihood, be a Negro slum child to begin with and, indeed, no problem would, in all likelihood exist. To say that " . . . he let himself be moved, guided and motivated by his feelings, that he tried to substitute his feelings for his mind"[157] is an excellent *description* of a social pathology but an extremely superficial *explanation* of how such a pathological condition evolved in the first place. Unfortunate though they may be, such "errors in logic" do not arise in a vacuum and cannot be exorcised as a miscarriage of some kind of amorphous and inviolable "volition" which exists independent of practical circumstances.

Free Will and Moral Choice

As the objectivists see it, evil (immorality) is, at basis, a conscious and intentional choice of a recognizable bad (i.e., irrational) act.[158] All evil is therefore based on volitional errors in cognition.

Man has free moral choice. His basic choice in life is always the choice *for* or *against* reason itself—the choice to think or not to think.[159] A person is always capable of willfully evading or suppressing knowledge.[160] The moral man is the man who is voluntarily committed to reason. The immoral man is, conversely, the man who is voluntarily committed to irrationality. As Barbara Branden states: "There *are* evil men in the world . . . . The world is not perishing because of the men who don't *know* the good, but because of the men who *refuse* to know it."[161]

Here, of course, we find overselves confronted with what is perhaps the basic weakness in Miss Rand's theory of value, her concept of free will. In essence, she finds herself trapped by her own rigorous definition of "objective truth." In a sense, she is faced with four possible choices:

1) There is no "objective" truth. All truths are simply inferences growing out of personal experience.

2) All knowledge is *relative* to personal experience (behavior), but personal experience itself is (as in Thomism) relative to certain objective conditions which invariably necessitate certain types of behavior which, in turn, predispose toward certain unavoidable conclusions with respect to the underlying nature of reality.

3) Knowledge about basic reality is objective, self-evident and certain. Such knowledge encompasses both the nature of ultimate truth (including both formal and/or empirical truths) as well as the nature of ultimate value.

4) Knowledge about basic reality is objective but encompasses only the nature of ultimate truth (including both empirical and/or formal truths), and not a knowledge of ultimate value.

With respect to all four of these positions, Miss Rand is faced with certain problems. If she were to accept the first position, she would undermine her entire "objectivist" philosophy by granting that her total philosophy is necessarily based on *a posteriori* interpretations of purely personal experience which are, by definition, beyond any sort of impersonal (objective) rational verification. She would, in effect, become either a "relativistic absolutist" or a "dogmatic relativist."

Position 1, unlike the other three, has the virtue of making cognitive error possible. Unfortunately, it removes any question of culpability, for, if knowledge is a matter of personal choice, one cannot be condemned for rejecting true (objective) knowledge. A man can choose to be irrational, but he can never be irrational by *intent*. Indeed, since all behavior is caused by prior knowledge, there can be no question of personal morality at all, and the terms "good" and "bad" must necessarily be restricted to a description of the consequences which an individual's acts have upon others.

Positions 1 and 2 actually vary more in *degree* than in *kind*. The difficulty with the second approach is, of course, that it is still basically a relativistic position. Thus, if *Being* is *objective,* but a *knowledge of Being is relative,* Being remains, *for all practical purposes,* relative by·

virtue of the fact that it is mediated, not only *through personal experience,* but largely on the basis of *pre-rational* and *non-rational* behavior.

If, on the other hand, Miss Rand were to subscribe to the third position, she would end up with her "objective" ontology intact but with absolutely no basis for subscribing to a doctrine of free will. This is true for several reasons.

1) If a person is capable of making a conscious and intentional choice to be irrational, he will first have to know what the rational alternative is. The *rational alternative* is however, by virtually any responsible definition, that course of action which "makes sense"—i.e., which is, in short, identified with, or "caused by," whatever beliefs the individual adheres to in the circumstances. Certain questions unavoidably arise then. Is it, for example, possible for a person to *believe* positions X to be true—i.e., to be the most effective course of action in the circumstances—and yet choose to act on the basis of position Y?

The answer is clearly no—unless one is willing to subscribe to the dubious position (a) that action is unrelated to belief (which would be a violation of the law of cause-effect at the psychological level) or (b) that a person may choose to act as he does not choose to act (which is a violation of the law of contradiction at the psychological level.)

2) It is not possible for a person to know that an act is both true (real) and valuable (good) and, at the same time, to choose to do otherwise.

Here again, we are faced with a question of semantics. All "knowledge" is, at basis, a form of commitment. To "know" something in any particular instance is always *to behave in terms of* such an assumption. To make a "statement" about one's beliefs is ultimately simply to explicate the ideological basis for one's behavior. A lie is, in this sense, a statement which does not correspond to the actual behavioral dispositions which are contained within one's professions of belief.

This is particularly true, of course, with respect to "objective" values. If the value of reason is self-evident, man cannot choose to reject reason without rejecting his own nature (which would also, of course, be logically impossible). If a knowledge of the fact that all value is natural (empirical) can be said to be objective and self-evident, it naturally follows that I cannot choose to believe in values which are supernatural without (1) not *knowing* that which I know as a practical condition for believing otherwise or (2) knowing that which I know to be true is not true (which is logical nonsense).

Put in another way, then, it is absolutely impossible for me to voluntarily reject or ignore an innate volition. If objective values (or objective truths, which function as general instrumental-values in the determination of effective behavior) are actually inherent, they cannot be denied. If they can be *denied*, they cannot be *inherent*. Indeed, if they are relevant to volition (choice) in any sense at all, they become contingent upon a variety of *subjective* factors and are no longer "objective" at all. (In a sense, of course, a value is always a volition, for if it did not affect motivated behavior, it would be irrelevant. To deny a recognized value would be to will *not to do* what one *wills to do*.)

The fourth position mentioned above is eliminated for much the same reason as the third. A statement of fact (truth) is always implicitly pragmatic, because it is always an elliptical "if-then" statement about the way in which certain experiences apply to the solution of real or incipient problems. The formal principle of identity in logic states, for example, *if* you desire to make accurate predictions about the characteristics of X on the basis of its membership of category Y, be sure that you continue to define category Y in the same way throughout the reasoning process.

In a sense, then, Miss Rand is faced with a dilemma. If man is free to choose rationality, he cannot be aware of the value of rationality to begin with, for this would preclude the act of choice altogether. Conversely, if the value of rationality is not self-evident, it becomes relative to knowledge which is, in turn, derived from experience (since it is not innate) and cannot be termed "objective" at all in the sense that it transcends the subjective and relativistic processes of human experience.

Objectivist Freedom and Psychological Determinism. According to Branden, the psychological determinists are quite wrong in maintaining that all behavior must be caused by the interaction of external forces—i.e., forces not identical with the behavior itself. Such a position is, as Branden sees it, an implicit denial of the possibility of human freedom. It eliminates all volitional behavior and assumes that man is a passive reactor who responds motor-mechanically to the dictates of external stimuli.

170

Without becoming sidetracked into a lengthy disquisition regarding the doctrine of psychological determinism, it is important to make two basic points with regard to the objectivist analysis of the psychological determinist's position.

1) Psychological determinism does not deny volitional behavior. It simply places such behavior within the context of objective cause-and-effect relationships.

2) The doctrine of psychological determinism does not deny freedom. It merely looks upon freedom as a particular type of volitional control exerted by the individual himself in choosing between alternative courses of action.

From the point of view of psychological determinism, for example, man is not free to perform two simultaneous acts. He is finite and must therefore choose. In a similar sense, once aware of rational processes, a man is free to choose between objective rational action and subjective non-rational action. He is not free, however, *to choose without choosing*, and, before any choice can occur, there must be at least two recognized alternatives.

To choose "reason," for example, a man must know what "reason" means in the sense of what it implies in terms of behavior. He must also know what "non-reason" means. To speak of an "enlightened choice" which is not contingent upon a prior knowledge of the other options available is absurd. A true choice always implies such information.

If this is true, however, how is it possible to speak of an *uncaused* commitment to reason? Is not the commitment to reason caused precisely by the choice to undertake such a commitment, which is, in turn, caused by a knowledge of the alternatives involved? Is not a knowledge of the alternatives, in turn, caused by some prior experience of those conditions which such alternatives indirectly represent?

To speak of an *irreducible choice*—a choice prior to experience—is to speak of a logical impossibility. We have, to use Branden's term, a "stolen concept." A choice is always contingent on knowledge, and knowledge—since it does not arise *in vacuo*—always demands prior experience with that which is known.

The objectivist attempts to sidestep these objections by the expedient of positing a special realm of "causeless causality." In effect,

171

man is capable of an undetermined and unmotivated choice of reason, because such a choice is (paradoxically) determined by man's nature as man. It is, at basis, man's nature to be uncaused.

Again, however, this brings up several difficulties. How can man choose without first having a knowledge of the options for choice? Where does such knowledge *come from*? If he is rational prior to choice—i.e., by nature, as in the philosophy of Aquinas—is he freely rational or rational only within a context of predetermined limitations?

If a person's choice is non-cognitive—i.e., if he "chooses" first and only subsequently desires the object of his choice—can he be said to have made a *moral choice* at all or merely to have *acted* on a precognitive basis? If cognition grows out of perception which, in turn, emerges out of a process of iterative (nonverbal) definition,[162] how can the choice to think be *cognitive* without also being *caused by* prior (ostensive) experience?

What this all adds up to, of course, is quite simple. The objectivist concept of free will is validated merely by assertion. Man is free *because he is free.* He cannot be *proven* to be free—i.e., his freedom cannot be shown to be necessitated (caused) by other conditions—because this would violate the very concept of freedom as gratuitous action. We are, in effect, then, faced with a statement of empirical identity: Man is free—self-evidently—because he is free.

Branden's objections to the Thomistic concept of free will are particularly interesting because they illustrate the peculiar extremes to which the objectivists' commitment in the ethical realm force them to go. Branden cannot accept St. Thomas' position because it would be a tacit admission of the fact that knowledge (and therefore behavior) is partially dependent upon environmental factors. For Aquinas, *truth* is essential (absolute), but the *apprehension of truth* on the part of each particular person is partially contingent upon the variable "accidents" of time and place. Branden rejects this position on the peculiar (and extremely dubious) grounds that, if man has a natural tendency to seek the truth—to be rational—he is, other things being equal, *determined* to do so and is not therefore totally *responsible* for his choices, which become, in effect, forced upon him by dint of his own psychological nature.

This all sounds very plausible until we remember that the objectivist's alternative is a creature who is by nature *compelled* to choose in a vacuum and who is therefore forced to suffer the inexorable consequences of his ungrounded decisions.

172

Still another sin which Branden ascribes to the psychological determinists is that of metaphysical agnosticism. "How," he enquires in his article "The Contradictions of Determinism," "did the advocates of determinism acquire *their* knowledge? What is its validation? Determinists are conspicuously silent on this point."[163]

According to Branden, all determinists are guilty of self-contradiction. They commit "the *fallacy of self-exclusion*."[164] "Those who expound determinism must either assert that they arrived at their theory by mystical revelation, and thus exclude themselves from the realm of reason—or they must assert that *they* are an exception to the theory they propound, and thus exclude their theory from the realm of truth."[165] "Only because man *is* a state of volitional consciousness—only because he *is* free to initiate and sustain a reasoning process, is knowledge in contra-distinction to irresistible, unchosen beliefs—possible to him."[166 A] In the absence of volitional consciousness, notes Branden, both science and reason are impossible.[166] "The very *concept* of logic is possible only to a volitional consciousness; an automatic consciousness would have no need of it and could not conceive of it."[167]

These criticisms are largely nonsense on at least several counts. To begin with, the psychological determinists are in no sense silent on the origins or validation of knowledge. The metaphysics of modern psychological determinism is clearly the metaphysics of science itself, and the underlying metaphysics of science *as science* rests upon the assumptions of pragmatic experimentalism. In addition, to say that the psychological determinists are barred from *objective knowledge* is, quite mistakenly, to equate *objective knowledge* with *absolute knowledge*. For the psychological determinists, knowledge is *objective* if and when it meets certain standards of verification which invest it with a degree of probability that enables it to function (within some meaningful context) as a *practical* certainty. The most *objective* knowledge is necessarily that which relates to the epistemological process of scientific inquiry itself. Even this, however, functions essentially as an absolute *procedural* guarantee against the establishment of substantive absolute knowledge which would fail to meet the test of experimental verification and is clearly not "absolute" in the traditional sense of word.

Psychological determinism is not, in short, "self-exclusive" in the sense that it denies the status of knowledge to certain types of evidence and not to others. Within the realm of science, certain facts are true

173

because they meet the criteria of successful verification. The criteria themselves are verified pragmatically on the basis of their assessed effectiveness in solving problems as compared with other available methods. The ultimate test is always the test of practical behavioral effectiveness.

Knowledge and Morality

At first glance, one of the most puzzling things about Miss Rand's philosophy is her adamant equation of the "reasoned" and the "reasonable." In a classic case of what Will James once termed "the philosopher's fallacy," she insists (in the face of overwhelming evidence to the contrary) that man is not merely *capable of reasoning* (in the usual sense of the word) but that he actually solves all of his significant problems *by reasoning*—i.e., by a process of conscious rational choice.

In Miss Rand's "psycho-epistemology," all men are consciously and volitionally committed to the realization of certain abstract intellectual principles. Men who do not appear to be motivated or who appear to be addicted to non-rational or irrational behavior are not in any sense absolved, however. Such individuals have merely chosen, through a subverting act of their own inalienable rationality, to be non-rational. This, too, however, has occurred consciously and reflectively. Like any other act, it is a free and conscious decision to be what the existentialists term "inauthentic."

It should be noted that, when Miss Rand speaks of man's faculty for rationality and moral responsibility, she is not *prescribing for men.;* she is *describing* how actual men do in fact behave in their ordinary day by day affairs. In other words, Rand, unlike her arch-opponents, the pragmatists, does not distinguish between how freedom, rationality and moral responsibility emerge and how they function *if* and *when* they come of age. Indeed, for Rand, this is a bogus distinction, for *her entire philosophy is based on the extremely radical assumption that reality-as-it-should-be (oughtness) and reality-as-it-is (isness) are precisely the same thing.* In short, and in what is clearly one of the central features of Miss Rand's entire philosophy, she holds that man is not merely perfectible (a vestige of pragmatic meliorism for which she has the utmost disdain) but, rather, in a far more radical sense, that he is in principle *already perfect*—a fact that will become quite evident if everyone will just leave him alone.

It is a great error to assume, as many do, that Miss Rand is *primarily* concerned with establishing the principle that reality is objectively logical. Nothing could be further from the truth. If this were so, Miss Rand's dispute with the pragmatists would be primarily procedural. There are very few pragmatists who are not also, if indirectly, committed to the idea that reality is logical.

Why the argument then?

The answer is really quite simple. Ayn Rand's philosophy *begins with ethics* and merely terminates with a theory of truth and knowledge. Her epistemology and her metaphysical assumptions—indeed, the vast bulk of her philosophy—are essentially an *a posteriori* rationalization for a fervent *a priori* commitment to the ethics of laissez-faire capitalism. Her basic argument with the neo-mystics—which, quite acutely, centers on pragmatists—has less to do with the *nature of metaphysical truth* than with the *nature of man as man.*

For Ayn Rand it is not enough that man be deemed *capable* of freedom and rationality. If he were only *capable* of reason, the development of this capacity might very well be contingent upon environmental conditions which could conceivably imply an objective dependence upon other people and which might even provide the foundation for an ideological commitment to an altruistic program of mutual aid. To grant the necessity of others would, in short, provide an opening for precisely that definition of man as a social being which could provide the rationale necessary to justify a fully developed altruistic ethic. The only way men can live a full and satisfactory life without benefit of others is if all men are fully endowed with reason and moral autonomy to begin with.

To say that any man is *to any degree* dependent upon others for the realization of his own personal happiness would be tacitly to invalidate the ethics of laissez-faire capitalism. It is not sufficient that man have the *potentiality* for free choice and rational action. An empty potentiality is, after all, dependent upon circumstances—other men—for its realization. In political and economic terms, any qualification such as this would immediately open the door to the logic of altruism and to its inexorable attendant evil of a "mixed economy."

At basis, then, Miss Rand's obdurate absolutism is well-founded. Happiness stems from self-gratification which, in turn, grows out of effective action. Effective action is, in turn, contingent on right reason and right values. If right reason and right values are not "self-evident"—if they are merely latent—they become partially contingent upon socially-conditioned experience. If this is the case, however, self-gratification becomes the cornerstone, not of laissez-faire capitalism, but of precisely that altruistic "social metaphysic" which Miss Rand abhors. Unless truth, reason and value are inviolable attributes of each person *as a person*, Miss Rand's entire house of cards collapses, and she finds herself confronted with that most dire of all objectivist anathemas, an egoistic defense of altruism as a condition necessary for the maximum realization of individual happiness.

On this basis, of course, Miss Rand's epistemological absolutism is an absolute necessity which is required to establish the validity of her laissez-faire ethics. This largely explains her obdurate refusal to countenance any sort of significant compromise. "Never fail to pronounce moral judgment,"[168] she states. "There can be no compromise on moral principles."[169] "To abstain from condemning a torturer, is to become an accessory to the torture and murder of his victims. The moral principle to adopt in this issue, is: 'Judge, and be prepared to be judged.' "[170] On the other hand, and as Rand indicates still elsewhere: " ... to pronounce moral judgment is an enormous responsibility ... one needs an unbreached integrity, that is: the absence of any indulgence in conscious, willful evil."[171]

In a profound sense, of course, Rand cannot afford to give ground on her epistemological assumptions without also endangering her system of values. Ideological integrity is always a key consideration, because her extreme position in the realm of ethics requires an equally extreme position in all supportive areas as well.

Moral Perfection

Rand rejects any sort of moral compromise. Good and bad are both absolute and categorical concepts. The barometer of goodness (virtue) and badness (vice) is wealth.[172A] Every act is either good or bad (in terms of the logical law of excluded middle) and no act can be both (for this would violate the formal principle of contradiction). Ultimately, then, moral ambiguity is not merely *illusory;* it is immoral as well.[172] It is always incumbent upon the truly moral person to make moral judgments,[173] and such judgments must necessarily be extreme[174] *if* they are to be consistent with "the absolutism of reality."[175]

* * *

There are perhaps two basic objections which can be leveled at Miss Rand's moral absolutism.

To begin with, she prescribes absolute moral judgment, but she provides no practical basis for making such judgments. The rich man, states Rand, is virtuous. The poor man is depraved. No man can be both rich and poor, both virtuous and depraved. The question naturally arises, then, as to precisely when a man is sufficiently *rich* to be virtuous or sufficiently *poor* to be depraved. Since no situation is, by definition, too complex to be evaluated and since there can be no ambiguous realm of moral grayness, there must be a clear-cut answer to every moral problem.

Unfortunately, these answers are not provided by Miss Rand's philosophy.

Secondly, while she provides us with a theory of "value"—pleasure derived by means of wealth[176 A]—she does not go on to define any sort of practical criteria for *choosing between values*. At basis, she leaves a large number of significant questions unanswered: Are some types of wealth (property relationships) preferable to others? Do material values differ in *kind* or only in *degree*? Is, for example, wealth derived by means of *production* of goods preferable to wealth derived by means of the *distribution* of goods? Faced with a decision between two profitable activities, should a person choose on the basis of the amount of probable net profit? Is *quantitative* profit the sole criterion for choosing between alternative courses of action?[176] What is the role and relative significance of egoistic love-relationships when it comes to choosing between alternative courses of action? If, for example, I have an opportunity for occupational advancement (and therefore significant monetary profit) which entails moving to Denver, but I can move to Denver only by jeopardizing the life of my young daughter who has a chronic heart condition, what am I to do? On precisely what basis (since purely *subjective* criteria are irrational) can I decide this question? In what way can I compare a *quantitative* value (money) with a *qualitative* value (love)? To what extent are such comparisons valid in the first place?[177]

Still another objection which might be raised against Miss Rand's ethical absolutism is precisely that which she herself levels against altruism[178]—i.e., that it is unreasonably idealistic, leading inexorably to disenchantment and, ultimately, to outbreaks of hostile reactive immorality. Why, for example, should the poor, who are depraved by definition, not ultimately turn to depravity itself as a goal which is infinitely more attainable than an impossibly exalted sort of virtue?

The Question of Moral Compromise. Compromise is anathema to

Rand, not only because her philosophy is a total and interlocking system but, perhaps even more important, because she realizes that any philosophy based on concepts of absolute truth is logically *extreme* by definition. If the truth is absolute and the recognition of truth is the *summum bonum,* it simply stands to reason that all rival positions are both categorically *untrue*—stemming either from volitional lies or inadvertent cognitive errors—and *immoral* as well—since they serve to undetermine the supreme ethical position of effective reason. "I most emphatically advocate a black-and-white view of the world .... There is no justification ever for choosing any part of what you know to be evil."[179]

Miss Rand's attitude toward compromise is particularly well-exemplified in her attitude with respect to the "mixed economy." Government authority, states Rand, is either limited or it is not, but it cannot be both.[180]

Those so-called "conservatives" who envision a mixture of private and governmental controls are, then, actually guilty of encouraging a gross and implicitly unethical misconception. "There can be no partnership between armed bureaucrats and defenseless private citizens who have no choice but to obey. What chance would you have against a 'partner' whose *arbitrary* word is law ... ?"[181]

A system of private property under governmental control is not true *capitalism* at all but, rather, a type of *fascism.* [182] A mixed economy "is an amoral, institutionalized civil war of special interests and lobbies, all fighting ... to extort some special privilege at one another's expense by an act of government—i.e., by force."[183]

In presenting this position, Miss Rand gives the impression of being an ardent champion of intellectualism and free inquiry. Actually, of course, nothing could be further removed from the facts. Close scrutiny reveals that Miss Rand's fervent opposition to "anti-ideologists"—those who choose not to determine their actions on the basis of intellectual (philosophical) principle—actually functions as an implicit anti-intellectualism.

It must be remembered that, for Rand, thought is equated with right reason—effective thinking. Right reason must, in turn, invariably terminate in ideology—specifically, the objective (rational) ideology of objectivism. We are, then, presented with an interesting sort of closed system characterized by tight circular logic in which thought (reason)—by definition—inevitably terminates in the objectivist *ideology.*

From the objectivist point of view, the term "ideology" is used quite incorrectly with reference to non-rational and even irrational systems of thought, such as those associated with religion, mystical and semi-mystical philosophies or anti-intellectualistic orientations. These are not properly characterized as true "ideologies," because they actually emerge, not out of reason, but either out of faith and/or mysticism (as is the case with religion and virtually all non-objectivist philosophies) or out of a volitional commitment to non-reason (as in the case of those individuals who refuse to intellectualize at all). The only true "ideology" is, then, properly speaking, objectivism, because objectivism is the only worldview derived by means of reason. All other "ideologies" are not really "ideologies" at all but invariably either *pseudo-ideologies* (which are not derived from reason) or *anti-ideologies* (which comprise either implicit or explicit refusals to think).

At basis, then, Miss Rand is not quite the devoted proponent of intellectual pluralism which she occasionally appears to be. By equating her own ideology with reason, her pro-ideology stance actually serves as an oblique assertion of the absolute truth of her own closed system of thought. Thus, her opposition to democracy—which is, after all, essentially *government by compromise*—is not motivated by a desire to *lessen freedom* but, quite the contrary, by a desire to *suppress unreason*. Democracy, is, after all, *anti-ideological* by its very nature. As Miss Rand suggests: "Anti-ideology has a new and very ugly name: it is called "Government by Consensus.""[184] Democracy is founded on the false premise that unrestricted individual reason is potentially fallible—that man does not have access to a hard core of self-evident truths and values which clarify all problems of polity. From the objectivist point of view, such a position is not only *untrue* but profoundly *immoral* as well. "The mainstream of thought," she observes, "is a stagnant swamp."[185] The sole function of voting, as Rand sees it, is to determine the proper *means* for instituting self-evident objectivist *ends.*[186] A society's basic principles, however, "are not determined by vote ... [but] by the facts of reality—as identified by those thinkers who chose the field of political philosophy."[187]

This is not to say, however, that Rand rejects *all* possibility of compromise with the non-objectivist world. On the contrary, certain compromises are possible. It is, however, "only in regard to concretes or particulars, implementing a mutually accepted basic principle, that one may compromise."[188] One may, for example, bargain with a buyer

179

over the price of some product and agree on a mutually satisfactory sum, but if one insisted upon obtaining the product for nothing, no compromise short of total surrender would be possible for the seller.

On the other hand, even such permissible compromises as these cannot be extended to the moral realm. "Today . . . when people speak of 'compromise,' what they mean is not a legitimate mutual concession or a trade, but precisely the betrayal of one's principles—the unilateral surrender to any groundless, irrational claim."[189] "There can be no compromise between a property owner and a burglar, offering the burglar a single teaspoon of one's silverware would not be a compromise, but a total surrender—the recognition of his *rights* to one's property."[190]

Phrased somewhat differently, then, it is Rand's contention that man is, by nature, both a reasoning animal and, by virtue of this reasoning ability, an animal who is possessed of a self-evident awareness of the fundamental meaning of life. Such being the case, he is invariably capable of acting on the correct moral principle. Whenever he makes a wrong decision, he cannot be absolved of responsibility on the grounds of ignorance, however. Such errors must always be properly ascribed to either misinformation or rational error.

The great difficulty, of course, is how to live in accord with such absolute and objective moral principles in an imperfect world. As Rand sees it, this is possible. One can always make a moral judgment provided "that one must know clearly, in full, verbally-identified form, one's own moral evaluation of every person, issue and event with which one deals, and act accordingly" and that one is willing to make his moral evaluation known to others "when it is rationally appropriate to do so."[191]

In effect, then, what Miss Rand advocates is that each person should recognize reality and act in accordance with it but that he should, at the same time, be fully aware that the collective misrepresentations and errors of others—i.e., of all those who suffer, to one degree or another, from the democratic-altruistic-collectivistic sickness—are an essential aspect of reality as it presently exists. It is not therefore a violation of objectivist principles—indeed, it may, on occasion, be a logical corollary of such principles—to compromise with nonobjectivist error whenever it becomes evident that one would be subverting one's own long-term objective self-interests and (in effect) undertaking a sort of self-sacrifice by doing otherwise.

What this means is, in effect, that Miss Rand is entirely opposed to *ineffective compromise.* She is not seriously disturbed by compromises which can be construed as *means* to more ultimate objectivist *ends. These* "compromises" are not *true* compromises, because they are ultimately consistent with the overall objectivist point of view. Indeed, to fail to compromise in certain circumstances would be to indulge in masochistic behavior and therefore to violate the enlightened ethics of selfishness through pointless acts of self-denial or self-destruction.

How all of this operates can be seen quite clearly by looking at some of Miss Rand's actual moral pronouncements. It is not, for example, inconsistent for an objectivist to accept such collectivistic emoluments as public scholarships, government research grants, social security benefits or unemployment insurance.[193] In such cases, a man merely receives his own money which was taken from him without his consent by political force. The victims of such immoral laws "have a clear right to any refund of their own money—and they would not advance the cause of freedom if they left their money, unclaimed, for the benefit of the welfare-state administration."[194]

In a similar sense, young men who view the military draft as a violation of their personal rights do not compromise their moral principles by agreeing to induction, for "unjust laws have to be fought ideologically; they cannot be fought or corrected by means of mere disobedience and futile martyrdom."[195A] "All of us are forced to comply with many laws that violate our rights, but so long as we advocate the repeal of such laws, our compliance does not constitute a sanction."[195]

Unfortunately, and as is perhaps quite obvious, Miss Rand leaves certain rather significant questions unanswered. Is it, for example, *moral* to submit to the "coercion" of an unjust government in the first place? Is it *moral* for an objectivist to take a position which *entails* involvement in social security? If so, who constrains the objectivist to do so?

In a similar sense: Does not voluntary participation in such immoral schemes signify tacit consent to such programs or at least a willingness to acquiesce to them? What, if anything, should restrain a wealthy capitalist whose wealth has been largely confiscated by unjust governmental taxation from *morally* knocking off one of the Federal Reserve Banks (providing, of course, that this could be done with a reasonable likelihood of success)? Indeed, wouldn't this kind of guerrilla warfare be precisely the *moral* thing to do in these circumstances?

The point is, of course, that it is precisely Miss Rand's extreme plasticity in rationalizing virtually *any* profitable action as the theoretically justified course of behavior—her remarkable ability to make any sort of compromise *a matter of principle*—which throws her entire theory of moral absolutism awry. Again, and to return to her views on how to live a rational life in a basically irrational society, she takes the position that it is morally justifiable to accept aid, such as public scholarships, from others, providing that it is extended as a gesture of good will in response to the receiver's objective merit by one who can afford it and who is not therefore making a sacrificial offering in response to mere need or incompetence.[196] She goes on to add that even objectivists are justified in receiving public (governmental) scholarships, because such a gesture is sanctioned by "the right of the victims to the property (or some part of it) which is taken from them by force."[197A] "The recipient of a public scholarship is morally justified *only so long as he regards it as restitution and opposes all forms of welfare statism.*"[197]

This is nonsense. Stripped of rhetoric, what Rand is saying is, in effect: "Do anything you like, but be sure that what you do is compatible with your own ultimate objectives. Never do business with the devil *unknowingly* and only when it serves your own best interests, providing these are broadly conceived." As she comments elsewhere: "When one pronounces moral judgment, whether in praise or in blame, one must be prepared to answer "Why?" and to prove one's case—to one's self and to any rational inquirer."[198]

The point is, of course, that those who oppose public scholarships still have every right to receive them, because, by receiving them and therefore withdrawing funds which would otherwise be left to the other nefarious activities of the evil "welfare state," they actually serve to weaken the existing social structure more by collaborating with it than they strengthen it by virtue of their willingness to comply. Also, of course, the objectivist has a moral obligation not to *sacrifice himself* by suffering the negative consequences which would arise from abstaining from the profits which are to be obtained from playing along with the enemy.

There are "limitations" to such compromises, however. One can only participate *morally* if one sustains grave *mental* reservations about the whole business. If one is *opposed in principle,* it is quite all right to concede in practice. One should never compromise oneself *enthusiastically,* however, and Miss Rand goes so far as to proscribe

182

participation in certain very aggravated areas—such as the FTC and FCC—altogether.

We are, then, presented with a virtual basket of moral paradoxes. A man "cannot accept a job in an undertaking which he considers immoral."[199] At the same time, however, "a man is not responsible for the moral and political views of his employers."[200]

Reduced to its essence, this comes amazingly close to St. Augustine's famous injunction, "Love God and do as you will." Miss Rand's position might be summarized "Be an objectivist and do as you will." She is able to justify virtually any sort of practical act as the logical requirement of some abstract and self-evident principle—as a rational requirement of enlightened self-interest. As she states, " . . . a man is morally in the clear only so long as he remains *intellectually* incorruptible."[201] " . . . so long as you . . . are prepared to give up any of [welfare statism's] momentary benefits in exchange for repeal and freedom . . . you are morally in the clear. The essence of the issue lies in your own mind and attitude."[202]

What makes so many of Miss Rand's statements with respect to compromise so puzzling is that they seem to be implicit denials of the entire objectivist position with respect to free will. Thus, she takes the position at one point that the moral principle involved in accepting a position from an employer whose political or economic views are less than congenial is basically ideological and not monetary: the crux of the matter consists "of defining as clearly as possible the nature and limits of one's own responsibility, i.e., the nature of what is or is not in one's power."[203A] "Minimizing the financial injury inflicted on you by the welfare-state laws does not constitute support of welfare statism . . . and is not morally reprehensible. Initiating, advocating or expanding such laws, is."[203] At still another juncture, however, she holds that "in a controlled or mixed economy, opposition becomes obligatory—since one is acting under force, and the offer of benefits is intended as a bribe."[204]

The contradictions implicit in these attitudes are well-exemplified in Rand's account of the history of American free enterprise. "It is," she states "important to note that the railroad owners did not start in business by corrupting the government. They had to turn to the practice of bribing legislators only in self-protection."[205] In order to organize his railroad empire, Vanderbilt was faced with the necessity of obtaining a franchise to enter New York City from a corrupt City

Council: "Should he be blamed for this, or does the blame rest on the fact that the government held an arbitrary, unanswerable power in the matter and Vanderbilt had no choice?"[206A] "What could the railroads do, except resort to bribery, if they wished to exist at all? Who was to blame and who was corrupt . . . .?"[206]

What Miss Rand overlooks, of course, is that, if man is endowed with free choice by nature—i.e., if this choice is not conditional and therefore relative to variable circumstances—no kind of social arrangement can *force* him to make any sort of decisions whatsoever. No one *forced* Vanderbilt to compromise with a corrupt legislature by bribing politicians. By bribing them, he not only strengthened the corruption of the system but corrupted himself by becoming a major force in sustaining and even promoting corrupt government. He made a choice. He could have chosen to pursue wealth in many other sectors of business which were not (at least at that time) closely controlled by government.

In other words, unless Miss Rand maintains, quite in contrary to her other assumptions about the prior and inviolable nature of free will, that objectivists are incapable of undertaking rational and productive action without the aid of governmental sanctions—i.e., in the more or less "private sectors" of our economy—how can she suggest that a man like Vanderbilt was, in effect, constrained to indulge in corruption? Clearly, if—and, as Miss Rand repeatedly suggests—an objectivist prefers to be as free as possible of external restraints, would any objectivist volitionally elect to become embroiled in public enterprise or significantly "mixed ventures" while other and far "purer" areas remain available for profitable individual venture?[207]

Perhaps the most striking example of Miss Rand's moral gymnastics are provided by her discomfited and discomforting support of Republican presidential aspirant Barry Goldwater during the national campaign of 1964. Her position on this issue is illustrative of her extraordinary skill in providing absolute moral reasons for supporting a man who was—by Miss Rand's own assessment—not only anti-ideological, inconsistent and self-contradictory but also a proponent of such altruistic myths as democracy and a "mixed economy."[209] "A voter's choice," comments Rand, "does not commit him to a total agreement with a candidate . . . . Under a two-party system, a voter's choice is and has to be merely an approximation . . . often, particularly in recent times, a voter chooses merely the lesser of two evils."[209A] "Some of Goldwater's specific steps may be wrong; his

184

direction is right."[209 B] A vote for a candidate, states Rand, is not an endorsement of the candidate's total platform. It merely signifies agreement with his fundamental political principles, his essential *political* philosophy: " . . . we have to judge him as we judge any work, theory or product of mixed premises: by his dominant trend."[209 C] "It is only *political* consistency that we demand of him; if he advocates the right political principles for the wrong metaphysical reasons, the contradiction is *his* problem, not ours."[209 D] "If his stand is mixed, we must evaluate it by asking: Will he protect freedom or destroy the last of it? Will he accelerate, delay or stop the march toward statism?"[209 E] Goldwater, notes Rand, "is the advocate of a mixed economy,"[209 F] but he differs from the other candidates in the sense that "they believe that some (undefined) element of freedom is compatible with government controls; he believes that some (undefined) government controls are compatible with freedom. Freedom is his *major* premise."[210]

There is really no point in belaboring this position. It speaks rather clearly for itself. It is, however, highly illustrative of the glib and offhand way that Miss Rand indulges in the fine old art of self-contradiction. To cite but two examples:

Principle: "There can be no compromise on moral principle."[211] There is always a good or bad, a black or white, answer to any question. To deny this is true is, in itself, an immoral gesture.

Violation of Principle: "Under a two-party system, the voter's choice is and has to be merely an approximation—a choice of the candidate whom he regards as closer to his own views; often, particularly in recent times, a voter chooses merely the lesser of two evils."[212]

Principle: Compromise is only defensible where two people are in agreement on basic moral principles. Politics is always contingent on prior philosophical assumptions about the nature of truth and value.

Violation of Principle: "One cannot expect, nor is it necessary, to agree with a candidate's total philosphy—only with his *political* philosophy (and only in terms of essentials) . . . if he advocates the right political principles for the wrong metaphysical reasons, the contradiction is *his* problem, not ours."[213]

In the final analysis, of course, one of the most fascinating things about Miss Rand's moral absolutism is not only that it is utterly unworkable but that she appears to be genuinely oblivious to the fact that it is. She is remarkably immune to all facts, inconsistencies and contradictions which pose any threat to her own sacrosanct premises. Like all absolutists—and this is, perhaps, the basic appeal of all absolutisms to begin with—she is totally and completely immune to any serious doubts once her mind has been made up. In firm, if uncomfortable, liaison with St. Thomas Aquinas, she holds staunchly to the position that any incompatibilities between *faith*—"self-evident truth"—and *reason* stem from merely ostensible differences which arise out of remediable errors and imperfections in whatever evidence is currently available. Objectivist reason will ultimately come to her rescue. A new *objectivist science,* replacing the old relativistic science, will ask the *right questions,* apply more enlightened techniques and obtain all of the necessary verifications which are required to substantiate objectivist contentions.

There are, then, no moral problems which are not amenable to solution on the basis of absolute (black-and-white) moral principles. Decisions should never be made by means of expediency (i.e., prudent compromise) but should always be founded on absolute moral principle mediated by reason.

Unfortunately, "there are many situations so ambiguous and so complex that no one can determine what is the right course of action."[214] *"That* is one of the evils of welfare statism: its fundamental irrationality and immorality force men into contradictions where *no* course of action is right."[215]

FOOTNOTES (CHAPTER VI)

1. Ayn Rand "The Psycho-Epistemology of Art," *The Objectivist Newsletter,* IV, 4 (April 1965), P. 15)
2. Nathaniel Branden, Review of the book *Human Action* by Ludwig von Mises, *The Objectivist Newsletter,* II, 9 (September 1963), p. 34.
3. Rand, "What is Capitalism?, Part II," *The Objectivist Newsletter,* IV, 12 (December 1965), p. 55.
4. *Ibid.*
5. Nathaniel Branden, "Emotions and Values," *The Objectivist,* V, 5 (May 1966), p. 1.
6. *Ibid.*

7. *Ibid.*, pp 1-2
8. *Ibid.*, p. 2.
9. *Ibid.*
10. Rand, "The Objectivist Ethics," in *The Virtue of Selfishness*, p. 25.
11. Nathaniel Branden, "Intellectual Ammunition Department," *The Objectivist Newsletter*, I, 1 (January 1962), p. 3.
12. Nathaniel Branden, "Alienation," *The Objectivist Newsletter*, IV, 9 (September 1965), p. 41.
13. Cf. Chapter III, pp. 36-6.
14. Cf. Chapter III, p. 40.
15. *Ibid.*
16. Cf. Chapter III, p. 41.
17. Nathaniel Branden, "Intellectual Ammunition Department," *The Objectivist Newsletter*, I, 1 (January 1962), p. 3.
18. Nathaniel Branden, "Emotions and Values," *The Objectivist*, V, 5 (May 1966), p. 7.
19. *Ibid.*, p. 2.
20. Nathaniel Branden, "Intellectual Ammunition Department," *The Objectivist Newsletter*, I, 1 (January 1962), p. 3.
21. Nathaniel Branden, "Emotions and Values," p. 3.
22. *Ibid.*, p. 7.
23. *Ibid.*, pp. 1-2.
24. *Ibid.*, p. 4.
25. *Ibid.*, p. 2.
26. *Ibid.*,
27. Leonard Peikoff, "Intellectual Ammunition Department," *The Objectivist Newsletter*, I, 2 (February 1962), p. 7.
28. Ayn Rand, "Philosophy and Sense of Life," *The Objectivist*, V, 2 (February 1966), p. 1.
29. *Ibid.*, p. 2; Nathaniel Branden, "Self-Esteem and Romantic Love," *The Objectivist*, VII, 2 (February 1968), p. 1.
30. Ayn Rand, "Art and Sense of Life," *The Objectivist*, V, 3 (March 1966), p. 1.
31. Nathaniel Branden, "Self-Esteem and Romantic Art," *The Objectivist*, VII, 2 (February 1968), p. 1
32. Rand, "Philosophy and Sense of Life," p. 1.
33. *Ibid.*, p. 3.
34. *Ibid.*, p. 5.
35. *Ibid.*
36. Nathaniel Branden, "Alienation," *op. cit.*, p. 41.
   Unfortunately, Miss Rand says very little about how the individual makes the transition from being directed by the "sense of life" to being directed by conscious reason except to note that it "takes many forms." (Rand, "Philosophy and Sense of Life," *op. cit.*, p. 3.) Assumedly, it is effected through a "choice to think." This is not *the* choice to think, however, for it is precisely the original choice to think or not to think which provides the implicit conceptual basis necessary for the sense of life to occur in the first place.

Strangely enough, the emphatically anti-Kantian Rand places herself in a strange position of espousing an epistemological position which is strongly redolent of Kantian idealism—which holds, that reason is not apprehended as a condition of things-in-the-world but is, rather, a perceptual category which exists prior to experience itself as a necessary precondition for any sort of experience to occur.

It is interesting to note how similar Rand's "choice to think" is to Sartre's idea of the "original choice." As Sartre sees it, the "original choice" comprises the basic *practical* response of the subjective self (the *for-itself*) as it attempts to realize the impossible demands of "the fundamental project" to be an absolute coincidence of self and nonself—what Sartre terms the attempt to be God. Thus, while every choice is encompassed by the basic demand of the God-ideal, each person *(for-itself)* must manifest this ultimate desire in his own unique fashion, by means of his own characteristic approach to existence. This initial and formative "manner" of encountering the external world (the *in-itself*) and others is designated the "original choice."

Sartre's original choice may be compared to a basic and all-encompassingg *Weltanschauung,* a manner of perceiving and responding to the world-in-general. In some respects, it is very much similar to the concept of self-image or even "ego" as broadly conceived. Through the original choice the subjective self "decides its past in the form of a tradition instead of allowing it purely and simply to determine its present." In this respect a different choice would invariably entail a radical conversion, a new choice of self and ends.

37. Rand, "Philosophy and Sense of Life," *op. cit.,* p. 2.
38. *Ibid.*
39. Rand, "Art and Sense of Life," *op. cit.,* p. 1.
40. Rand, "Philosophy and Sense of Life," *op. cit.,* p. 6.
41. Nathaniel Branden, "Self-Esteem and Romantic Art," *The Objectivist,* VII, 1 (January 1968) p. 3; *Ibid.,* VII, 2 (February 1968), p. 4; and Rand, "Of Living Death," *"The Objectivist,* VII, 10 (October 1968), pp. 2-3.
42. *Ibid.,* p. 5.
43. *Ibid.*
44. Rand, "Philosophy and Sense of Life," *op. cit.,* p. 6.
45. Rand, "Our Cultural Value-Deprivation, Part II," *The Objectivist,* V, 5 (May 1966), p. 11; Rand, "What Is Romanticism?" VIII, 5 (May 1969), p. 1.
46. Rand, "The Psycho-Epistemology of Art," *op. cit.,* p. 16.
47. *Ibid.*
48. *Ibid.*
49. *Ibid.*
50. *Ibid.*
51. *Ibid.*
52. *Ibid.*
53. *Ibid.,* p. 15.
54. *Ibid.,* p. 16.
55. Rand, "Art and Sense of Life," *op. cit.,* p. 3.

56. *Ibid.*, p. 2.
57. *Ibid.*
58. *Ibid.*
59. Rand, "Psycho-Epistemology of Art," *op cit.*, p. 16.
60. *Ibid.*
61. *Ibid.*
62. *Ibid.*
63. Rand, "Art and Sense of Life," *op. cit.*, p. 7.
64. Rand, "Art and World Treason," *The Objectivist Newsletter*, IV, 3 (March 1965), p. 14.
65. Rand, "Art and Sense of Life," *op. cit.*, p. 7; Rand, "Basic Principles of Literature," *The Objectivist*, VII, 8 (August 1968), p.5.
66. *Ibid.*
67. Rand, "Bootleg Romanticism," *The Objectivist Newsletter*, Iv, 1 (January 1965), p. 2.
68. Leonard Lyons, The New York Post, January 23, 1964, quoted in "The Horror File," *The Objectivist Newsletter*, IV, 6 (June 1965), p. 25.
69. Rand, "Bootleg Romanticism," *op. cit.*, p. 3.
70. Rand, "Art and Sense of Life," *op. cit.*, p. 6.
71. Rand, "Our Cultural Value-Deprivation, Part II," *op. cit.*, p. 11.
72. Rand, "Art and World Treason," *op. cit.*, p. 14. With respect to the usual classifications of literature, Miss Rand describes herself as a "romantic realist." (Ayn Rand, "The Goal of My Writing," *The Objectivist Newsletter*, II, 10, October 1963, p. 38.)
73. Rand, "Art and the Sense of Life," *op. cit.*, p. 8. Miss Rand's most complete analysis of romantic literature is to be found in her most recent work, *The Romantic Manifesto: A Philosophy of Literature* (New York: World Publishing Co., 1970).
74. Rand, quoting from her introduction to the novel *Ninety-Three* by Victor Hugo, *The Objectivist Newsletter*, I, 10 (October 1962), p. 42.
75. Rand, "The Esthetic Vacuum of Our Age," *The Objectivist Newsletter*, I, 11 (November 1962), p. 49.
76. Ibid.
77. Ibid. p. 50.
78A Rand, "What is Romanticism?" *op. cit.*, p. 1.
78. Rand, "The Goal of My Writing," *The Objectivist Newsletter*, II, 10 (October 1963), p. 37.
79. Rand, "Art and Moral Treason," *op. cit.*, p. 10; Rand, "Introduction to *The Fountainhead*," *The Objectivist*, VII, 3, (March 1968), p. 3.
80. Rand, "Art and Moral Treason," *op. cit.*, p. 14.
81. Rand, "The Goal of My Writing," *op. cit.*, p. 37.
82. Rand, "Psycho-Epistemology," *The Objectivist Newsletter*, III, 3 (April 1965), p. 15.
83. *Ibid.*
84. Rand, "Bootleg Romanticism," *op. cit.*, p. 1.
85. *Ibid.*
86. *Ibid.*
87. *Ibid.*, p. 2.

88. Rand, Review of the book *The Girl Hunters* by Mickey Spillane, *The Objectivist Newsletter*, I, 10 (October 1962), p. 46; Rand, "Basic Principles of Literature," *op. cit.,* pp. 5-6.

   Miss Rand's enthusiasm for Spillane does not extend to some of his more recent efforts. As she states in *The Objectivist Newsletter* (Volume III, Number 10) for October 1964, her expressed admiration for Spillane's works does not extend to his more recent novel, *Day of the Guns.* As she notes: "I feel obliged to state for the record that I object emphatically to the political views expressed in this novel, which are shocking and rationally indefensible." (Ayn Rand, "Book Report" *The Objectivist Newsletter,* III, 10, October 1964, p. 43.)

89. Rand, Review of *The Girl Hunters* by Mickey Spillane, *op. cit.,* p. 42.
90. Rand, "Bootleg Romanticism," *op. cit.,* p. 1.
91. As Miss Rand points out, romantic art may be the source of a pre-conceptual and largely subconscious "moral sense of life," but it is not the source of *morality as such* — i.e., "an abstract, conceptual code of values and principles." (Ayn Rand, "Art and World Treason," *op. cit.,* p. 10.) The latter is not the product of art but of active rational cognition.
92. Rand, "Art and Moral Treason," *op. cit.,* p. 10.
93. Nathaniel Branden, "Volition and the Law of Causality," *The Objectivist,* V, 3 (March 1966), p. 8.
94. Rand, *"Playboy's* Interview with Ayn Rand," *op. cit.,* p. 6.
95. Nathaniel Branden, "The Objectivist Theory of Volition," *The Objectivist,* V, 1 (January 1966), p. 12.
96. Nathaniel Branden, "Intellectual Ammunition Department," *The Objectivist Newsletter,* III, 1 (January 1964), p. 3.
97. Rand, "Altruism as Appeasement," *The Objectivist,* V, 1 (January 1966) p.7.
98. *Ibid.*
99. Rand, "The New Fascism," *The Objectivist Newsletter,* IV, 5 (May 1965), p. 17.
100. Rand, *Conservatism: An Obituary* (New York: The Nathaniel Branden Institute, 1962), pp. 12-13.
101. Nathaniel Branden, "The Contradictions of Determinism," *The Objectivist Newsletter,* I, 5 (May 1963), p. 17.
102. Nathaniel Branden, "Intellectual Ammunition Department," *The Objectivist Newsletter,* III, 4 (April 1964), p. 15.
103. Nathaniel Branden, "The Contradictions of Determinism," *op. cit.,* p. 17.
104. Rand, *Atlas Shrugged,* quoted in Nathaniel Branden, "The Contradictions of Determinism," *op. cit.,* p. 17.
105. Nathaniel Branden, "Volition and the Law of Causality," *The Objectivist,* V, 3 (March 1966), p. 12.
106. Nathaniel Branden, "The Objectivist Theory of Volition," *op. cit.,* p. 14.
107. Nathaniel Branden, "Psycho-Epistemology," *The Objectivist Newsletter,* III, 10 (October 1964), p. 41.
108. *Ibid.*
109. Nathaniel Branden, "The Contradictions of Determinism," *op. cit.,* p. 17.
110. Nathaniel Branden, "Volition and the Law of Causality," *op. cit.,* p. 12.

111. *Ibid.*, pp. 12-13. What Branden means when he states that awareness is a primary" is difficult to say. Assumedly, he means that, since experience is a concomitant of behavior, experience (awareness) is unavoidable and unchosen, providing the necessary context for all thought (except, of course, for the "choice to think" itself). Since he denies the existence of any sort of innate knowledge, he must refer to preperceptual sentiency.

112. Nathaniel Branden, "Intellectual Ammunition Department," *The Objectivist Newsletter,* III, 4 (April 1964), p. 15.

113. Nathaniel Branden, "Intellectual Ammunition Department," *The Objectivist Newsletter,* III, 1 (January 1964), p. 3.

114. Nathaniel Branden, "Social Metaphysics," *The Objectivist Newsletter,* I, 11 (November 1962), p. 47.

115. Nathaniel Branden, "The Objectivist Theory of Volition," *op. cit.,* p. 9.

116. *Ibid.,* p. 8.

117. Nathaniel Branden, "Intellectual Ammunition Department," *The Objectivist Newsletter,* I, 1 (January 1962), p. 1.

118. Nathaniel Branden, "Emotions and Values," *The Objectivist,* V, 5 (May 1966), p. 4.

119. Nathaniel Branden, "Volition and the Law of Causality," *op. cit.,* p. 11.

120. Nathaniel Branden, "The Contradictions of Determinism," *op. cit.,* p. 17.

121. Nathaniel Branden, "Intellectual Ammunition Department," *The Objectivist Newsletter,* III, 4 (April 1964), p. 15.

122. Nathaniel Branden, "Volition and the Law of Causality," *op. cit.,* p. 12.

123. *Ibid.,* p. 11.

124. *Ibid.,* p. 10.

125. *Ibid.,* p. 12.

126. Nathaniel Branden, "The Contradictions of Determinism," *op. cit.,* p. 17.

127. *Ibid.*

128. Nathaniel Branden, "The Objectivist Theory of Volition," *op. cit.,* p. 10. My italics.

It might be remarked in passing that Branden seems to have an extremely naive concept of what constitutes a "capacity." If a "capacity" is not a *predisposition* to respond to real circumstances under certain conditions, what is it? It would, after all, be odd to refer to a person as having a capacity to do something which is either logically or empirically impossible. This is simply not what the term means. A "capacity" is always, in other words, a predisposition to perform certain potential acts and, in this sense, always serves as at least an incipient determinant of behavior. It is difficult to see how it would be possible to exercise a "non-capacity" volitionally. Capacities are structural components which are logically required for any sort of effective behavior to occur.

130. Nathaniel Branden, "Volition and the Law of Causality," *op. cit.,* p.10.

131. Rand, "Art and Moral Treason," *op. cit.,* p. 14.

132. Nathaniel Branden, "The Objectivist Theory of Volition," *op. cit.,* p. 11.

133. *Ibid.,* pp. 8-9.

134. *Ibid.,* p. 8.

135. Nathaniel Branden, "Intellectual Ammunition Department." *The Objectivist Newsletter,* III, 4 (April 1964), p. 15.

191

136. *Ibid.*
137. *Ibid.*
138. Nathaniel Branden, "Volition and the Law of Causality," *op. cit.,* p. 12.
139. Nathaniel Branden, "Psycho-Epistemology," *op. cit.,* p. 41.
140. Nathaniel Branden, "Intellectual Ammunition Department," *The Objectivist Newsletter,* I, 1 (January 1962), p. 3.
141. Nathaniel Branden, "Emotions and Values," *op. cit.,* p. 1.
142. *Ibid.,* p. 5.
143. *Ibid.*
144. *Ibid.*
145. *Ibid.,* p. 8.
146. Nathaniel Branden, "Emotions and Repressions," *The Objectivist,* V, 8 (August 1966), p. 9.
147. *Ibid.*
148. *Ibid.,* p. 8.
149. *Ibid,.* p. 10.
150. Nathaniel Branden, "The Concept of Mental Health," The Objectivist, VI, 2 (February 1967), p. 11.
151. *Ibid.,* p. 8.
152. Nathaniel Branden, "The Objectivist Theory of Volition," *op. cit.,* p. 8.
153 *Ibid.,* p. 11.
154A. *Ibid.*
154. *Ibid.*
155. *Ibid.,* p. 13.
156. *Ibid.*
157. *Ibid.*
158. Cf. Chapter III, pp. 40-41.
159. Cf. Chapter III, pp. 40-41.
160. Cf. Chapter III, pp. 40-41.
161. Barbara Branden, review of Allen Drury's novel *Capable of Honor, The Objectivist,* V, 10 (October 1966), p. 10.
162. Nathaniel Branden, "The Stolen Concept," *The Objectivist Newsletter,* II, 1 (January 1963), p. 2. At one point Branden states: "All perceptions are initially ostensive definitions—that is the beginning of cognition." (Nathaniel Branden, "The Stolen Concept," *op. cit.,* p. 2).
163. Nathaniel Branden, "The Contradictions of Determinism," *op. cit.,* p. 19.
164. *Ibid.,* p. 20.
165. *Ibid.*
166A. Nathaniel Branden, "The Contradictions of Determinism," op. cit., p. 20.
166. *Ibid.*
167. *Ibid.*
168. Ayn Rand, "Intellectual Ammunition Department," *The Objectivist Newsletter,* I, 4 (April 1962), p. 15.
169. Ayn Rand, "Intellectual Ammunition Department," *The Objectivist Newsletter,* I, 7 (July 1962), p. 29.
170. *Ibid.,* p. 15.
171. *Ibid.*
172A. See Chapter IV, pp. 30 and 47-8.

172. *Ibid.*
173. *Ibid.*
174. *Ibid.*
175. *Ibid.*
176A. *Ibid.*
176. Miss Rand seems to be aware of these problems, and she voices concern over some of them in her writings. Unfortunately, she ends up by merely disparaging the fact that satisfactory hierarchies of values are frequently lacking and says virtually nothing about what these hierarchies should be or precisely how they should be determined.
177. In her "Introduction to Objectivist Epistemology" (Rand, *The Objectivist,* V, 9, September, 1966, p. 5), Miss Rand indicates that it is possible to measure love, but she offers no practical way to do so. In the *Playboy* interview she suggests that any attempt to place human relationships above productive labor is improper. As she states, "If [men] place such things as friendship and family ties above their own productive work . . . then they are immoral. Friendship, family life and human relationships are not primary in a man's life." (Rand, *"Playboy's* Interview with Ayn Rand," *op. cit.,* p. 7.)
   At still another point in this same interview she comments that "the only man capable of experiencing a profound romantic love is the man driven by passion for his work—because love is an expression of self-esteem, of the deepest values in a man's or a woman's character." *(Ibid.)* "One falls in love with the person who shares these values." *(Ibid.)*
178. Cf. Chapter IV, pp. 63-5.
179. Rand, *"Playboy's* Interview with Ayn Rand," *op. cit.,* p. 9.
180. Rand, *Textbook of Americanism* (New York: The Nathaniel Branden Institute, 1946), p. 4.
181. Rand, "The New Fascism: Rule by Consensus," *The Objectivist Newsletter,* IV, 6 (June 1965), p. 24.
182. Rand, "The New Fascism: Rule By Consensus, Part II," *op. cit.,* p. 23.
183. Rand, "The New Fascism: Rule by Consensus, Part I," *op. cit.,* p. 20.
184. Rand, "The New Fascism: Rule by Consensus, Part I," *op. cit.,* p. 19.
185. Rand, *"Playboy's* Interview with Ayn Rand," *op. cit.,* p. 15.
186. It can be maintained, of course, that the democrat is not compromising with his basic premises if it is understood that one of his basic premises is the value of compromise itself. Miss Rand would not accept this argument—quite properly within the context of her own assumptions—on the grounds that the principle of democratic compromise violates man's self-evident awareness of certain absolute truths and values, truths and values which exists apart from any particular circumstances whatsoever and which are therefore legitimately immune to any sort of subjective popular determinism.
187. Rand, "Intellectual Ammunition Department," *The Objectivist Newsletter,* IV, 2 (February 1965), p. 8.
188. Rand, "Intellectual Ammunition Department," *The Objectivist Newsletter,* I, 7 (July 1962), p. 29.
189. *Ibid.*

190. Rand, "Intellectual Ammunition Department," *The Objectivist Newsletter*, I, 7 (July 1962), p. 29.
191. Rand, "Intellectual Ammunition Department," *The Objectivist Newsletter*, I, 4 (April 1962), p. 15.
192. *Ibid.*
193. Rand, "The Question of Scholarships," *The Objectivist* V, 6 (June 1966), pp. 13-14.
194. *Ibid.*
195A. Rand, "The Wreckage of the Consensus," *The Objectivist*, VI, 5 (May 1967), p. 8.
195. *Ibid.*
196. Rand, "The Question of Scholarships," *op. cit.*, p. 12.
197A. *Ibid.*, pp. 12-13.
197. *Ibid.*
198. Rand, "Intellectual Ammunition Department," *The Objectivist Newsletter*, I, 4 (April 1962), p. 15.
199. Rand, "The Question of Scholarships," *op. cit.*, pp. 14-15.
200. *Ibid.*
201. *Ibid.*, p. 15.
202. *Ibid.*
203A. *Ibid.*
203. *Ibid.*
204. *Ibid.*
205. Rand, *Notes on the History of American Free Enterprise* (New York: The Nathaniel Branden Institute, 1946), p. 7.
206A. *Ibid.*, p. 5 and 7.
206. *Ibid.*
207. In a recent issue of *The Objectivist* Nathaniel Branden warns his readers of unauthorized groups of individuals who have been forming organizations and publishing materials of an ostensibly "objectivist" nature which frequently deviate in significant respects from the orthodox position. He mentions one group in particular who advocate withdrawing to an island and forming an objectivist society *de novo*. Interestingly enough—while Branden (and, assumedly, the objectivist hierarchy) do not lend official sanction to such a proposal—it actually makes much better sense (and seems to be far more consistent with Miss Rand's own basic principles) than her own proposals for "uncompromising compromise" with an already corrupt society.
208. Rand, "How to Judge a Political Candidate," *The Objectivist Newsletter*, III, 3 (March 1964), p. 10. More recently, Miss Rand has transferred her affections to Ronald Reagan whom she views as the most promising figure at the present time. (Rand, "The Wreckage of the Consensus," *The Objectivist*, VI, 5, May 1967, p. 7.)
209. Rand, "How to Judge a Political Candidate," Part III, *op. cit.*, p. 10.
209A. *Ibid.*
209B. *Ibid.*
209C. *Ibid.*, p. 9.

209D. *Ibid.*
209E. *Ibid.*
209F. *Ibid.*
210. *Ibid.*
211. Rand, "Intellectual Ammunition Department," *The Objectivist Newsletter,* I, 7 (July 1962), p. 29.
212. Rand, "How to Judge a Political Candidate," *op. cit.,* p. 10.
213. See page 184. Miss Rand's willingness to make common cause with Goldwater does not extend—or, at least, extends only under certain conditions—to making common cause with those who are committed to traditional religious beliefs. She would seem to be in basic agreement with Barbara Branden that "a rational advocate of capitalism *can* cooperate with religious people who share his political principles, but only . . . in a movement that does not claim religion as the base and justification of its political principles." (Barbara Branden, "Intellectual Ammunition Department," *The Objectivist Newsletter,* I, 3, March 1962, p. 11.)
214. Rand, "The Question of Scholarships," *op. cit.,* p. 15.
215. *Ibid.*

CHAPTER VII

THE ETHICS OF OBJECTIVISM: AN ANALYSIS

There is much in Ayn Rand's ethical theory which would be fully acceptable to many modern philosophers. Her basic position that happiness (and pleasure) is always at basis a personal experience and that man is, and therefore should be, objectively egoistic (or self-interested) is not a position with which many philosophers, and the overwhelming majority of contemporary psychologists would be inclined to quarrel. In a similar sense, there are few scientifically-oriented theorists who would take exception to her position that social values can ultimately be determined teleologically (on the basis of their contribution to more basic *personal* needs) and verified psychologically through the criterion of individual pleasure and happiness.

In addition to these points, many responsible thinkers would probably also be predisposed to concur with many of her additional contentions: that personal happiness is a product of effective behavior (which is, in turn, a corollary of rational thought); that the rational act is ultimately synonymous with the moral act; that a natural (or objective) code of moral behavior logically evolves out of a formal equation (identification) of moral and rational action. Finally, there would seem to be no strong objection on the part of many scientifically-oriented theorists to her position that the operational *summum bonum* of rational action implies the goal of intellectual freedom—the freedom to make and form rational decisions—which, in turn, necessitates the existence of certain prerequisite political and economic conditions within society as a whole.

Beyond this rather extensive area of agreement, however, most scientifically-disposed philosophers[1] would be inclined to object rather strenuously to certain other aspects of Miss Rand's moral theory. Perhaps the most pronounced objections would be leveled at the following five areas:

1) her identification of value with property relationships;
2) her concept of creativity (or productiveness);
3) her concept of altruism;
4) her definition of "human rights"; and
5) her political and economic theory.

For purpose of clarity, each of these topics will be considered in turn.

The Materialization of Value
For Ayn Rand, value is defined in terms of property relationships.[2] Values are invariably realized through objects and are expressed in terms of the power over, and control of, things.[3] Life itself is looked upon as fundamentally an acquisition of and control over property.[4] "Property rights" are ultimately synonymous with "human rights."[5] Theft is a primary form of enslavement,[6] and progress is, in turn, a byproduct of surplus (which is only possible under a capitalistic system).

Miss Rand's position here is vulnerable to criticism on several counts. To begin with, she confuses two different concepts of value: (1) "value" defined as the objective *conditions* necessary to facilitate the experience of pleasure and (2) "value" defined as the *value-experience* of pleasure *per se.*

Since she occasionally takes the position that value (as value-experience) is necessarily apprehended subjectively (i.e., personally, psychologically) and is therefore a private phenomenon, it must be assumed that she does not actually intend to reify value by equating the value-experience with value-objects (or value-conditions) and, in all likelihood, subscribes to the point of view that the *experience of value* inheres, not in objects or conditions as such, but, rather, in the individual's response to such objects or conditions. By extrapolation, then, and in terms of her total theory, it seems evident that what Miss Rand actually intends to convey is that, while the *experience of value* is necessarily a *personal response* which is attached to a particular sort of cognitive relationship to the object-world, such a response is always contingent upon the possession of, or control over, actual material objects (or property).

At basis, then, Miss Rand rejects the position which holds that value lies in the eye of the beholder and maintains, instead, that, regardless of how value may be experienced *psychologically,* it can never be a *true* value-experience—i.e., an experience which yields pleasure—if it does not derive from enhanced power over actual objects and events.

From the objectivist point of view, it is quite erroneous to assume that happiness may be realized *either* by enhancing possessions *or* by diminishing desires. Rather, true value emerges *only* by satisfying desires through the acquisition of goods. All other prescriptions for living the good life—commitment to the realization of abstract truth, psychological identification of self with others, and so on—are looked upon as radically false and ultimately misdirective.

Miss Rand's position here is both clear and unequivocal. From a purely scientific point of view, however, it is unacceptable for several reasons.

Her position that value can derive solely from material relationships with the object-evironment can be criticized on two counts: (1) It is not consistent with certain other aspects of her ethical theory. *If* pleasure is always apprehended *subjectively,* it is primarily a *perceptual relationship* and not a series of *objective conditions.* (2) Miss Rand's contentions about the objective bases necessary for subjective pleasure are not scientifically-verified and are, in fact, inconsistent with the best psychological evidence which is currently available. Contemporary scientific research in the behavioral sciences does not support her contentions, and her theory does not reflect the consensus of informed opinion among responsible experts in the appropriate areas of research. In addition, her theory cannot be said to be the most plausible or probable explanation of human behavior with respect to those things which meet the usual scientific criteria for acceptability in the areas to which she addresses herself.

Creativity and Productiveness

From the objectivist point of view, rational action (productive intelligence) is always and invariably a personal attribute of the individual. There is no collective thought. All thought is therefore the personal property of its creator. As Rand states: "Men learn from one another. But all learning is only the exchange of material. No man can give another the capacity to think."[7]

Miss Rand is open to criticism here on several counts, but primarily on the basis of her exceedingly narrow concept of what constitutes the cognitive process.

Contrary to what Miss Rand may say, rational thought does not characteristically emerge independent of others. Man possesses no inherent knowledge and is possessed of no significant range of predetermined behavior, such as instincts. Those determinative potencies which the human being does possess at birth merely serve to keep him alive and to make him more fully available to the "new common nonbiological heredity"[8] of culture. In a sense, then, man may be said to possess two heredities, a biological one and a cultural one. All other organisims have merely a biological heritage.

At basis, human nature is arranged hierarchically on three interdependent levels:

1) a primary biophysical nature (which expresses itself in terms of)
2) a secondary sociocultural nature (which is reflected in)
3) a tertiary symbolic nature.[9]

As biologist Theodore Dobzshansky has said, "Human genes have accomplished what no other genes succeeded in doing. They form the biological basis for a superorganic culture, which has proved to be the most powerful method of adaptation to the environment ever developed by any species."[10]

Ultimately, then, man is born with the sort of neurological apparatus which provides him with the potential (or capacity) for rational action. The practical *function* of rational action—the actual application of rational procedures—demands more than capacity, however. It must also be *developed* through a particular sort of social experience which makes provision for the development of the appropriate sort of rational and linguistic skills.

It is precisely man's capacity for symbolic experience which makes practical (operational) intelligence a *cultural* (collective) and not merely a *personal* attribute. If symbolic cues were excluded, men would be only slightly better at solving the kinds of problems we ordinarily pose to laboratory animals. It is through symbolism that men become capable of sharing experience—of acquiring language and of assimilating precisely the kind of logical procedures and established patterns for productive enquiry which are required to think effectively. Through symbolism, semanticist Alfred Korzybski has said, man becomes a "space-binder" and a "time-binder."

> ... the results of the process of abstracting are communicable. In this particular character of the process lies its value as a time-binding mechanism: A means of enabling one person to

benefit from the knowledge of other persons, of enabling each new generation to bind into its own time, so to speak, the wisdom of times past, so avoiding the blunders and extending the achievements of previous generations . . . . By virtue of the communication of symbols it is possible for one person to use other nervous systems as well as his own.[11]

Miss Rand is radically wrong about the etiology of rational thought. Man is *potentially* rational by nature. He is *operationally* (or practically) rational by means of culture. Knowledge is both cumulative and transferable. Even the most "creative individual *initiates* far less than he *acquires* as a social legacy by virtue of his membership in the cultural collective.

Altruism and Egoism

Man, states Rand, is (and therefore should be) objectively egoistic—rationally selfish. The traditional goal of altruistic behavior is not only erroneous, it is also profoundly self-subverting, because it is based on a negation of personal happiness and a paradoxical exaltation of pain as the highest possible pleasure. The ultimate resolution of man's ethical dilemma resides in a recognition of the fact that the trader is the paradigmatic moral man and that the only *moral* society is that society which is committed to the fullest expression of free and self-seeking rational acquisitiveness.

In large degree, Miss Rand is guilty of destroying her customary straw man. Her attacks on altruism are not attacks on the type of rational altruism which is founded upon enlightened self-interest as is represented, for example, in the utilitarianism of John Stuart Mill. Instead, she concentrates her fire on the outdated metaphysical altruism of Kant, explaining that " . . . it is Kant's version of altruism that people, who have never heard of Kant, profess when they equate self-interest with evil."[12] "The ultimate monument to Kant and to the whole altruist morality," she continues, "is Soviet Russia."[13]

This is nonsense. Kant's intuitive altruism is basically a dead letter today and has very little influence which extends beyond small pockets of professional philosophers. In refuting absolute altruism Miss Rand does not validate absolute egoism, she simply beats a dead horse.

The type of altruism which is significant today is a rational altruism based on psychological egoism—the sort of altruism which says, in effect, "It is good to aid others, because we live in a world in which we are necessarily interdependent and in which we must therefore help others in order to help ourselves and in order to guarantee the satisfaction of our own broader and more sustaining interests." This kind of altruism does not require "categorical imperatives" or divine sanctions, it can be verified on quite objective grounds.

Miss Rand's definition of the term "altruism" is both untenable and slanted. To begin with, she sets up a totally artificial dichotomy between *egoism* and *altruism*. There are few modern philosophers who are willing to accept the basic findings of contemporary empirical psychology who would not agree with Miss Rand's basic contention that man is at basis self-seeking and capable of realizing value only through the medium of subjective (and therefore personal) satisfaction. To say, however, that subjective satisfaction precludes a realization of pleasure through some sort of ego-identification with the well-being of others simply does not follow.

In still another sense, of course, the way she defines the term "altruism" is designed to preclude any sort of realistic appraisal. Thus, as Rand sees it, altruism "makes suffering the most important part of life."[14] It is "the placing of others above self, of their interests above one's own."[15] It is a negation of life, a voluntary self-annihilation.[16] For the altruist, states Rand, pain is pleasure and pleasure pain. Indeed, the ideal of altruism has "tied man irrevocably to other men and left him nothing but a choice of pain: his own pain borne for the sake of others or pain inflicted upon others for the sake of self."[17]

These statements are quite true—*if* one is willing to buy Miss Rand's rather warped notion of what the term "altruism" means in the first place. If, on the other hand, one adopts a more conventional (and somewhat less slanted) concept of altruism—if, for example, one thinks of "altruism" in a somewhat more contemporary way as a particular expression of psychological egoism, in which the ego is organized in such a way as to encompass the welfare of others as a significant aspect of its own identity—the entire issue becomes a bit less obvious.

At basis, Miss Rand's concept of altruism is defective on three grounds:

1) Altruism is neither the *opposite* nor the *contrary* of egoism. It is merely one way in which egoism manifests itself. It is, in essence, that type of self-gratification which is achieved by identifying oneself with,

201

and subsequently participating in, the well-being of others on a psychological level.

2) The goal of altruism is neither "suffering" nor "pain" but the active *elimination* of suffering and pain—which is a substantially different thing altogether.

3) Altruism does not require the creation of suffering (pain) as a condition for its alleviation, because suffering is a continuing aspect of the human condition. In addition, altruism does not exclude a concern with additional non-altruistic (or extra-altruistic) values. Since it is basically a manifestation of egoism, it in no sense excludes non-contradictory types of purely personal commitment, and there is no particular reason why altruism cannot be supplemented by other, and essentially non-altruistic, types of behavior as well.

In a purely psychological sense, of course, much of what Miss Rand says about altruism is fundamentally untenable. Most of it is also inconsistent with her own assumptions about the intrinsic value of pleasure, for, if pleasure is in fact a self-evident (intrinsic) value, it provides a necessary condition for any sort of normative experience at all and must therefore act as an irrefutable motive behind all behavior, whether altruistic or otherwise. If this is true, however, it is pointless to talk about a volitional commitment to pain, for, unless such "pain" is experienced subjectively as pleasurable, such a course of action is simply implausible on the basis of Miss Rand's own hedonistic assumptions. In this sense, Miss Rand is faced with a dilemma: either (1) all altruism is motivated by egoistic hedonism (and is therefore an expression of man's basic drive toward pleasure) or (2) there is, in fact, no such thing as "altruism" at all, and her entire point is both misleading and irrelevant.

There is no reason why altruism cannot be defined as an expression of a more profound egoism—indeed, as an ego-involvement with the well-being of others.

The objectivists do not successfully refute the theory of psychological hedonism—what they term the "everyone is selfish" fallacy[18]—they simply dismiss it (quite incorrectly) as a tautology, which holds "that all purposeful behavior is motivated."[19] To make such a distinction, however, notes Branden, is "to equate *'motivated* behavior' with *'selfish* behavior'; it is to blank out the distinction between an elementary fact of human psychology and the phenomenon of *ethical choice.*"[20]

Actually, the doctrine of psychological hedonism can be broken down into three basic points:

1) All behavior is motivated—i.e., all behavior is initiated and sustained by the need to equalize psychological (and therefore physical) tensions.

2) All motivation is based implicitly on personal needs and/or values which are the basis for such tensions.

3) Therefore, all behavior is indirectly initiated and sustained by the attempt to realize personal values.

Regardless of Branden's comments, this theory is neither "crude" nor an "equivocation." It is "tautological" only in the sense that all definitions are necessarily tautological in analytical regress. It does not equate *motivated* behavior with *selfish* behavior (at least in the usual senses of these terms). Rather, it suggests, quite clearly, that "selfish behavior" (in the sense of behavior which is directed at the satisfaction of the narrowly-conceived organism-self) as well as "altruistic behavior" are merely sub-varieties within the far more encompassing category of *motivated behavior.* It does not "blank out the distinction between an elementary fact of human psychology and the phenomenon of *ethical choice.*" It merely grounds ethical choice in a coherent and scientifically-verifiable theory of cognition, a theory which makes it quite apparent that this "distinction" is far less *apparent* than is frequently thought to be the case. Finally, it does not "evade the central *problem* of ethics." It addresses itself quite clearly and explicitly to precisely this question.

Even Miss Rand is, in one instance, for example, willing to concede that a concern for loved ones is selfish.[21] The interesting thing is that, while she is willing to concede that sacrifices for loved ones, or even, on occasion, for the sake of one's own basic intellectual identity, can be justified on purely egoistic grounds, she tends to regard any extensions of egoistic self-generalization to encompass more distant types of interpersonal relationships or to include larger groups of people as being fundamentally pathological on the grounds that only "parasites" *need* others.[22]

Ultimately, of course, Miss Rand's contention that capitalism and altruism are incompatible,[23] as well as her position that trade provides the only just ethical basis for all human personal and social relationships,[24] are derivative ideas which are necessarily contingent upon the acceptability of her more basic premises.

The Nature of Rights

A "right," according to Ayn Rand, is any condition required to realize the self-evident value of rational action. The most basic "right" (or condition) implied by the objectivist commitment to rational action is "liberty"—i.e., freedom from coercion by others. This right, in turn, implies two corollary (or supportive) rights: (1) the right to private property and (2) the right to free trade.[25] There are no social (or collective) rights,[26] and the powers of society are legitimately subordinated to "natural law" which is a logical outgrowth of clearly-defined individual self-interest.[27]

In more specific terms, there are three inalienable "human rights." These are life, liberty and the pursuit of happiness.[28] "The Right of Life means man cannot be deprived of his life for the benefit of another man nor of any number of other men."[29] "The Right of Liberty means Man's right to individual action, individual choice, individual initiative and individual property."[30] "The Right to the Pursuit of Happiness means Man's right to live for himself . . . so long as he respects the same right in others."[31]

These rights are *inalienable* in the sense that they are totally unconditional. They are not a "conditioned favor or privilege granted to him by society (by 'the people' or the collective)—a privilege which he has to purchase by performing some sort of duty *in return . . . . This is the basic principle of collectivism and statism.*"[32] Rights which are not inalienable are not truly "rights." "Either man's rights are inalienable, or they are not . . . . . When you begin making conditions, reservations and exceptions, you admit that there is something or someone above man's rights, who may violate them at his discretion."[33]

Rights are also invariably personal. They relate to man as an individual and are "unconditional, private, personal, individual possessions of each man."[34] They are objective metaphysical facts which are neither *from* nor *for* but, rather, which provide the individual with protection *against* the group.[35]

A right can only be violated by means of physical force. "Whenever a man is made to act without his own free personal, individual, voluntary consent—his right has been violated."[36]

Coercion, then, always provides objective evidence of the violation of human rights.

NO MAN HAS THE RIGHT TO INITIATE THE USE OF PHYSICAL FORCE AGAINST ANOTHER MAN

> ... you cannot expect or demand any action from another man, except through his free, voluntary consent.[37]

Individual rights are not only self-evident values, however. They also provide the sole means for determining the best interests of society-at-large. "Without individual rights, no public good is possible."[38] Majority good can never be achieved by restricting the good (i.e., the rights) of minorities.[39]

On the other hand, the entire concept of "public good" is fundamentally illusory. Indeed " ... there is no such thing as the 'public interest' (other than the sum of the individual interests of individual citizens.)"[40] Such terms as "public interest" and "public property" have never been satisfactorily defined. They merely serve as verbal sanctions for the establishment of totalitarian power and the restriction of individual freedom.

"Public property," states Rand, is "a collectivist fiction."[41] The "public" is a bloodless abstraction. Only individuals exist, and the "public interest" (or the "common good") is therefore a meaningless term.

In actual practice, of course, the "public interest" becomes the special province of whatever small set of government managers decides to set themselves up as its ultimate arbiter with respect to some particular type of activity. If, for example, the airwaves are defined as "public property," the definition and identification of public interest in an area like television becomes the special province of a small group of men termed the FCC. These men are then empowered to protect "the public" by coercing broadcasters into conforming to *their* ideas of what constitutes the "public interest."

In a similar sense, there is no such thing as the "rights" of special groups—the "rights" of Negroes, the "rights" of labor and so on—for the existence of such "rights" would not only violate the very meaning of the term but would also imply a double standard of ethics in which your "right" as a member of such a group would become my "responsibility" (as a non-member) for insuring your welfare. Thus, and as Miss Rand indicates, "Today's 'liberals' recognize the workers' (the majority's) right to their livelihood (their wages), but deny the businessmen's (the minority's) right to *their* livelihood (their profits)."[42]

This is perhaps best exemplified by the position which Miss Rand takes *vis-a-vis* the late President Kennedy's pronouncements regarding the "rights of the consumer": the right to safety, the right to be informed, the right to choose, and the right to be heard. Such "rights," she states, are apparently " . . . something other than the rights possessed by *all* men, and belong only to consumers or to men in their capacity as consumers. Since the only other human capacity relevant in this context is that of *producers,* it appears that consumers possess these rights, but producers do not."[43] In point of fact, notes Rand, ". . . there is no such thing as 'consumer's rights,' just as there can be no 'rights' belonging to some special group or race and to no others. There are only the *rights of man*—rights possessed by every individual man and by all men as individuals."[44A] Such rights are adequately protected by the criminal code: " . . . the precedent which Mr. Kennedy is here attempting to establish is the legal hallmark of dictatorship: *preventive law* . . . . "[44]

In a sense, then, governmental intervention in the guise of consumer protection actually works against the best interest of the consumer himself by destroying the automatic mechanisms of the marketplace. An objectivist economist Alan Greenspan indicates " . . . it is precisely the 'greed' of the businessman . . . his profit-seeking, which is the unexcelled protector of the consumer . . . it is in the self-interest of every businessman to have a reputation for honest dealings and a quality product."[45] "Protection of the consumer by regulation is thus illusory. Rather than isolating the consumer from the dishonest businessman, it is gradually destroying the only reliable protection the consumer has: competition for reputation."[46]

* * *

Miss Rand's concept of rights, like so many of her other basic ideas, is susceptible to attack on a number of different points.

For one thing, of course, her definition of "rights" is extremely difficult to sanction. Instead of establishing a concept of "public good"

206

and regarding "individual rights" as the conditions necessary for the fulfillment of such a goal, Miss Rand posits her rights as self-evident absolutes which are simply true by definition. As she states: "You cannot say a thing such as 'semi-inalienable' and consider yourself either honest or sane."[4][7]

What makes this position particularly difficult to go along with is that Miss Rand finds it virtually impossible to establish any sort of *operational* morality within the context of her own metaphysical assumptions. As a result, she consistently violates her own definitions. Thus, she defines the inalienable right of the *pursuit of happiness* as "man's right to live for himself . . . so long as he respects the right of others." If this is not the *qualification* of an *absolute*, the *conditionalizing* of a *right*, it would be difficult to say what it is. In a similar sense, she defines the *right of life* to consist of the fact that man "cannot be deprived of his life for the benefit of another man nor of any number of other men." She then proceeds to advocate a criminal code which sanctions the use of physical force to restrict the actions of those who violate ethical standards. Again, if this is not a violation of the *transgressor's* life, liberty and pursuit of happiness on behalf of society, what is it? As Miss Rand sees it, of course, this course of action is *not* a violation of the transgressor's rights at all, because it is not *society* which acts against him. Instead, the transgressor is being struck down by the *logical consequences of his own behavior* which are the natural consequences of his violation of the rights of others. It is not, in other words, *society* but *reality* which has struck back. From the objectivist point of view, executing a murderer is not a violation of the *murderer's* right to life. It is, rather, a logical and necessary expression of the *victim's* right to life, because even physical force is justified in defense of inalienable rights. Indeed, the murderer, by killing has proven his irrationality. He is therefore no longer a *human being* in the full sense of the word and can no longer be said to participate in the inalienable rights accorded to a *reasonable* creature. Two facts remain, however.

1) The collective has been legitimately invested with the power to execute the transgressor. It is *social retribution* which Miss Rand advocates and not personal retaliation on the part of the victim's family and friends.

2) Unless all criminals are to be *defined* as subhuman and therefore

exempted from the usual inalienable *human* rights, the victim's right to life has been violated regardless of whether this augments the rights of others or not, and this, by Miss Rand's own definition, is immoral.

At basis, Ayn Rand's position with respect to such questions as capital punishment and war may be summarized as follows:

1) Rights are inalienable.
2) They can only be restricted morally in the name of other rights. (One man's pursuit of happiness can, for example, be restricted only to augment the effective functioning of another man's pursuit of happiness.)
3) A right restricted by the objective requirements of the rights of others is not compromised. It merely serves the higher purpose of augmenting freedom-in-general.

What all of this means, of course, is that, despite her professed aversion to "conditional rights," Miss Rand repeatedly "conditionalizes" her own *absolute* rights in the most flagrant way. The collective, she indicates, ". . . cannot decide what is to be the purpose of a man's existence nor prescribe his choice of happiness."[48] Where, then, does the "criminal law" which Miss Rand advocates come from? Are these laws to be authored and enforced on a purely individual basis? Is each person to be his own judiciary, police force and army? If *not*—and this is clearly not what Rand has in mind—how can she sanction such "preventive laws" as those providing for public safety and those guarding against fraud without, at the same time, imposing frozen collective decisions on the dynamic process of purely individual action? Are these not *collective* decisions which serve to prescribe a particular choice of happiness? Are not the police and the soldiers who are hired to enforce such decisions empowered to apply physical force—not in retribution for direct violations of their *own* personal liberties—but to ensure the welfare of others and, indeed, of society-in-general?

This, of course, brings us to still another point of contention. Only physical force, states Rand, is capable of restricting individual freedom. What, then, constitutes "physical force?" Is it restricted to murder, physical injury and actual dispossession of property? Or does it extend to more subtle forces of deprivation—the socio-economic sins of omission—which *indirectly* control and determine behavior? Miss Rand opposes *nonvolitional* slavery. What about the more *volitional* types of

208

slavery, however? The wage-slavery, for example, which is *voluntarily sought* by the victim himself in order to alleviate the poverty which has been *involuntarily bestowed* upon him by virtue of a lack of education or an absence of opportunity?

What precisely is *voluntary* in such circumstances? How *objective* after all *is* the criterion of physical force? Is there, for example, no physical force involved in the power to restrict or deprive others of opportunities by denying them the basic intellectual and material resources required to deal with opportunities constructively? Is there not, in a finite world, a very real and necessary relationship between the unlimited power of some to acquire and the corresponding loss of power on the part of others, who find that which has already been monopolized (and which has, therefore, been forcibly curtailed) non-acquirable? Does not Miss Rand's obsessive concern for the possible depredations of governmental statism simply leave the door ajar for the private imperialism which (barring governmental restrictions) appears to be the unavoidable consequence of any sort of *unrestricted* personal acquisition?

Still another point where objections can be raised to Miss Rand's theory of rights is with respect to her rejection of the concept of the "public good." She is here open to two basic criticisms:

First, she rejects the concept of *public good*, but she not only continues to use it; she even uses it, on occasion, to bolster her own position with respect to "inalienable" individual rights. It is, in short, one thing to deny the *existence* of public good. It is scarcely defensible, however, to then make such a statement as *"Without individual rights, no public good is possible."*[49]

In addition, she makes two basic errors in her discussion of the "public good." For one thing, she states that the term "public interest" has never been defined and is incapable of definition—a statement which is patently absurd even within her own frame-of-reference. In addition, she states that the only "public interest" is "the sum of the individual interests of individual citizens"[50]—a peculiar statement considering that this is precisely what virtually everyone means when they speak of "public good" in the first place. If Miss Rand means that there is no such thing as "public interest" in the Platonic sense—i.e., as a disembodied abstraction which possesses reality apart from its concrete referents in the actual people—she is quite correct. The question more appropriately, however, is "Who ever said there *was*?" Miss Rand, again, is simply sticking pins into her own voodoo dolls.

Still another objection with respect to Miss Rand's theory of rights can be leveled against her contention that there is no such thing as a "minority right." Again, Miss Rand is tilting against windmills. "Minority rights," in the sense Rand uses the term, are simply implausible and have no reputable champions at all.

To be more specific, Miss Rand is actually arguing against the validity of two kinds of so-called "minority rights": (1) rights relating to special groups—e.g., the "rights" of Negroes or the "rights" of Catholics—and (2) the rights relating to *all* men in one or more of their essential *subfunctions as men*—e.g., the "rights of the consumer." In both cases, of course, Miss Rand wins her paper battle very handily through the simple expedient of context-dropping. What is meant, for example, by the "rights of the Negro?" The answer is quite obvious. The "rights of the Negro" are merely "human rights"—life, liberty and the pursuit of happiness—which are denied to the Negro *as a man* on the basis of his race. The same principle applies, of course, to such phrases as "the rights of labor" or "the rights of Jews."

In a similar sense, what is ordinarily meant by the "rights of the consumer?" The answer is apparent, it means, quite simply, the "human rights" of life, liberty and the pursuit of happiness as these apply to *the universal human function of consumption*. "Consumer rights" do not imply a double standard of morality, relating only to members of the class "consumers" and discriminating against the class "producers." This is true for the simple reason that *all* men are members of the class "consumers" and, therefore, *in their function as consumers*, no one is discriminated against. Indeed, and to follow Miss Rand's own line of reasoning, since the consumer's rights mentioned in her example—rights which enjoin honesty and which protect the consumer from physical injuries—are also violations of inalienable *human rights* as well as violations of the *criminal code*, they could *not* serve to violate the rights of producers without also violating the prepotent rights of man as man. In line with this, it seems interesting to note that Miss Rand does not seem to disagree with Kennedy's actions so much as she disagrees with his rhetoric. She is quite content to accept the rights of the consumer against fraud and threats to health, providing that these are recognized as violations of the *criminal code* and not as *conditional rights* which are based upon the broader interest of the entire community.

In a peculiar sense, then, it becomes evident that, while Miss Rand unequivocally favors inalienable human rights, she just as unequivocally opposes virtually any sort of legislation which would prevent the abuse of these rights. She justifies this position in three ways:

1) While agreeing to the necessity of protecting the individual against violence, she restricts her definition of physical force to questions of bodily integrity or to the actual dispossession of material property *once this has been acquired.*

2) She argues that, given the proper sort of laissez-faire conditions, men are basically sane and moral and that the successful capitalist (who is, by definition, both rational and productive) exists in a state of moral grace and therefore transcends the need for any sort of external regulation whatsoever.

3) She maintains that external regulations reduce individual incentive and responsibility and therefore exert a negative effect on the automatic processes of rational production.[51]

Political and Economic Theory

Miss Rand's economic and political theory might be described as an elaborate and interlocking system of self-supporting error. It is founded upon a series of extremely dubious assumptions (many of which have already been examined) which are looked upon either as self-evident assumptions or as logical implications growing out of such self-evident assumptions.

In essence, Miss Rand's position may be outlined in three basic points:

1) Wealth (i.e., the acquisition of, or control over, property) *is* value.

This is, of course, an excellent example of a "self-evident" metaphysical truth. It is true by assertion (identity) and thereby precludes the necessity for any sort of *a posteriori* verification.

2) Wealth cannot be uncaused.

Again, this is true by definition and is backed up by no empirical verification.

3) The cause of wealth is rational productivity, i.e., intelligent labor. (All value is an outgrowth of rational behavior. Those goals which are *not* the product of rational choice are therefore incapable of yielding value.)

One difficulty which arises, of course, is how to dispose of those goals which have emerged *prior* to the development of the rational

211

processes on the basis of inherent need—the *values,* for example, of food and shelter. The question arises, in short, as to whether food can be legitimately termed a "value" if it has not been "chosen" as such on the basis of conscious and rational volition. At basis, Miss Rand is faced with two alternatives: (1) Food assumes value prior to the development of rational choice and is *not* therefore a value. (2) Food is not chosen rationally but can be subsequently subjected to rational analysis and *made* a value.

What confuses the issue even more, of course, is the fact that the objectivists on occasion violate their own labor theory of value by accepting inherent needs as objective values. Thus, according to Nathaniel Branden, the human organism requires certain things (such as food and water) for survival, and these needs are "objectively demonstrable."[52 A] "The same principle applies to man's psychological needs. It can be shown that man has a need of self-esteem—a need to be confident of his judgment and his capacity to deal with reality."[52]

In either case, of course, the objectivists are faced with something of a dilemma. Either (1) values include certain things which are not *selected* rationally (however "rational" they may be recognized to be *after the fact*) but which are nevertheless capable of eliciting pleasure—in which case they violate their own "rational labor" theory of value—[53 A] or (2) all value is a product of rational labor (and such prerational objects as food and shelter are logically excluded as sources of *true* value).

In a sense, then, Miss Rand paints herself into a corner. If all wealth is *not* the product of rational productivity, it is quite possible to possess wealth (as, in the case of food and shelter) gratuitously—that is, purely by virtue of possessing that which is categorically (factually) good for man as man. If this is true, however, Miss Rand is not justified in asserting that all wealth is *caused* by rational action and that good ends (values) can only result from good means (rational action). Indeed, on this basis, it would naturally follow that certain values (food, shelter, and so on) necessarily evolve *pre-rationally* and even provide the *conative* (volitional) basis for all subsequent sorts of *normative* choice.

Ultimately, then, Miss Rand's contention that value in the guise of wealth signifies rational productivity can only be justified if one is willing to go along with her highly truncated view of what comprises true wealth to begin with. When Miss Rand states that all value (wealth) must be caused, she does not mean caused by *natural* necessity. She means, quite explicitly, caused by *rational human action* through a

212

personal act of valuation. In essence, then, value is always a means-ends relationship. True value is always (1) *caused* (and not merely inherent in the human situation *per se*) and (2) caused by *rational action.*

This means that, to accept Miss Rand's contention that wealth signifies rational action (and therefore virtue), we must first be willing to subscribe to her dubious theory that value is always the product of rational labor—that value inheres, not in property-relationships as such, but, rather, only in those things which emerge out of enlightened production.

Miss Rand is forced to reject the possibility of unearned wealth for two reasons: (1) because she looks upon such a possibility as a violation of the logical principle of cause-and-effect and (2) because she limits her concept of causation to the province of human action. Ironically, then, Miss Rand cannot logically and without self-contradiction accept the position that food is a value prior to all rational choice (and as a condition for any sort of rational choice at all), because, if she does, she would also be saying, by implication, (1) that value can be caused by natural necessity and is not entirely contingent on human reason and effort and (2) that the existence of value (wealth) does not, therefore, inalterably signify the presenc of rational productivity but may merely denote the accidental acquisition of natural value.

At basis, then, it is only by adhering strictly to the position that all value is caused by rational human effort that Miss Rand can conclude that unearned wealth is irrational (unreal) and therefore both evil and incipiently self-destructive.

In a similar sense, Miss Rand must necessarily make the assumption that all true productivity (rational action) is purely *personal* and based upon *individual* effort. If rationality were not *self*-derived—if it were dependent upon culture and, hence, were largely the product of the rational effort of others—it would, by definition, be *uncaused* (i.e., unmerited on the basis of individual rational effort) and therefore be both dishonestly possessed and incipiently self-negating.

The same principle applies, of course, to the whole question of symbolic wealth. From the objectivist point of view, true wealth is never indirect and vicarious. Symbolic wealth—paper money, checks, credit cards, letters of credit, and such—is never a *true* standard of wealth, because it depends upon the confidence and, therefore, upon the incipient support of others. Ultimately, all symbolic wealth is rooted in the collective consciousness (the belief system) of others and does not correspond directly to its own material basis in actual property. In addition, of course, symbolic wealth is a social creation of the group and is not therefore caused by contemporary rational action on the part of the individual. It is always therefore second-hand wealth which is based upon the beliefs of others rather than upon the objective conditions of purely material possession and control.

It is difficult to say just how far Miss Rand's distrust of symbolic wealth extends. Certainly, her statements in this area are not entirely consistent. She holds that wealth is objectified value,[53] but, at the same time, she appears to be edgy about paper money[54] and seems committed to the position that only gold constitutes non-arbitrary value.[55] This, of course, brings up a number of interesting points. Why, for example, gold? Does not the value of gold itself reflect an (illegitimate) reliance upon the prior rational effort of generations long dead as well as a dependence upon the attitudes and the collective belief systems of all "gold-standard" cultures? Is not the actual barter of material goods the only legitimate basis for trade?

The objectivist position with respect to gold is well-summarized by objectivist economist Alan Greenspan in his article "Gold and Economic Freedom" which appeared in *The Objectivist* for July of 1966. According to Greenspan, a money economy is clearly superior to a barter economy, because it enables a far more extensive type of trade. Gold has become the predominant commodity to be used as a medium of value for a number of reasons but primarily because it has traditionally been a relatively scarce luxury good which is durable, divisible, easily transportable and homogeneous.[56]

A banking system which operates on the gold standard is able to issue currency and to extend credit in relationship to its total deposits in gold as reserves. In all events, however, "the amount of loans which [the banker] can afford to make is not arbitrary: he has to gauge it in relation to his reserves and to the status of his investments."[57]

A free banking system which utilizes the gold standard is limited in extending credit by the tangible assets of the economy. The use of the gold standard is incompatible with chronic government deficit spending in which the government borrows money by the expedient of issuing government bonds. Such spending is "the hallmark of the welfare state."[58] Under the gold standard, "a free banking system stands as the protector of an economy's stability and balanced growth."[59]

In a sense, of course, the whole question of organized society and its self-perpetuating cultural residue is one which complicates matters immensely for Miss Rand, for if value is defined as the product of contemporary personal effort in the rational mode, one is necessarily confronted by the embarrassing problem of how to dispose of that wealth which has already been produced by the past rational activity of others who are now dead. Miss Rand's answer is, of course, brief and to the point and can be summarized as follows:

1) All wealth (value) which is not the product of individual rational effort in the present—i.e., in the individual's own lifetime—is not "caused" and is therefore both irrational and evil when possessed by another who has not earned it.

2) Evil (in the guise of false wealth) cannot cause good (value). For it to do so would be a violation of the basic principles of identity and cause-and-effect.

3) Therefore, unearned wealth (as an evil) is automatically self-negating since it is, by definition, inconsistent with true value.[60 A]

(Miss Rand does not explain in this regard whether false wealth is eliminated as wealth—i.e., is self-eliminating—or is merely voided as a source of subjective value (pleasure). If the latter is the case, the possession of false wealth—as, for example, through the unmerited inheritance of money or through winning a lucky bet—might not subjectively enrich the possessor but it would deprive the potentially meritorious of the opportunity to acquire such wealth (value) in the arena of free competition.'

4) Value cannot be effectively transmitted from producer to consumer. It can only be earned directly in the present mode on the basis of individual rational effort.

5) Each generation, then, must either recreate its own value through the *acquisition* of wealth, or it must *revalidate or redeem* (through contemporary rational action) the value-potential inhering within whatever wealth has been bestowed upon it by others. Thus, as Rand indicates, wealth can be left to heirs, but it cannot be kept as a merely static possession; it must be either consumed by the heirs or earned as a result of the heir's own productive efforts.[60 B] The greater the value of the property, the greater the effort demanded of the heir. In a free, competitive society, no one could long retain the ownership of a factory or of a tract of land without exercising a commensurate effort."[60]

* * *

Ultimately, then, no one can fall heir to real wealth or suffer from a lack of such wealth, for the simple reason that both wealth and poverty

215

(as sources of value or disvalue) are invariably the product of personal effort in the lives of particular individuals. Inherited wealth does not convey grace, and congenital poverty cannot be construed as a type of original sin. True wealth (wealth as a source of value) is always and necessarily redistributed each generation on the basis of simple merit (i.e., rational effort), and this redistribution is facilitated by two conditions:

1) There is (by logical implication) sufficient wealth with which to endow all of the meritorious.

2) There is no advantage which accrues to initially possessing wealth (or power), and that person who begins life under conditions of poverty is just as likely to accede to a position of wealth and power, if truly meritorious, as that individual who is forced to earn the right to possess whatever wealth he acquires by virtue of inheritance. Indeed, since fortuitous wealth cannot be merited without rational effort, it may very well be that the (logically) negative consequences of possessing unearned wealth actually serve to augment the difficulties involved in retaining it and thereby tend to equalize conditions between those who initially "have" and those who "have not."

In the case of inherited wealth, the primary right is not that of the heir but of the original producer of the wealth. The worthiness of the heir is irrelevant. The producer of the wealth has the right to use and subsequently to dispose of the products of his own labor. " . . . just as the man who produces wealth has the right to use it and dispose of it in his lifetime, so he has the right to choose who shall be its recipient after his death."[61] "The heir's is a *derived* right . . . . But if the future heir has no moral claim to the wealth, except by the producer's choice, *neither has anyone else*—certainly not the government or 'the public.' "[62]

In a free economy, wealth is not a static, limited quantity. Rather, it is produced, "its potential quantity is virtually unlimited."[63] Under free capitalism, inherited wealth is not an impediment to others, for a worthy heir creates more wealth and, in so doing, raises the general standard of living. In this way, he expedites the economic advancement of others. The greater the wealth, the wider the market for ability. Successful producers are forced by economic necessity to develop their own future competitors. A free and competitive market will not tolerate stagnation. "If the heir is not worthy of his money, the only person threatened by it is himself . . . he will not be able to maintain it for long; he will not be equal to the competition."[64] "The personal luxuries or drunken parties that the incompetent heir may enjoy on his father's money, are of no *economic* significance."[65]

Miss Rand rejects any sort of limitations on personal freedom. She holds that value accrues to the acquisition of and control over objects (property) and never over people.[66] ". . . economic power is exercised by means of a *positive*, by offering men a reward, an incentive . . . political power is exercised by means of a negative, by the threat of punishment, injury, imprisonment, destruction."[67] Ironically, however, she then proceeds to equate property rights with human rights on the principle that man is a material organism who finds his realization in his relationship to the material world. What she fails to indicate, of course, is that, if the acquisition of property curtails the opportunities of others (who *are,* at basis, nothing more than their property relationships), it also and by logical implication curtails their freedom *as individuals* and amounts to an indirect control over people *as people.* In a sense, then, material success also signifies an indirect power over others through the redistribution of objective value (property). If property is an objective necessity of man as man, that man who monopolizes property has no need to coerce others *directly* because he already influences them at first remove by controlling certain of the conditions under which their lives are lived.

At basis, then, Miss Rand's categorical rejection of all violence, with the exception of justified retaliation in response to actual threats to one's own person or property, is not quite as ingenuous as it first sounds. Indeed, in a society which would, in all likelihood, be characterized by a snowballing monopolization of economic and therefore political power, there would be no *incentive* for anyone to resort to physical violence or confiscation except for those deprived of economic opportunity. The poor, in Miss Rand's vision of the world, would be faced with but two logical alternatives: (1) submission to immoral poverty or (2) revolt against the moral rich. Since they would already be both deprived and depraved, it seems reasonable to assume that they would opt for the latter course of action if they were given half an opportunity.

This being the case, Miss Rand is, once again, faced with two alternatives: (1) the maintenance of a police state (a sort of free enterprise Sparta, characterized by the passive elimination of the helots as a logical and therefore unavoidable consequence of progressive penury) or (2) the active elimination of the depraved poor in a morally-legitimized purge in retaliation against real or threatened revolution. In either case, of course, the end-result would be a clear victory for the reigning elite of economic *Ubermensch*.[68]

From the objectivist point of view, then, the right to political freedom (liberty) should be absolute *except where it violates more significant rights*. Civil disobedience—i.e., direct action in willful violation of the law (as contrasted to appeals for change conducted by "due process" through established legal channels)—may occasionally be justified in cases where the individual is primarily concerned with obtaining a legal decision with respect to some particular action and where his behavior does not violate the rights of others. Under appropriate circumstances, such behavior implies a profound respect for the *deeper* significance of the laws and actually represents an attempt to correct some perceived injustice within the established context of legal morality.[69]

Mass civil disobedience, however, is never justified where these conditions do not hold true. "The end does *not* justify the means. No one's rights can be secured by the violation of the rights of others.."[70] "The forcible occupation of another man's property or the obstruction of a public thoroughfare is so blatant a violation of rights that an attempt to justify it becomes an abrogation of morality."[71]

The only time when civil disobedience is justified—as, for example, in the strike of the leaders of production in *Atlas Shrugged*—is when society has reached the stage of dictatorship characterized by "one-party rule, executions without trial for political offenses, expropriation or nationalization of private property, and censorship."[72] Censorship is the most important characteristic of a dictatorship. Without censorship, internal reforms are still possible. "When censorship is imposed, *that* is the sign that men should go on strike intellectually, by which I mean, should not cooperate with the social system in any way whatever."[73]

In the absence of dictatorship, the proper means for resisting oppression are intellectual means. "It is *ideas* that determine social trends, that create or destroy social systems. Therefore, the right ideas, the right philosophy, should be advocated and spread."[74]

Perhaps the best example of illegitimate mass civil disobedience is that provided by the so-called "campus revolt" at the University of California in Berkeley. From the objectivist point of view, this revolt was essentially a sort of spontaneous exercise of ill-formulated anarchism—"a social movement that began with the ponderous, brain-cracking, dialectical constructs of Hegel and Marx, and ends up with a horde of morally unwashed children stamping their feet and shrieking: "I want it now!' "[75] Indeed, comments Rand, "if [a] dramatist were writing a movie, he could justifiably entitle it 'Mario Savio, Son of Immanuel Kant.' "[76]

In a sense, of course, perhaps the most interesting feature of the Berkeley situation was that it presented a philosophical problem which the existing society was virtually incapable of coping with.[77] "The most ominous aspect of the situation," states Rand " . . . is the fact that it has not met any *ideological opposition* . . . that such criticism as it did evoke was, with rare exceptions, evasively superficial."[78]

According to Rand, the real point in contention at Berkeley was not *free speech* but *power*. A radical core of activists employed a legitimate issue to manipulate a large and divergent group of followers for the sake of political aggrandizement.[79] The revolt itself, however, was an implicit attack on the entire notion of private property. It was, in effect, the attempt to enlarge student control over public property in the cause of "guild socialism"—i.e., to replace the tyranny of the larger collective (the state) with that of a smaller collective (which has subsequently come to be known as the "Free Student Union.)"[80]

In a far more specific sense, the students who instigated the revolt were guilty of making three basic "ideological" errors.

1) They were guilty of making a totally erroneous distinction between "force"—the proper and peaceful exertion of pressure on others—and "violence"—duress arising from literal physical contact.[81] Thus, comments Rand " . . . if the rebels occupy the administration building, that is 'force'; if the policemen drag them out, that is 'violence.' "[82] The upshot of such a spurious distinction "is to establish a moral inversion: to make the *initiation* of force moral, and resistance to force immoral—and thus to obliterate the *right of self-defense.'*[83]

2) The campus rebels assume, again erroneously, that freedom of speech implies and even requires a corollary freedom of action. They go on to suggest that the difference between these two is vague or even indefinable and that the freedom to speak which exists without a corresponding freedom to act (particularly, of course, as this is expressed through the freedoms to associate, to organize or to

assemble) is empty and meaningless. Such an idea, states Rand, is clearly implausible, for no organized society can afford to equate freedom of expression with freedom to commit crimes unless it is also willing to concede that free speech is altogether impracticable.[84]

3) They mistakenly assume that the right to free speech includes the right to *unrestricted free speech on someone else's property.* The misconception here is quite obvious. The University of California does not belong to the students. It is—although inadvisedly in terms of more basic objectivist precepts—the property of the taxpayers of the state of California and is properly administered and controlled by their managers-in-residence, the University administration.[85]

Education

Miss Rand's position with respect to education is remarkably consistent with her underlying objectivist philosophy. From the objectivist point of view, for example, education is not a "natural right" of man. "There *are* no such free gifts."[86] In addition, education is not properly the prerogative of the state, and state control over education is fundamentally inconsistent with basic objectivist principles. As Nathaniel Branden indicates, "the disgracefully low level of education in America today is the predictable result of a State-controlled school system."[87] The American public school system has come to resemble "a vast civil service, in which the trend is toward a policy of considering everything about a teacher's qualifications . . . *except his teaching ability;* and of considering everything about a student's qualifications . . . *except his intellectual competence.*"[88]

The steps which must be taken are clear. The state should not be allowed to take children forcibly from their homes in order to subject them to educational training of any sort whatsoever, and this should be true quite regardless of parental approval or permission.[89] No citizen should have any portion of his wealth appropriated to support any sort of educational program or to pay for the education of other people's children.[90]

The solution to the existing disgraceful state of education is to de-collectivize it, *"to bring the field of education into the market-place."*[91] "Education should be liberated from the control or intervention of government, and turned over to *profit-making* private enterprise, not because education is unimportant, but because education is so *crucially important.*"[92] "When the economic principles

220

that have resulted in the superlative efficiency of American industry are permitted to operate in the field of education, the result will be a revolution, in the direction of unprecedented educational development and growth."[93]

With respect to ultimate objectives of education, Miss Rand is equally explicit. Ideally, they are the general objectives of objectivism itself. On an individual level, the goal of education is the fullest expression of the self-interests (ego-needs) of each student. On a broader social scale, this would clearly imply a commitment to the ethics of laissez-faire capitalism. In a more specific sense, these ends would be attained by acquainting each student with the underlying nature of objective reality and by providing him with the rational skills necessary to deal with the real world effectively.[94]

At basis, of course, all education "consists of acquiring knowledge, which requires the development of [the child's] capacity to grasp and deal with an ever-widening range of abstractions."[95] This involves, states Rand, two related but distinguishable patterns of intellectual development, " . . . the *cognitive* and the *normative*. The first deals with knowledge of the facts of reality—the second, with the evaluation of these facts. The first forms the epistemological foundation of science—the second, of morality and of art."[96]

In contemporary schools, the cognitive development is hampered by a variety of anti-rational assumptions and influences, but the child's moral development is totally subverted. Conventional morality is not concerned with positive life-values, "it is concerned with imposing a set of rules upon him—concrete, arbitrary, contradictory and, more often than not, incomprehensible rules, which are mainly prohibitions and duties."[97] "The child whose valuing capacity survives the moral barbarism of his upbringing, has to find his own way to preserve and develop his sense of values."[98]

At the elementary level, the basic problem is that of weaning the child away from the world of concrete-specifics to the broader realm of abstract concepts. This goal of concept-formation is best attained through the sort of instructional approach which demands clarity, precision and intellectual rigor. The problem with most contemporary educational methods is that they tend to work against these ends and that they therefore tend to subvert the child's future intellectual development. This is particularly apparent in the chaotic modern methods of teaching reading, where explicit understanding has frequently been subordinated to vague approximations, "substituting memorizing for understanding, and adopt [ing] something as close to a parrot's psycho-epistemology as a human brain can come."[99]

In addition to clear and abstract conceptualization, however, the elementary school should exercise the normative function of developing the child's "moral ambition."[100] This is possible only through the instrumentality of romantic art, which offers the child an image of the ideal, which, contrary to his home environment, teaches him to associate morality not with pain but with pleasure.[101]

At the secondary and college levels, much the same process would continue but increasing emphasis would be placed on such purely intellective matters as how to think and how to integrate and systematize knowledge along objectivist lines. Actually, Miss Rand has very little to say about the process of education at the secondary level. She does, however, offer five major criticisms of contemporary American *higher* education at the college and university levels. These are as follows:

1) It does not teach the student how to think

2) It lacks any coherent and hierarchized curriculum which includes a defined and ordered series of subject-matter steps.

3) The content taught is largely unsystematized and therefore largely unintelligible and meaningless to the students.

4) The professors are guilty of intellectual cowardice; they are uncommitted and therefore fail to profess.

5) The administrators are guilty of moral cowardice; they refuse to take sides on significant problems and issues.

In all likelihood, all of these criticisms would also apply (with certain modifications) to the secondary level of instruction as well.[102]

Political and Economic Theory

Miss Rand does not favor anarchy.[103] She does, however, favor restricting governmental authority to protecting the citizenry against arbitrary force. The role of government is to place force under objective (rational) control through the use of a police force, an army, and a system of courts which would (ideally) be supported by means of voluntary taxation.

Contrary to popular opinion, collectivist statism does not eventuate in the elimination of all conflict as represented by wars and aggressions. Indeed—quite in contrast to its professed dedication to such noble ideals as peace, cooperation, security and brotherhood—collectivism is nothing more than gang rule founded upon the omnipresent threat of violence.[104] "In a full dictatorship, statism's chronic 'cold' civil war takes the form of bloody purges .... In a mixed economy, it takes the form of pressure-group-warfare .... "[105]

Miss Rand devotes very little attention to the question of foreign policy, but she is quite explicit on what the nature of a fully-developed objectivist foreign policy would be. [106] As she states in her article "The Roots of War": "The essence of capitalism's foreign policy is *free trade* ... the opening of the world's trade routes to free international exchange and competition among the private citizens of all countries dealing directly with one another."[107]

In a similar sense, objectivist writer Edith Efron in a review of Ludwig von Mises' book *The Anti-Capitalistic Mentality* approvingly quotes von Mises' observation that our foreign aid, which seems intent upon offering a "fair share" of American wealth to less fortunate nations, makes sense only if one assumes that "the Lord presented mankind with a definite quantity of machines and expected that these contrivances would be distributed equally among the various nations."[108]

It is certainly clear the Miss Rand is not in favor of such ventures in international altruism as the Peace Corps which are, as she indicates, set up by statists "to send young Americans into unpaid (though tax-supported) servitude to foreign nations."[109]

There are, from Miss Rand's point of view, two basic types of coercion: direct (such as murder, theft, or military agression) and indirect (encompassing all forms of compulsory, or coerced, altruism—such as social welfare legislation.)[110] A free society protects itself against both forms of violence, and, indeed, objective natural law demands retaliation in the face of such evil abuses of power.

By implication, then, Miss Rand would utilize the powers of the state in two ways: (1) to prevent or suppress unjust violence *against people* (as in the case of murder or war) and (2) to prevent or suppress unjust violence *against property*—which would ultimately encompass *any* restraints on private property or the exchange of private property (trading) and which would ultimately preclude all *positive* social legislation which purports to provide for the equalization of wealth and which, in the long run, would ultimately lead to the elimination of all involuntary taxation as well.

Such an ideal state would from Miss Rand's point of view provide for absolute social justice, and this justice could not be abused for three reasons:

1) Value (property) ultimately derives from productive action (rational labor) as this has been applied to real (material) problems.[111] In essence, Miss Rand's position may be summarized as follows:

Property is good (an application of the law of identity).
A good cannot be (i) uncaused or (ii) caused by an act which is bad (an application of the laws of causality and contradiction).
Property is therefore always caused by good action—i.e., productive (rational) action.

In terms of Miss Rand's own peculiar variant of the labor theory of value, then, all *value* (property) is caused by *labor* (defined as rational productive action applied to the acquisition of, or control over, property.)[112] As Rand states: "The entity involved in production and trade is *man.*"[113]

Neither capital nor pure physical labor is sufficient to create wealth, however. As Ludwig von Mises indicates in several passages which are quoted approvingly by Nathaniel Branden in one of his reviews contained in *The Objectivist Newsletter:*

It is not the capital employed that creates profits and losses. Capital does not "beget profit" as Marx thought. The capital goods as such are dead things that in themselves do not accomplish anything. If they are utilized according to a good idea, profit results. If they are utilized to a mistaken idea, no profit, or losses, result. It is the entrepreneurial decision that creates either profit or loss. It is mental acts, the mind of the entrepreneur, from which profits ultimately originate. Profit is a product of the mind, of success in anticipating the future state of the market. It is a spiritual and intellectual phenomenon.

               * * *

The American worker is badly mistaken when he believes that his high standards of living is due to his own excellence. He is neither more industrious nor more skillful than the workers of Western Europe. He owes his superior income to the fact that his country clung to "rugged individualism" much longer than Europe. It was his luck that the United States turned into an anti-capitalistic

224

policy as much as forty or fifty years later than Germany. His wages are higher than those of the workers of the rest of the world because the capital equipment per head of the employee is highest in America and because the American entrepreneur was not so much restricted by crippling regimentation as his colleagues in other areas. The comparatively greater prosperity of the United States is an outcome of the fact that the New Deal did not come in 1900 or 1910, but only in 1933.[114]

In a similar sense, and as Rand states: " . . . the man who discovers new knowledge—is the permanent benefactor of humanity . . . the value of an idea . . . can be shared with unlimited numbers of men, making all sharers richer at no one's sacrifice or loss . . . . "[115]

2) Unearned value (wealth) is "irrational" and is not therefore true value.[116] The ultimate effects of possessing unearned wealth are evil and self-defeating. An honest man cannot consume more than he produces.[117]

The possessor of unearned wealth is fundamentally dishonest. He seeks the benefit of unearned value—a violation of the logical/moral law of causality which is the source of all property rights—and is bound to be inexorably destroyed by the logic implicit in his own behavior.[118]

Wealth is objectified value.[119] It is the base of moral existence as well as the barometer of a society's virtue. It follows, then, (1) that those who possess wealth are virtuous and (2) those who do not possess wealth *lack* virtue, do not *merit* wealth to begin with, and would in fact, be *destroyed by it* even if it were to be provided to them.

3) An honest man—i.e., one who is rational and productive—cannot be compelled to work. True labor can only be commanded by means of volitional assent in a context of free enterprise.[120] In a similar sense, those who *can* be coerced to work are (1) dishonest (and therefore unintelligent and unproductive) and (2) incapable of producing real wealth.[121]

Again, of course, Miss Rand engages in a type of circular and persuasive definition. Her position might be summarized as follows:

a) Sanity consists of seeing the world *as it is.*

b) Anyone who has such a "reality-orientation" recognizes that value consists of the acquisition of, and control over, material property—recognizes, in short, that the sole legitimate motive for human behavior is economic.

c) Such a person necessarily subscribes to "free enterprise" psychology and acts solely on the basis of free and volitional personal acquisitiveness.

d) Such a person cannot be forced to "work," then, for real work is, by definition, both (a) personal and (b) rational (sane). Coerced effort violates objective necessity and demands the subordination of personal acquisitiveness to the interest of others. It therefore violates both of the conditions required for true labor to exist.

Actually, of course, when all of these ideas are put together and shaken up a rather interesting theory emerges which might be summarized as follows:

Value is wealth.

Wealth is caused by productive rational action in the realm of property relationships.

Wealth signifies productive rational action in the area of practical property relationships and therefore serves as a visible sign of personal merit.

In any given instance, then, it necessarily holds that (1) the wealthy are virtuous; (2) the poor are depraved; and (3) everyone is either virtuous or depraved.

This being true, it stands to reason that coerced humanitarianism in the guise of such things as unemployment relief-assistance or free medical care for the aged is bad for two basic reasons:

1) Unearned wealth will ultimately work against, and slowly destroy, those who receive it.

2) The confiscation of wealth from the virtuous can only eventuate in a curtailment of true labor by the productive (virtuous) and therefore can only terminate in a decrease in the amount of real wealth (and therefore of real virtue) available within the culture at large. "The small minority of adults who are *unable*, rather than unwilling to work, have to rely on voluntary charity; misfortune is not a claim to slave labor . . . ."[122] "Any type of *non-sacrificial* assistance, of social bonus, gratuitous benefit or gift value possible among men, is possible only in a free society, and is proper so long as it is non-sacrificial."[123] "I regard

charity as a marginal issue. What I am fighting is the idea that charity is a moral duty and a primary virtue."[124] "I regard compassion as proper *only* toward those who are innocent victims, but not toward those who are morally guilty."[125]

The objectivist position with respect to charity is particularly evident with respect to the question of medicare. Medicare, states objectivist spokesman Leonard Peikoff, "is a proposal to enslave the doctors."[126] Medical care may be extended to the improvident as a form of voluntary charity, but it is never a human "right." Indeed, no man ever has a "right" to "the unrewarded services of others."[127] No man has the right "to help the sick by making life impossible for the healthy."[128]

Government aid always and necessarily entails government controls, for "he who pay the money for a service is *morally obligated* to see that he receives full value in return; he must set the terms, conditions and standards governing his expenditures. If he does not, he is an irresponsible wastrel."[129]

In a similar sense, public works programs are as ineffective as a dole. True labor—i.e., rational, productive action—cannot be coerced, and no real wealth is forthcoming outside the context of free enterprise. As a result, public works programs function as indirect subsidies for unproductive effort and act indirectly as a dole with the result that (a) the poor are destroyed by the effects of misguided charity and (b) the wealthy are encouraged to resist confiscation by curtailing their productive effort and thereby reducing the total amount of real wealth available.

Voluntary charity, on the other hand, does not provide an adequate answer either. Like social welfare legislation, it ultimately acts to reward and thereby to encourage vice and depravity and serves in the long run to destroy precisely those to whom it is tendered through the inexorable logic of objectivist economics.

The answer, then, is clear. It can only lie in a society regulated by non-altruistic laissez-faire capitalism in which the rich are (by social and philosophical definition) good, and the poor are bad. In such a society—with allowance for a certain amount of unavoidable "suffering" on the part of the depraved poor during the era of transition—there would be a progressive elimination of vice and depravity. The poor would no longer be protected against the natural consequences of their own depraved ways. They would, as a result,

227

either become virtuous—i.e., rich—or they would be allowed to suffer the logical consequences (hunger, starvation, disease and death) of their refusal to become contributive members of a truly rational society. In this way, there would be a progressive purification and moral regeneration of society as a whole directed by the inexorable logic of free economic enterprise.

FOOTNOTES (CHAPTER VII)

1.   A "scientific philosopher" is, for all practical purposes, a philosopher who subscribes to the scientific method, or to some common-sense modification of the scientific method, as a basis for establishing the nature of empirical truth.

2.   Cf. Chapter III, pp. 35-6: IV. pp. 45-9, 49-52, 60-61; VI, pp. 148-150.

3.   *Ibid.*

4.   *Ibid.*

5.   *Ibid.*

6.   *Ibid.*

7.   Rand, *The Fountainhead,* in *For the New Intellectual,* p. 79.

8.   Theodore Dobzshansky, *The Biological Basis of Human Freedom* (New York: Columbia University Press, 1956), p, 8.

9.   This is a rough adaption of a scheme outlined by Erich Fromm in his book *Beyond the Chains of Illusion* (New York: Pocket Books, 1962, p. 94.) Fromm distinguishes between *economic basis, social character,* and *ideas and ideals.*

10. Dobzshansky, *op. cit.,* p. 121.

11. Alfred Korzybski, as quoted in Wendell Johnson, *People in Quandaries* (New York: Harper, 1946), p. 162.

12. Rand, *Faith and Force: The Destroyers of the Modern World,* p. 7.

13. *Ibid.,* p. 8.

14. Rand, *The Fountainhead* as quoted in *For the New Intellectual,* p. 81.

15. Rand, "For the New Intellectual," in *For the New Intellectual,* p. 36.

16. Cf. Chapter IV, p. 34.

17. Rand, *The Fountainhead,* as quoted in *For the New Intellectual,* p. 81.

18. Nathaniel Branden, "Intellectual Ammunition Department," *The Objectivist Newsletter,* I, 9 (September 1962), p. 40.

19. *Ibid.*

20. *Ibid.*

21. Cf. Chapter IV, pp. 64-5.

22. Miss Rand is quite correct in attacking the sort of "crisis ethics" which restricts moral consideration to black-and-white—and therefore atypical and abnormal—situations which demand the most imperative

action in response to rigidly dichotomized ethical options. To take her own example of the life boat crowded with the survivors: Should one jump over the side and save the provisions for the others or not?

The rational altruist is no more likely to have an absolute answer for this kind of situation than is the rational objectivist. Indeed, Miss Rand's own answer might very well be deemed acceptable by many contemporary champions of the altruistic ethic. They would, in all likelihood, ask much the same question as Miss Rand: Could the individual remain in the boat and sacrifice the others without violating his own ultimate sense of personal identity? How, and to what extent, do the others in the boat relate to this identity? Are the others loved ones or merely strangers? To what extent, if any, is the individual normatively committed to the well-being of strangers *as strangers* (i.e., to others *per se*)? Could the person in question continue to live without anguish for the rest of his life if he were to remain alive and suffer his own cowardice? Would the probability of such continuing anguish overbalance the probability of future pleasures which would derive from remaining alive?

To take another of the Objectivist examples: Would it be morally defensible to rescue a drowning tyrant like Adolf Hitler? (Nathaniel Branden, "Benevolence vs Altruist," *The Objectivist Newsletter*, I, 7, July 1962, p. 27.) Again—and assuming for the sake of clarity that we are talking about Hitler at the height of his destructive powers—there are probably few rational altruists who would answer in the affirmative. For many, it would seem far more benevolent to let him drown on the basis (1) that his past behavior makes the likelihood of an evil career overwhelmingly probable and (2) that the sheer probability of such behavior would make his demise a more satisfactory means to ultimate altruistic ends than his continued existence.

23. Cf. Chapter IV, pp. 49-51.
24. Cf. Chapter IV, pp. 47-8.
25. Cf. Chapter IV, pp. 45-6.
26. Cf. Chapter IV, pp. 47-9.
27. Cf. Chapter IV, pp. 45-9.
28. Rand, *Textbook of Americanism*, p. 5.
29. *Ibid.*, pp. 5-6.
30. *Ibid.*
31. *Ibid.*
32. Rand, "Check Your Premises," *The Objectivist Newsletter*, I, 6 (June 1962), p. 21.
33. Rand, *Textbook of Americanism*, p. 12.
34. *Ibid.*, p. 5.
35. *Ibid.*
36. *Ibid.*, p. 6.
37. *Ibid.*
38. *Ibid.*, p. 10.
39. *Ibid.*, p. 11.
40. Rand, "The Property Status of Air Waves," *The Objectivist Newsletter*, III, 4, (April 1964), p. 14.
41. *Ibid.*, p. 16.

42. Rand, "America's Persecuted Minority: Big Business," quoted in *The Objectivist Newsletter,* I, 1 (January 1962), p. 2.
43. Rand, "Check Your Premises," *The Objectivist Newsletter,* I, 6 (June 1962), p. 17.
44A. *Ibid.,* p. 20.
44. *Ibid.*
45. Alan Greenspan, "The Assault on Integrity," *The Objectivist Newsletter,* II, 8 (August 1963), p. 31.
46. *Ibid.*
47. Rand, *Textbook of Americanism,* p. 12.
48. *Ibid.,* p. 6.
49. *Ibid.,* p. 10.
50. Rand, "The Property Status of Air Waves," *op. cit.,* p. 14.
51.   These are not, of course, *all* of the objections which can be leveled against Ayn Rand's position with respect to "human rights." Among other things, it is based on an erroneous concept of intelligence (creativity, productiveness) a concept which is, in turn, imbedded in a fallacious theory of knowledge. Rational action, Miss Rand contends, in the face of overwhelming scientific evidence to the contrary, is a purely private phenomenon which is not contingent upon existing cultural conditions. She seems to assume that operational intelligence emerges spontaneously as the natural outgrowth of unregulated activity. In effect, then, she maintains that a *freedom from* interference by others is a sufficient basis for effective practical intelligence. Accordingly, she expresses no concern with *positive freedoms,* such as the traditional freedoms of speech, association and religion, and clearly regards such ostensibly "liberating" social services as compulsory education and child welfare legislation as tacit expressions of political coercion against personal rights. (Cf. Chapter IV, pp. 47-9).

    In a sense, of course, Miss Rand is quite consistent in rejecting any sociological correlates of practical intelligence, because her entire philosophy rests on a theory of pure (non-egological) knowledge in which cognition is in no significant sense dependent upon personality variables but, rather, stems from spontaneous awareness of certain apodictic and self-evident truths.

    Still another objection to Miss Rand's concept of human rights is, of course, that it is based upon a fundamentally dubious identification of value with property relationships—an equation which is mirrored in her reduction of all rights to the two basic categories of property rights and free trade.
52A. Nathaniel Branden, "Intellectual Ammunition Department," *The Objectivist Newsletter* III, 1 (March 1962), p. 11.
52. *Ibid.*
53A. Cf. Chapter IV, pp. 50-1.
53. Cf. Chapter IV, pp. 45-6, 49-51 and 60-61.
54. Cf. Chapter IV, pp. 60-61.
55. Cf. Chapter IV, pp. 60-61.
56. Alan Greenspan, "Gold and Economic Freedom," *The Objectivist,* V, 7 (July 1966), pp. 12-13.

57. *Ibid.*, p. 13.

58. *Ibid.*, p. 15.

59. *Ibid.*, p. 13.

60A. Rand, "Intellectual Ammunition Department," *The Objectivist Newsletter,* III, 5 (May 1964), p. 19.

60B. *Ibid.*

60. *Ibid.*

61. Nathaniel Branden, "Intellectual Ammunition Department," *The Objectivist Newsletter,* II, 6 (June 1963), p. 22.

62. *Ibid.*

63. *Ibid.*

64. *Ibid.*

65. *Ibid.*

66. Cf. Chapter IV, pp. 45-6, 49-51 and 60-62.

67. Rand, *America's Persecuted Minority: Big Business,* p. 6.

68. Miss Rand's position with respect to the question of Negro civil rights appears to be reducible to the following position:

   1) The value of legality (institutionalized morality) always transcends the value of particular ends within such an established legal (moral) context.

   2) The proper role of legality is the defense of property rights.

   3) Property rights take precedence over all others.

   4) All violations of property rights are therefore immoral as such. There is no justification for such action; no endeavor justifies such extreme means.

   The Negro is, then, fully equal, but he has no right to violate the laws or appropriate the property of others as a means of expressing such equality.

69. Rand, "The Cashing-In Part III," *The Objectivist Newsletter,* IV, 9 (September 1965), p. 40.

70. *Ibid.*

71. *Ibid.*

72. Rand, *"Playboy's* Interview with Ayn Rand," *op. cit,*

73. *Ibid.*

74. *Ibid.*

75. *Ibid.*, p. 45.

76. Rand, "The Cashing-In, Part II," *The Objectivist Newsletter,* IV, 8 (August 1965), p. 33.

77. *Ibid.*, p. 38.

78. Rand, "The Cashing-In, Part II," p. 44.

79. Rand, "The Cashing-In, Part I," *The Objectivist Newsletter,* IV, 7 (July 1965), p. 28.

80. Rand, "The Cashing-In, Part III," p. 43.

81. *Ibid.*, pp. 40-41.

82. *Ibid.*

83. *Ibid.*

84. *Ibid.*, p. 40.

85. *Ibid.*

231

86. Nathaniel Branden, "Intellectual Ammunition Department," *The Objectivist Newsletter*, II, 6 (June 1963), p. 22.
87. *Ibid.*
88. *Ibid.*
89. *Ibid.*
90. *Ibid.*
91. *Ibid.*
92. *Ibid.*
93. *Ibid.*
94. Rand, "Introducing Objectivism," *The Objectivist Newsletter*, I, 8 (August 1962), p. 35.
95. Rand, "Art and Moral Treason," *The Objectivist Newsletter*, IV, 3 (March 1965), p. 10.
96. *Ibid.*
97. *Ibid.*
98. *Ibid.*
99. Rand, "Introduction to Objectivist Epistemology, Part II," *The Objectivist* V, 8 (August 1966), p. 2.
100. Rand, "Art and Moral Treason," *op. cit.*, p. 13.
101. *Ibid.*, p. 12.
102. Rand, "The Cashing-In, Part II," *op. cit.*, p. 34.
103. Cf. Chapter IV, pp. 47-8.
      Actually, there is much in Miss Rand's philosophy that is very similar to traditional anarchistic theory. Like the anarchist, Rand would like to deemphasize politics radically and move into an era of automatic social self-regulation on the basis of pure individual freedom. As she comments: "When I came here from Soviet Russia, I was interested in politics for only one reason—to reach the day when I would not have to be interested in politics .... I am interested in politics only in order to secure and protect freedom." (Rand, *"Playboy's* Interview with Ayn Rand," *op. cit.*, p. 14).
104. Rand,, "The Roots of War," *The Objectivist*, V, 6 (June 1966), p. 2.
105. *Ibid.*
106. Where she does speak about foreign policy, Miss Rand is quite explicit and outspoken. For example, she favors withdrawing from the United Nations and severing diplomatic relations with the Soviet Union. (Rand, *"Playboy's* Interview with Ayn Rand," *op. cit.*, p. 13). She also advocates abolition of the military draft, since it is a "violation of fundamental rights, of a man's right to his own life." (*Ibid.*, p. 12.) She holds that armies should be strictly voluntary. (*Ibid.;* Rand, "The Wreckage of the Consensus," *The Objectivist*, VI, 5, May 1967, p.2.)
      In their article "The Consitution and the Draft," attorneys Henry and Phyliss Holzer hold that conscription is a denial of the right to life and therefore a violation of the Ninth Amendment of the Constitution. (Henry Mark Holzer and Phyllis Holzer, "The Constitution and the Draft, Part II," *The Objectivist*, VI, 11, November 1967, p. 14.)
107. Rand, *"Playboy's* Interview with Ayn Rand," *op. cit.*, p. 10.

108. Ludwig von Mises, quoted in Edith Efron's review of his book *The Anti-Capitalistic Mentality, The Objectivist Newsletter,* I, 5 (May 1962), p. 18.
109. Rand, "Choose Your Issues," *The Objectivist Newsletter,* I, 1 (January 1962), p. 1.
110. Cf. Chapter IV, pp. 47-53.
111. Cf. Chapter III, p. 52.
112. Cf. Chapter IV, p. 53.
113. Rand, "What is Capitalism?" *The Objectivist Newsletter,* IV, 11 (November 1965), p. 52.
114. Ludwig von Mises, quoted by Nathaniel Branden in his review of von Mises' book *Planning for Freedom,* The Objectivist Newsletter, I, 9 (September 1962), p. 38.
115. Rand, "What is Capitalism?, Part II," *The Objectivist Newsletter,* IV, 12 (December 1962), p. 60.
116. Cf. Chapter IV, pp. 60-61.
117. *Ibid.*
118. *Ibid.*
119. Cf. Chapter IV, pp. 59-60.
120. Cf. Chapter IV, pp. 59-62.
121. *Ibid.*
122. Rand, "What is Capitalism?, Part II," *op. cit.,* p. 59.
123. Rand, "Intellectual Ammunition Department," *The Objectivist Newsletter,* III, 2 (February 1964), p. 8.
124. Rand, *"Playboy's* Interview with Ayn Rand," *op. cit.,* p. 10.
125. *Ibid.*
126. Leonard Peikoff, "The Doctors and the Police State," *The Objectivist Newsletter,* I, 6 (June 1962), p. 25.
127. Rand, "How *Not* to Fight Against Socialized Medicine," *The Objectivist Newsletter,* II, 3 (March 1963), p. 12.
128. Rand, *Atlas Shrugged,* as quoted in Leonard Peikoff, "The Doctors and the Police State," *op cit.,* p. 26.
129. Peikoff, "The Doctos and the Police State," *op. cit.,* p. 25.